Strategic Studies: Issues and Policies

n

1

...rategic Studies provides a bridge between the use of force or diplomacy and the
political objectives. This series focuses on the topical and timeless issues relating
...uding the nexus of political, diplomatic, psychological, economic, cultural, his-
...ry affairs. It provides a link between the scholarly and policy communities by serv-
...gnized forum for conceptually sophisticated analyses of timely and important

...ormation: The New U.S. Nuclear Doctrine
...s J. Wirtz and Jeffrey A. Larsen

...Weapons of Mass Destruction in the Middle East: Directions and
...n the New Century
...s A. Russell

...of the Cold War: The Deployment and Negotiated Elimination of Intermediate
Forces in Europe
...itman

...Facing the Middle East: Security, Politics and Economics
...s A. Russell

CRITICAL ISS
THE MIDI

Initiatives i

James J. Wirt
General Edit

Jeffrey A. La
T. V. Paul
Brad Roberts
James M. Sm
Series Editors

Initiatives in
achievement
to strategy, i
toric and mili
ing as the re
strategic issue

Nuclear Tra
Edited by Jar

Proliferation
Policy Option
Edited by Jar

The Last Batt
Range Nucle
Maynard W.

Critical Issue
Edited by Jar

CRITICAL ISSUES FACING THE MIDDLE EAST

SECURITY, POLITICS, AND ECONOMICS

Edited by
James A. Russell

CRITICAL ISSUES FACING THE MIDDLE EAST
© James A. Russell, 2006.

First published in 2006 by
PALGRAVE MACMILLAN™
175 Fifth Avenue, New York, N.Y. 10010 and
Houndmills, Basingstoke, Hampshire, England RG21 6XS
Companies and representatives throughout the world.

PALGRAVE MACMILLAN is the global academic imprint of the Palgrave Macmillan division of St. Martin's Press, LLC and of Palgrave Macmillan Ltd. Macmillan® is a registered trademark in the United States, United Kingdom and other countries. Palgrave is a registered trademark in the European Union and other countries.

ISBN-13: 978–1–4039–7246–0
ISBN-10: 1–4039–7246–X

Library of Congress Cataloging-in-Publication Data

Critical issues facing the Middle East : security, politics, and economics / edited by James A. Russell.
    p. cm.—(Initiatives in strategic studies—issues and policies)
    Includes index.
    ISBN 1–4039–7246–X
    1. National security—Middle East. 2. Middle East—Defenses.
3. Middle East—Politics and government—21st century.
4. Middle East—Economic conditions—21st century. I. Russell, James A. (James Avery), 1958–II. Series.

UA832C75 2006
355′.033056—dc22   2005058615

A catalogue record for this book is available from the British Library.

Design by Newgen Imaging Systems (P) Ltd., Chennai, India.

First edition: July 2006

10 9 8 7 6 5 4 3 2 1

Printed in the United States of America.

CONTENTS

LIST OF TABLES AND FIGURES

TABLES

FIGURES

ACKNOWLEDGMENTS

The chapters in this volume emerged from a two-year project examining security and stability in the post-Saddam Middle East funded by the National Intelligence Council and the Defense Intelligence Agency. Over this period, a series of one-day symposiums cohosted by the Center for Contemporary Conflict at the Naval Postgraduate School and the Strategic Studies Group at the Center for Naval Analyses in Alexandria, VA, served as the venues to discuss the emerging multidimensional view of regional security that resulted in the structure of this volume. Dr. Paul Pillar, since retired from the NIC, provided critical support for the symposium series as did RADM (Ret.) Michael A. McDevitt from the Center for Naval Analyses. The symposiums would not have been possible without the support and hard work of Alexia Suma, Mary Ellen Connell, and Celinda Ledford at the Center for Naval Analyses. Special thanks are also due to Jeff Larsen and his team at Larsen Consulting Group for their assistance in preparing the manuscript. Finally, thanks to Heather VanDusen at Palgrave-Macmillan for her assistance in bringing the ideas in this volume to print.

1

INTRODUCTION

James A. Russell

Most scholarly written work examining the generic topic of "security" understandably deals first and foremost with military and strategic issues in the context of global interstate relations. The study of international relations in political science has developed a variety of elaborate theoretical constructs to explain a state's quest for security. Indeed, various prominent scholars have put forth the proposition that this quest for security constitutes a defining feature of interstate relationships in the wider international system.[1] The so-called realist and neorealist schools of thought believe that interstate competition and friction, manifesting itself in armed conflict, is an immutable feature of the international system. As states pursue security through armaments and supporting interstate and/or alliance frameworks devoted to achieving security, other states seek to counter these actions through acquisition of armaments and a balancing set of political relationships. According to this theory, an important and underlying foundation of the international system is the never-ending quest by states for security, which forms a perpetual and indelible cycle that drives the wider international system.[2] A supporting associated body of impressive scholarly work surrounds the interactions between states that involve the threat and actual use of force as bargaining instruments in a coercive framework as part of their quest for security.[3]

A competing set of arguments to the realist and neorealist paradigm called "neoliberalism" emerged during the 1970s. This theory focused on the growing importance of non-state actors and the increasing and complex interdependence between different levels of actors throughout the international system.[4] This argument rejected the realist arguments about the primacy of the state in the international system, suggesting a more complicated systems-level approach to explaining the configuration of the international environment. According to this view, the motivations and actions of states are much more complicated and more difficult to explain than the realist focus on the never-ending quest for security. This view of the world saw the quest for rules-based international regimes as a logical extension of the search by states to help manage complex interdependence.

Theoretical literature in the field of comparative politics in political science likewise treats the concept of security in a variety of different ways. For example, specialists in comparative politics commonly address the concept of security within the context of the structure of the state itself—as a tool of internal control and governance that can change on a case-by-case basis depending on a variety of internal and external variables.[5] A variation on this theme is suggested by the idea of "omnibalancing," which attempts to address the contradictions ruling elites face in balancing the requirements of external security while simultaneously pursing their most important objective: maintaining their hold on power.[6] The idea of omnibalancing seems particularly applicable to the Middle East, in which states such as Libya, Saudi Arabia, Egypt, Syria, Iran, and the Gulf States are dominated by a relatively small circle of defined elites—all of whom face complicated internal and external factors playing into their respective regimes' pursuit of security.[7]

Whereas each of these theoretical approaches suggests interesting and analytically useful lines of inquiry, political scientists have yet to formulate an all-inclusive theory of their discipline that unifies structural characteristics of the international system, whether those characteristics are focused on the state, non-state actors, international regimes, or the environment. The search for a unified theory or set of theories is going on in other disciplines. In physics, for example, interesting explorations surrounding something called string theory suggest the potential for a unified theory of the universe that reconciles the internal forces of the atom with the external forces created in the universe after the big bang.[8] The process of paradigmatic examination, change and evolution now being openly debated in scientific circles is indeed a heartening and healthy phenomenon. A similar effort aimed at paradigmatic evolution and change is long overdue in political science to bridge the divide between the views in each of its subfields. This could lead to the development of an integrated definition of "security" that includes internal and external variables and transnational phenomenon associated with globalization. One leading scholar recently noted that structural changes in the international system brought about by globalization mean that "the definition of what is a 'security' issue is also becoming more and more fluid and fungible—including the dislocations of economic development; the destabilizing effect of transitions to democracy; the undermining of traditional cultures, beliefs, and loyalties; threats to the public environmental and public health; and the like."[9]

Consistent with such a formulation, popular definitions of the term "security" in fact suggest a multifaceted concept that encompasses a variety of internal and external variables. For example, *Webster's Ninth New Collegiate Dictionary* defines the term security as "the quality or state of being secure as: a: freedom from danger; b: freedom from fear or anxiety; c: freedom from want or deprivation."[10] The *Webster's* definition, not surprisingly, suggests that the concept of security consists of internal and external factors—freedom from external threats and freedom from internal threats that can provoke a sense of insecurity in both the state and the individual. But despite the

Webster's definitional link, with a few exceptions as noted above, security studies writ large as a field within political science and international relations tends not to attempt to link these factors in any kind of systematic or theoretical models. Attempting to bridge this divide by suggesting a unified but variegated concept of security is the objective of the collection of essays in this volume. The authors address sources of insecurity in the Middle East from the perspective of the fields of economics, politics, history, international relations, and religion.

TWENTIETH-CENTURY SECURITY IN THE MIDDLE EAST

The intellectual and paradigmatic divide between external and internal views of security is reflected in the approach that governments traditionally take toward protecting themselves from external threats and using their national instruments of power to secure their interests around the world. The Middle East is no exception to this generalization. Outside powers in the twentieth century seeking to exert influence and protect their interests in the Middle East uniformly considered the pursuit of security a military and geostrategic problem. In the period between World Wars I and II, for example, a weakened British empire relied largely on the Royal Air Force deployed in a series of dispersed air bases throughout the Middle East and Persian Gulf to coordinate communications, movements of forces, and, when necessary, would use machine guns on the locals to maintain some semblance of order.[11] In hindsight, the British pursuit of regional security appears extraordinarily economical in terms of monetary cost and manpower compared to the billions of dollars lavished by U.S. taxpayers on the region during the last 15 years.

Following the British withdrawal from the Gulf region in 1972, the United States slowly but inexorably reinserted itself into the role that had been played by the British for the previous century. Like the British, the United States developed a series of military facilities that over time has grown into a sophisticated network of operational military hubs stretching from the Gulf into Central Asia.[12] Reflecting the region's growing importance, from the 1980s onward, regional military and operational contingencies became a primary assumption driving defense planning and budgeting in the Defense Department. Gulf Wars I and II only confirmed to many the efficacy of the approach taken by the United States to defense planning and budgeting to ensure regional security and stability, which was centered on defense cooperation agreements, forward deployed forces, pre-positioned military equipment, foreign military sales, and training and military exercises.

It is thus no accident that the United States came to regard security in the Middle East as primarily a military problem. In fact, most scholars and policy professionals understandably regard the Middle East as one of the world's ideal laboratories to study the impact of armaments and the use of force on interstate relationships and the regional environment. Throughout most of the twentieth century, the region has been beset by armed intra- and interstate conflict, ranging from the insurgencies associated with the postcolonial wars of national liberation to the Arab–Israeli wars to the Iran–Iraq War and Gulf Wars I and II. In short, the study of security in the Middle East has justifiably focused on the threat and actual use of force. Seen against a backdrop spanning the last century, the insurgency in Iraq simply represents the latest iteration in this long-running saga.

Although focusing on purely military aspects of security is understandable and a fruitful line of inquiry for scholars, it seems equally clear that the concept of security needs to be broadened and deepened—particularly as it applies to the Middle East. It is abundantly clear that the sources of "insecurity" in the Middle East are vast and varied, demanding a more complicated framework than the usual focuses on interstate rivalries, military capabilities, and armaments.[13] Expanding the consideration of the sources of insecurity is of vital importance if regional and international actors are to devise effective security strategies to manage this troubled environment. Moreover, if the concept of security is to be broadened and deepened, it suggests that instruments of state power developed to manage the security environment must be similarly altered. It is apparent that in today's Middle East various threats to security stem from underlying structural problems that transcend the particular characteristics of certain states. The problems of authoritarian governments, Islamic extremism, structural unemployment, terrorism, drug trafficking, human trafficking, and organized crime are transnational problems and region-wide phenomena not confined to geographic units defined by states' borders.

In short, security must be viewed as a multidimensional construct that demands multilevel and interdisciplinary levels of analysis. Development of a different paradigm to consider differentiated elements of security also suggests a parallel effort to bring instruments of state power and its organizations into some kind of alignment with this new marketplace of security. In his book *The Pentagon's New Map*, Tom Barnett suggests that for the United States the global environment represents a kind of new marketplace for security. According to Barnett, the United States needs to think of using force in the context of "exporting security" along the global fault lines separating those states participating in globalization and those that are not.[14] It seems clear, for example, that the United States now lies suspended in a state of paradigmatic, institutional, and intellectual disconnect as it seeks to apply its traditional instruments of state power that are wholly unsuited to today's security environment in an approach inadequately described by the meaningless phrase "global war on terrorism."[15] Fleshing out the sources of the disconnect is important not just for the United States but for the international community.

STRUCTURAL SOURCES OF INSECURITY

Today's regional security environment in the Middle East and the Persian Gulf remains highly unstable, an instability that due to its intensity and duration suggests deep-rooted structural problems that go beyond the interstate disputes associated with the Arab–Israeli Wars and intraregional rivalries that have also resulted in the Iran–Iraq War and Gulf Wars I and II. Various forces have been identified by the National Intelligence Council as providing the environment for the "perfect storm" that will almost certainly result in pervasive future instability.[16] The security environment is only a manifestation of the region's deep systemic problems, including those that follow.

Governments and Governance

As documented by the three successive Arab Human Development Reports, the region faces a basic and overriding crisis in governance. The terms and conditions of citizenship and the development of basic elements of civic society are being addressed as the region navigates its way toward developing new societies.[17] Today, the region confronts the wreckage of the failed secular Arab nationalist movement, Arab socialism, and Pan-Arabism, as well as leftover anachronistic forms of governments essentially run as businesses by familial elites. The era of these governmental forms is drawing to a close, and it remains unclear what forms of governance will emerge to take their places. The process of transition to new governmental structures may be violent and result in region-wide instability, and the types of governments that emerge may be revolutionary in nature. Whereas the postcolonial secular elites successfully repressed political Islam and the Islamists throughout much of the twentieth century, Islamists remain a powerful domestic political constituency in most Middle Eastern societies.

The era of political Islam is arriving in the Middle East, a result of generational change and the inevitable, gradual collapse of the postcolonial secular order in countries such as Syria, Egypt, Libya, and Iraq. It remains unclear whether Islamists across the Diaspora will adopt the intellectual and ideological radicalism articulated by Osama bin Laden and Ayman al Zawahiri or some other more moderate frames.[18] Iran's discredited model of Islamic governance presents another possibility.

Other competitors for the space of governance are appearing in the Gaza Strip and the West Bank, where Hamas has emerged as viable contender to the Palestinian authority's attempt to introduce some semblance of democracy to the Palestinians. In the Gulf, various familial elites are attempting to forestall the development of Islamism by encouraging political reforms that create circumscribed forums for more widespread political participation.[19] In Iraq, it appears that the Shi'ites and the clerical order headed by Ayatollah Sistani will have a chance to test their hand at heading some form of federated governance, which could provide yet another model for regional governments.

There is common intellectual and spiritual ground between the Islamists and bin Laden; however, it seems clear that there is not yet a broadly based social movement embracing bin Laden's idea of a unification of the Ummah and a return to the days of the Caliphate. Characterized by some as the struggle for the soul of Islam, it is this struggle to develop a coherent political philosophy that can guide the development of different ways of governance that may be the single biggest determinant of stability and security. What makes the impending crisis of governance so important is the host of pressing problems that will challenge the ability of governments to deliver competent "governance" for all the region's populations.

Urbanized, Youthful, and Unemployed Populations

Although projections depict slowing population growth, the region's population is expected to more than double by 2050 to reach 649 million. Saudi Arabia and Yemen are expected to grow almost fourfold by 2050, from 24 to 91 million, and from 19 to 71 million, respectively. Egypt and Iran are predicted to have populations of over 100 million in 2050. Only 25 percent of the population was urban in 1960, compared with 57 percent in 2001. This rate is expected to climb to 70 percent by 2015, with about one-quarter of the population living in cities of one million or more. Regional populations are also increasingly youthful. A "youth explosion," age 20–24—the key age group entering the job market and political society—has grown steadily from 10 million in 1950 to 36 million today, and will grow to at least 56 million by 2050, according to the United Nations. These youths are entering societies that are already shouldering profound structural unemployment, in the range of 20–30 percent in some Middle Eastern countries, which only promise to become worse as populations continue their inexorable increase.

Water

Fresh water shortages, already below World Bank minimums, will only grow more acute due to the lack of renewable freshwater sources as populations increase and present new challenges to governance. Increasing reliance on expensive desalinated water will help in the oil rich Gulf States, but is more of a problem for the non-oil rich countries such as Jordan.

Economics

Despite the region's large oil reserves, economic growth rates generally lag behind much of the developing world. The lack of global competitiveness flows from a general lack of private sector development and nondiversified economies, which is manifested by high structural unemployment throughout the region. Perhaps the region's most critical stumbling block in building competitive economies revolves around the human capital inefficiencies resulting from the lack of women in the work force. Societies that deny women basic human rights are consequently denied access to the human capital that resides in roughly 50 percent of their populations.

"Traditional" Sources of Insecurity

These long-term sources of insecurity provide the tectonic plates of geologic strata underneath which the shorter-term sources of insecurity boil like magma. As previously noted, short-term sources of insecurity seem abundantly consistent with various theories of realism. Historic and enduring interstate rivalries and the quest of states for security still represent powerful and enduring sources of conflict. The quest for nuclear and other nonconventional weapons by a variety of states must certainly appear at the top of any list of sources of insecurity. Continued unpredictable intrastate dynamics also play a significant role in influencing how states pursue their security.

The Arab–Israeli Dispute

The historical legacy of the postcolonial era still exerts a destabilizing influence on the regional landscape. One of its main leftovers—the Arab–Israeli dispute—continues to be cited by many regional leaders as a leading source of instability and radicalization among the region's restive publics. The festering dispute has led to the creation of groups on both sides that embrace violence as a tactic to achieve their respective objectives. The Palestinian groups Hamas and Islamic Jihad both make liberal use of terrorist tactics such as suicide bombings as an asymmetric tactic to counter Israel's overwhelming conventional superiority. In Israel, a variety of right-wing groups have grown in strength over the last decade and exert powerful political leverage. Their efforts to continue expanding settlements in the West Bank, for example, provides another enduring source of conflict and violence. The cycle of violence between Palestinians and Israelis seems endless at this point, providing daily video feeds and news headlines that help perpetuate negative public sentiment against the United States and legitimizes the use of violence as part of the backdrop of daily life.

Nuclear Proliferation

The potential of nuclear proliferation casts a further pall over the region. Iran seems to be marching inexorably toward development of a nuclear fuel cycle that could produce weapons-grade fissile material. Coupled with repeated hostile statements toward Israel (and vice versa), the region is presented with an unstable coercive framework between two or more states, both of which possess unconventional military capabilities. The unfolding of this regional dynamic promises to exacerbate the security dilemma of all regional states. The major regional states of Israel, Saudi Arabia, and Iraq might all feel compelled to take some sort of corresponding step to ensure their own security. In the case of Saudi Arabia, it would make sense for the ruling House of Saud to turn to Pakistan for some sort of equivalent capability to respond to Iran's acquisition of nuclear weapons, much like the House of Saud responded to the war of the cities in the Iran–Iraq War by acquiring long-range missiles from China in the late 1980s. For its part, Israel might feel compelled to take military action, raising the possibility of escalation and a wider regional conflict involving Israel, Syria, Iran, and the United States.

Iraq

Events in Iraq will dramatically affect interregional relationships and the effort of regional states toward ensuring their security. In some ways, Iraq's successful transition to a functioning democracy represents a threat to all the regional states—much like the Islamic revolution did to the region in 1979. Other aspects of developments in Iraq will affect a variety of states, which could in turn prompt additional conflict: Turkey and Iran fear a semi-independent Kurdish entity in Iraq; Saudi Arabia fears a Shi'ite-dominated Iraq that could destabilize its own Shi'ite minority and those communities in Bahrain and Kuwait; all regional states fear the prospect of an Iraq with strong ties to the clerical establishment in Iran and its surrogate enforcers— the Iran Revolutionary Guard Corps, the Badr Corps, and other Shi'ite militias; and all regional states fear the prospect of an Iraq that becomes a haven for terrorists and religious extremists.

Saudi Arabia

Saudi Arabia in particular finds itself on the horns of a security dilemma. The Kingdom faces a variety of contradictory forces, including an uncertain U.S. security partnership meant to address external threats at a time when the region is highly unstable. The principal threat to security arguably now comes from internal sources and from an increasingly complicated domestic political landscape that includes powerful elements that are opposed to maintaining the U.S. security partnership.[20]

Iran

Iran finds itself in an uncertain environment: surrounded by the United States on all sides, with daily pronouncements from Tel Aviv, Washington, and a variety of European capitals, all saying something different but all unified about their opposition to Iran pursuing a nuclear weapons capability. The uncertain state of Iranian domestic politics and Iranian domestic political institutions add another layer of uncertainty, with the development of competing centers of gravity in the Iranian political landscape.

CONCLUSION

Structural long-term sources of instability will inexorably gather momentum over the next decade and beyond. Populations will increase and will be concentrated mainly in urban areas; fresh water will become scarcer; structural unemployment and slow economic growth is unlikely to go away; and aging transportation, housing and communications infrastructures will face increasing strain due these underlying systemic forces. These long-term forces will collide with the enduring sources of inter- and intrastate conflict, promising to create a "perfect storm" of instability and conflict.

The purpose of the essays in this volume is to disaggregate the sources of this impending storm using an interdisciplinary focus that will illuminate for policy professionals, academics, and students the challenges faced by the regional states and outside powers in coping with a variegated security environment. Breaking up these sources of potential instability and conflict into their constituent components can help all these communities develop a more integrated definition of security—one that broadens the focus from armaments and the use of force.

NOTES

1. For a good summary of different schools of realism see Charles W. Kegley, Jr. and Eugene Wittkopf, *World Politics: Trend & Transformation*, 9th ed. (Belmont, CA: Wadsworth/Thomson, 2004), especially chapter II: "Theories of World Politics," 29–57. The authors cogently note that in the post–World War II era, "As the historical imperatives of 'power politics' required unceasing attention to the threat of war, the logic of Realpolitik asserted that military security was the essence of world politics" (38).

2. Kennth Waltz, *Theory of International Politics* (Reading, MA: Addison-Wesley, 1979). In this and in his later work, Waltz wrote extensively on the internal and external efforts of states to ensure their survival through armaments and alliance relationships aimed at balancing and/or domination over rivals in the international system.

3. Thomas Schelling, *Arms and Influence* (New Haven, CT: Yale University Press, 1966); Lawrence Freedman, ed., *Strategic Coercion: Concepts and Cases* (Oxford: Oxford University Press, 2003); Robert Pape, *Bombing to Win: Air Power and Coercion in War* (Ithaca, NY: Cornell University Press, 1996); and Daniel Byman and Mathew Waxman, *The Dynamics of Coercion* (Cambridge: Cambridge University Press, 2002).

4. Best expressed in Robert Keohane and Joseph Nye, *Power and Interdependence*, 3rd ed. (New York: Addison Welsleyan-Longman, 2001).

5. Perhaps the defining example of this view is Charles Tilly, *Coercion, Capital and European States, AD 990–1990* (Cambridge, MA: Basil Blackwell, 1990).

6. Steven David, *Choosing Sides: Alignment and Realignment in the Third World* (Baltimore, MD: Johns Hopkins University Press, 1991).

7. Paul D. Hoyt, " 'Rogue States' and International Relations Theory," *The Journal of Conflict Studies*, vol. 20, no. 1 (Fall 2000). Although not specific to the Middle East, Hoyt's treatment of the rogue state issue is appropriate, since several of the so-called rogues (Libya, Syria, and Iran) are in the region.

8. Brian Green, *The Elegant Universe* (New York City: Vintage Books, 2000).

9. Phil Cerny, "Terrorism and the New Security Dilemma," *Naval War College Review*, vol. 58, no. 1 (Winter 2005), 12–13. On this particular point, Cerny's piece refers back to Lyn Davis, *Globalization's Security Implications*, RAND Issue Paper IP-245-RC (Santa Monica: RAND Corporation, 2003).

10. *Webster's Ninth New Collegiate Dictionary* (Springfield, MA: Merriam-Webster, 1990), 1062.

11. Details provided in J.E. Peterson, *Defending Arabia* (New York: St. Martins Press, 1986), chapter II, "Power and Empire in the Arabian Peninsula," 13–58.

12. For a description of the locations and roles of these hubs see James A. Russell, "Strategy, Policy, and War in Iraq: The United States and the Gulf in the 21st Century," *Cambridge Review of International Affairs* (Summer 2005).

13. Emphasized regularly by Anthony Cordesman, the Arleigh Burke Chair for Strategy at the Center for Strategic and International Studies, Washington D.C., over the last several years in his congressional testimony and voluminous written work. For one of his latest pieces emphasizing these themes, see his testimony before the Senate Armed Services Committee, Middle East and Africa Threat Panel, "Evolving Threats in the Middle East: Their Implications for Defense Planning," September 28, 2005.

14. Thomas Barnett, *The Pentagon's New Map* (New York: Berkley Books, 2004).

15. Thomas Johnson and James A. Russell, "A Hard Day's Night: The United States and the Global War on Terrorism," *Comparative Strategy* (June 2005).

16. National Intelligence Council Report 2020.

17. For example, issues of citizenship and the relationship between the governed and the government in Saudi Arabia are addressed by Gwen Okruhlik, "The Irony of Islah (Reform)," *Washington Quarterly* (Autumn 2005).

18. Described eloquently by Gilles Kepel, *The War for Muslim Minds* (Cambridge, MA: Harvard University Press, 2004).

19. Joseph Kechichian, "Democratization in the Gulf Monarchies: A New Challenge to the GCC," *Middle East Policy*, vol. 11, no. 4 (Winter 2004).

20. James A. Russell, "Saudi Arabia in the 21st Century: A New Security Dilemma," *Middle East Policy*, vol. 12, no. 3 (Fall 2005).

POLITICAL ECONOMY

2

LONG-TERM SOURCES OF INSTABILITY
IN THE MIDDLE EAST

Alan Richards

Americans think that instability is somehow exceptional. Too often, they imagine that the intricate web of the modern twenty-first-century polity, economy, and society has always been. They believe that it not only defines a normal country, but also can be constructed, rather like building a bridge or a computer—all you need is a good manual. They continue to be surprised when violent social movements spread rapidly and imagine that they can stop them simply by "standing up for our values."

It is hard to conceive of a more deeply dangerous perspective from which to view the escalating violence in the Middle East. This chapter argues that the instability and violence so obvious there are, when viewed historically, exactly what should be expected. Instability is unsurprising, and is unlikely to end anytime soon. The region is enmeshed in the modernization process, always a vast, deeply unsettling, multidimensional, and violent social transformation. Specific features of the region also contribute to the difficulties of these complex changes, and much of the chapter focuses on these particularities. Both a comparative historical perspective and an analysis of specific issues suggest that humility is essential for any policymaker approaching these challenges. Quick fixes do not exist. Indeed, solutions often do not exist. There may only be policies and actions that are slightly more or slightly less likely to contribute to instability and violence.

After situating the current crisis in the Middle East from a comparative historical perspective, this chapter examines ten of the most pressing challenges facing the countries of the region. They are broadly grouped as either demographic—including the critical impact of youth—or as a natural resource, particularly water. Although improved governance will be necessary for better management of these challenges, it is unlikely to come from existing regimes without significant reform. These regimes fear such change because they understand how deeply unpopular they are with their own people. They avoid change and desperately try to deny the main opposition forces—largely those of political Islam—any participation in governance. Such an approach radicalizes the opposition, exacerbating governance deficiencies. Given America's close alliance with many unaccountable regimes, and the realities of American military power, the stage is set for many years of profound, violent instability.

A HISTORICAL PRELUDE: INSTABILITY IS NORMAL

William Faulkner once said, "The past is not dead. It is not even past." A glance at history is necessary if we are to understand the instability that now plagues the Middle East. History also offers us the only available guide to the longer-term possibilities for improvement.

Current analysts of instability often ask, "Why do they hate us?" Too frequently the question is misleadingly posed, as when highly visible students of the current crisis in the Muslim world ask, "What went wrong?"[1] The question implies that, somehow, developments in the Muslim world have been fundamentally different from those in other parts of the world, such as Europe or East Asia. Such a view is often popular because it allows us to indulge our very human tendency to think of ourselves as superior.

From the perspective of understanding violence and instability, however, the historical record suggests a very different interpretation. Today's Middle East finds itself enmeshed in the modernization process, an enormous, hugely complicated transformation of society. Simply stated, the transformation is from one kind of society to another—from a society where most people are illiterate farmers, ruled by a small elite of warriors and priests, to a society where most people are educated, living in cities, and making their living from manufacturing and service industries. This process began in Western Europe and has extended, to varying degrees, across the entire planet.

Such a change has always been traumatic and violent. The transformation poses huge economic, political, social, demographic, and cultural challenges. Some people do very well, whereas others are ruined. Yet, nearly everyone is profoundly disoriented. Our all-too-human propensities for conflict and violence are exacerbated by the strains of the transition to modernity, as the historical record amply demonstrates. As has been argued at least since the days of Emile Durkheim, such transformations are breeding grounds for violence.

Consider the histories of the two parts of the world where this transformation has been most successful—Europe (and its North American offshoot) and East Asia. Their histories often read like a horror novel: World Wars I and II; Stalin's Gulag; Hitler's Holocaust; Japanese fascism; the Chinese revolution; the Great Leap Forward and its attendant famine; and the Cultural Revolution. The American experience has also been bloody: the extermination of Native Americans; the racial violence of slavery and Jim

Crow; and the more than half-million casualties of its Civil War. A historical perspective forces us to ask, "Why should we expect Middle Easterners to do better than Europeans, Americans, the Japanese, or the Chinese?" A glance at history suggests that the answer should be, "We shouldn't, and they haven't."

Much of the violence of this transition has been inflicted by utopian fanatics—fascists, Nazis, Stalinists, Maoists, members of al Qaeda, and so on—who believe that they enjoy a monopoly on truth, and that those who disagree with them "are not merely mistaken, but wicked or mad."[2] Ideologues have their greatest appeal when the dislocations of the transition to modernity are most acute. Only the slaughter of World War I and its chaotic aftermath allowed the Bolsheviks to seize power in Russia. Hitler is inconceivable without the massacres of the trenches, the Treaty of Versailles, the hyperinflation that destroyed the German middle class, and the despair of mass unemployment during the Great Depression. In China, waves of famine, governmental collapse, and the horrors of the Japanese invasion set the stage for Mao. The appeal of fanatics becomes most seductive when economic, political, social, and cultural crises combine and when people have been repeatedly humiliated.

Today's Middle East faces just such a crisis. The utopian fanaticism of radical Islamists is nourished by the deep despair of huge numbers of young Middle Easterners, two-third of whom are below the age of 30, half of whom are younger than 20, and 40 percent of whom have yet to reach their fifteenth birthday. There are 150 million people from Morocco to Iran who are younger than 20. Fifteen years from now, another 100 million are likely to be born. Middle Easterners increasingly means young people.

What are their lives like? For the first time in history, many of these youths have received some education, although its quality may be questioned. They no longer are satisfied with the old, difficult, dirty jobs, but too often they lack the skills needed to perform successfully in the modern, hyper-competitive global economy. The combination of their rapidly growing numbers, the nature of their education, government economic mismanagement, and the vagaries of the global economy have spawned massive social dislocations. Unemployment rates throughout the region are usually in double digits, and real wages and living standards have declined for a generation. After ten to fifteen years of governments tinkering with economic policies, no country has a rate of economic growth sufficient to reduce unemployment and to raise living standards significantly.

Most of these kids now live in cities—cities that are crumbling. For example, the population of Karachi has mushroomed from 1 million people at independence to 11 million. It will grow to perhaps 20 million by 2015. Urban planners throughout the region are completely overwhelmed. Housing, transportation, water and sewage, health care, and all other services are in short supply. In many poor neighborhoods, only the mosque provides some refuge from the heat, filth, and chaos of the streets. Crises in public finance have forced governments to retreat from providing such public goods, leaving this function to private—often Islamist—schools, clinics, hospitals, and welfare agencies.

In short, huge numbers of semi-educated young people can't find rewarding jobs or decent housing and live in squalid surroundings. This situation alone would be enough to spark profound discontent. But, of course, economic failure is only one facet of today's regional crisis. Youth politics everywhere focuses not merely on material goods, but also on questions of identity, justice, and morality. Impatience and Manichean thinking are among the burdens of youth politics everywhere. And, as criminologists tell us, the resort to violence is also overwhelmingly a youth phenomenon.

The young look around and see not only economic failure, but also corruption and tyranny. They see national failures—Arab states in the protection of Palestinians or Pakistani governments in the protection of Muslim Kashmiris. Not surprisingly, they often despise their governments, their representatives, and their foreign supporters—including the U.S. government. For all of these reasons, the utopian schemes of religious firebrands have broad and growing appeal.

Throughout Islamic history, Islam has provided the language of opposition to tyrannical rule and of calls for justice.[3] This remains the case today and helps explain the power of the appeal of Islamist ideas. Inequity and oppression are ubiquitous, and young people naturally look for explanations, analyses, and programs from the same sources as previous generations—religious ideas, concepts, and language. Islamism is a protest against injustice, tyranny, and national humiliation. Delivering neither material goods nor a sense of dignity, the old ideologies, forms of secular nationalism, are understandably widely perceived as failures. Nationalism has not vanished—far from it. Instead, it has been assimilated into the Islamists' discourse. The combination of a deep, multidimensional crisis of transition to modernity and the specific cultural idiom of political protest has produced a very heady mixture, indeed.

It is the height of folly for outsiders to imagine that they can alter this significantly, least of all by direct military intervention. Only an authentic, indigenous response to the problems of modernity—which, in this case, means an Islamic response—has any chance of providing long-term stability to the region.[4] American direct military intervention in the Middle East is no more likely to facilitate this transition than it did in China. Only changes from within China, deploying Chinese idioms and fostering Chinese interests, could overcome the legacy of the worst days of Mao. As was the case in China, foreigners can do very little in the Muslim Middle East. In fact, there is considerable danger that our mistakes may make the transition even bloodier than history suggests it will likely be. Perhaps if we understand the magnitude of the challenges, and the attendant high probability of ongoing violence, we can refrain from counterproductive actions that undermine our own national interests—even as we imagine we are promoting them.

AN INVENTORY OF CHALLENGES

The current transformation to modernity in the Middle East faces a series of daunting challenges, including:

- Restoring economic growth
- Restraining population expansion
- Providing jobs
- Educating the young
- Alleviating poverty
- Coping with urbanization
- Saving water
- Obtaining food
- Halting environmental destruction
- Attracting money for investment, from foreigners and, more importantly, from domestic savers

The first six of these may loosely be grouped as demographic and human resources challenges, and the next three are natural resource issues. The final challenge encompasses all of the others. Success will require changes in governance, itself a significant task facing the region. The prospects for future stability are decidedly mixed. This is not surprising since by their nature transformations are deeply destabilizing. Changes in governance always provoke conflict.

Restoring Economic Growth

For the past two decades, the economies of the region have been running faster to stand still, with economic growth only slightly more than the growth of population. This is a lackluster performance when compared with economically advanced countries that have seen their per capita incomes rise at about 1.5 percent per year during the same time period. East Asia, excluding Japan, has grown much faster at 5.8 percent per year, a rate that doubled per capita incomes in 12.5 years. Even Latin America, with its notorious lost decade of the debt-ridden 1980s, saw per capita incomes rise at just under 1 percent annually during the past 20 years.

In the Middle East and North Africa, the story is stagnation during the 1980s and only sluggish growth during the 1990s. During the 1980s, gross domestic product (GDP) per capita stagnated at 2.4 percent per year. Growth during the 1990s was only marginally better at 3.1 percent per year, and it has remained roughly at that level.[5] Since population growth rates have fallen to about 2 percent, output per person has grown at slightly more than 1 percent per year since Gulf War I.

These numbers are based on conventional national income accounting. They fail to include two important phenomena: (1) the informal or underground economy, whose inclusion would improve the statistics and (2) the

costs of resource depletion and environmental degradation, whose inclusion
would make the situation look considerably worse. For example, in 1994, the
World Bank estimated that the yearly cost of environmental destruction in
the region was approximately equal to 3 percent of GDP. There is no evidence that such costs have fallen during the past decade and some evidence
that they have risen. When we account for wasting assets, it is quite possible
that regional economies—and per capita wealth—are actually shrinking.[6]

There are, of course, considerable differences among the countries,
although they are not significant from a political perspective. (See table 2.1.)
Reducing unemployment and raising real wages even modestly would require
growth between 6 and 7 percent per year. No country in the region has
achieved anything like this performance. As we shall see in more detail later,
sluggish growth implies a combination of rising unemployment and falling
real wages—an increase in poverty. For an entire generation, anxieties over
jobs and incomes have been endemic.

What accounts for this lackluster performance? Geography and history
have conspired to undermine economic growth. The region has been cursed
by a geographical inheritance of little water, much oil, and strategic location.
Despite the enormous sums of foreign exchange that oil revenues have

Table 2.1   Economic growth performance: per capita GDP
growth rates (% per year) for selected countries in the MENA
region

	1975–99	7990–99
UAE	−3.7	−1.6
Lebanon	—	5.7
Saudi Arabia	−2.2	−1.1
Oman	2.8	0.3
Turkey	2.1	2.2
Jordan	0.4	1.1
Tunisia	1.9	2.9
Iran	−0.9	1.9
Syria	0.8	2.7
Algeria	−0.4	−0.5
Egypt	2.9	2.4
Morocco	1.4	0.4
Pakistan	2.9	1.3
Yemen	—	−0.4
Global South (LDCs)	2.3	3.2
Arab countries	0.3	0.7
East Asia	6.0	5.9
Latin America	0.6	1.7
South Asia	2.3	3.4
Sub-Saharan Africa	−1.0	−0.4
Middle income	1.8	2.3
Low income	1.7	1.2
World	1.3	1.1

Source: World Bank.

supplied, legions of analysts have pointed out that oil has been a mixed blessing.[7] Whether stressing problems of the Dutch Disease, of corruption, or of other features of rentier state behavior, analysts agree that oil revenues weakened the competitiveness of non-oil traded goods and reduced pressures toward more accountable governance. Oil also contributed to a continuation of destructive nineteenth-century legacies of strategic location, which arguably distracted elites from the tasks of economic development.

History has also been unkind. All of the states of the region have suffered either directly or defensively from the baleful legacies of European colonialism and its shadow, the independent monarchical or republican statist apparatus—the so-called *mukhabarat* state. This predatory rule has actively blocked the development of the rule of law and the transparency of governance, essential drivers of economic growth and prosperity.[8] The result has been a set of states that were obsessed with national security, narrowly based, repressive, generally unaccountable, and reliant on oil and strategic rents for much of their revenue.

Whether republican or monarchical, the resulting large state sectors spawned inefficient production, rigid labor markets, skewed educational systems, and recurrent balance-of-payment difficulties.[9] Whether in Washington or Davos, the necessity of economic reform and enhanced accountability in governance as a key to restoring economic growth and promoting regional stability has become the new orthodoxy.

American elites seem wedded to a dangerous delusion—that economic growth and democracy are easily fostered and always produce stability. Unfortunately, neither assertion is reasonable. Rapid economic growth by itself exacerbates some problems, such as environmental difficulties and water shortages. Moreover, rapid economic growth will very likely require significant, destabilizing changes in governance. Winners from such a process may deny the legitimacy of entrenched power holders, the latter are unlikely to go quietly. We have known for a long time that economic growth can be, and often has been, profoundly destabilizing. Karl Marx was wrong about many things, but his insight that economic growth was often socially and politically destabilizing was correct.

Restraining Population Expansion

Demography is a second factor affecting medium-term instability, not so much because of any Malthusian phenomenon, but because the impact of past population growth on the labor market and the age structure of the population. There is both bad news and good news: the population continues to grow, but the rate of increase is decelerating markedly.

The population of the region was slightly greater than 300 million in 2000. It is expected to increase to about 400 million by 2015 (U.S. Census Bureau), growing at about 2 percent per year, according to World Bank estimates, or at 2.3 percent (UN Population Division). Only sub-Saharan Africa has a faster rate of population growth. This increase in the number of people by nearly one-third in but a decade will, of course, place further strains on housing, water use, and educational systems.

The good news is that population growth rates have fallen quite sharply in many countries during the past 10 years—from 3.2 percent in the mid-1980s to 2.7 percent in the early 1990s to 2–2.3 percent today. Reduced fertility caused this change. There are reasons to expect further declines because of increased female education and the availability of contraceptive technology.

However, deceleration in the fertility decline rate is also possible. Evidence suggests that shifts from high rates of decline (total fertility rates [TFRs] of 6–7) are more rapid than changes from more moderate levels (TFRs of 3–4) to replacement levels (TFRs of 2.1). The most plausible explanation for this phenomenon is that the initial declines happened because families were having more children than they desired. When contraceptive technology became available, fertility rates fell quickly. By contrast, shifts in fertility rates to near replacement levels involve deep social changes that may take much longer. It is possible, therefore, that the rapid changes of the recent past are relatively poor indicators of the immediate future.

This overall picture masks significant national differences. Fertility has fallen sharply in Egypt, Iran, and Tunisia, for example, but has remained stubbornly high in Gaza, the West Bank, Yemen, and Saudi Arabia, whose rates (over six children per woman) are among the highest in the world. Given the central role of Palestine and the Arabian Peninsula in regional instability, these figures are particularly worrisome.

In most countries fertility remains well above replacement levels (TFRs of about 4.2), and prior rapid growth means that the largest generation of young women in the region's history will soon enter their childbearing years. Despite a deceleration in fertility rates, demographic momentum alone ensures that the number of people in the region will grow dramatically during the coming decades. Most people in the region are young: half of all Arabs, Iranians, and Pakistanis are younger than 20 years of age. Two-thirds of all Middle Easterners are younger than 30. The bottom line is simple: expect more of the same.

Providing Jobs

Population growth from the past fuels the growth of the labor force today. Consequently, the Middle East region has the most rapidly growing labor force in the world at 3.4 percent per year, twice the rate of the rest of the global South. In some countries, the situation is even more serious—Algeria at 4.9 percent, Syria at 4.8 percent, and Yemen at 5.6 percent. The region needs to provide an additional 4 million jobs every year just to keep up with additions to the labor force. When compared with the 0.8 percent labor force growth rate in the United States and the 0.4 percent rate in the European Union (EU), the Middle East must produce four times as many jobs as the United States and eight times as many as the EU. The inevitable result is increasing unemployment and stagnant or falling real wages.

The employment problem may be the most politically volatile economic issue facing the region during the coming two decades. Unemployment is particularly concentrated among the young who are looking for jobs and hoping to start families. Their aspirations have been raised by education, but they don't have adequate skills to qualify and compete for the relatively scarce jobs in the modern private sector. Taking an informal-sector job often reduces their status and harms their marriage chances. Accordingly, their families finance them while they wait for government jobs.

Decades of government job guarantees for graduates underlie this situation. Governments alone cannot provide the necessary jobs. But, politically driven regulations and polices—combined with rising political risk—impede the private sector investment necessary to create jobs. Even relatively good economic performers such as Tunisia and Morocco are at best barely keeping up. No country's economy is growing quickly enough to reduce unemployment significantly or raise real incomes appreciably.

Current levels of unemployment are high. Methodologies for estimating unemployment vary widely. Although not comparable to the kind of monthly labor force surveys used in the United States, there is a consensus that unemployment stands at 15–20 percent of the labor force. (See table 2.2.) In some countries, unemployment is at a level not seen in the United States since the worst days of the Great Depression in the 1930s.

Unemployed, frustrated young men form a huge, rich pool for recruitment by political radicals. Of course, unemployment is only one of many forces that fuels the sense of humiliation that may be the most important proximate cause of violence in the region. Nevertheless, a vast, swelling tide of unemployed

Table 2.2 Unemployment in the Middle East: a compendium of estimates

Country	Unemployment rate (%)	Remarks
Algeria	30	1999
Egypt	12	2000
		Some estimates show 20%
Iran	20–25	2001
Jordan	15	Official rate. CIA gives 25–30 (1999)
Lebanon	18	1998
Libya	29	2000
Morocco	15–22	2000
Saudi Arabia	14–18	Higher among graduates
Syria	12–15	1999
Tunisia	16	1999
Yemen	35	1999

Sources: Saudi Arabia, US Embassy, Riyadh, and NYT, August 26, 2001; Iran, Eric Rouleau, *Le Monde Diplomatique*, www.en.monde-diplomatique.fr/2001/06/05iran; all others: MEDEA Institute (European Institute for Research on Mediterranean and Euro-Arab Co-operation), and *CIA World Fact Book*.

young men, with little prospects of improvement on the horizon, augurs poorly for long-term stability in the region.

Educating the Young

Many Arabs remain illiterate. Only in Jordan and Lebanon can more than four out of five adults read and write, mostly at the fourth grade level. Whereas more than three-quarters of adults are literate in Kuwait, the figure is only one-half to two-thirds in Algeria, Iraq, Libya, Tunisia, Saudi Arabia, and Syria. Half, or fewer, are literate in Egypt, Morocco, and Sudan. By comparison, the average literacy rate for lower-middle income countries is nearly 90 percent. Literacy rates in Iran, Israel, and Turkey are considerably higher. The rapid improvement in Iranian literacy since the revolution is especially notable—from just over 40 percent to over 75 percent today. Low levels of literacy contribute to a host of socioeconomic ills, ranging from high fertility rates to low foreign direct investment (FDI) and low international competitiveness. Literacy in economically competitive countries such as Mexico, Korea, or Thailand is at 90, 98, and 95 percent, respectively.

The picture for women is gloomier still. Adult illiteracy is concentrated among women. In only seven counties of the region can a majority of adult women read and write. By contrast, in Southeast Asia and Latin America, most women are literate (exceptions include Cambodia, Guatemala, and Haiti). Egypt and India are about equal, but lower than Rwanda.

As with population growth, however, there is a glass-half-full aspect to educational developments in the region. The past generation has seen a dramatic increase in school enrollments of both boys and girls. Nearly all boys are enrolled in primary school and the same is true of girls in some countries—Algeria, Egypt, Jordan, Lebanon, Libya, Syria, and Tunisia. Though not as high in other countries of the Arab world, the enrollment of girls in primary school has increased dramatically during the past generation.

The glass is less full elsewhere. For example, in Saudi Arabia and Oman, 25 percent of girls are not enrolled. Worse still, the figure is more than 30 percent in Morocco, 53 percent in Sudan, and 60 percent in Yemen. The waste of human resources, although decreasing, remains appallingly vast.

The uneven yet dramatic push to expand school enrollment over the past generation has spawned a deep generation gap in many societies, simply because the youth can read, whereas many of their parents cannot. Those between the ages of 15 and 24 have a much higher literacy rate than the adult population as a whole. For the Middle East North Africa (MENA) region in 2001, youth literacy has been estimated to be 81 percent, still below the 86 percent average for the global South. In some countries—Saudi Arabia, Iran, Jordan, Lebanon, Libya, Oman, and Tunisia—more than nine out of ten young people are literate. Yet here too, there is wide variation and some key laggards, notably, Egypt at 70 percent, Morocco at 68 percent, Yemen at 66 percent, and Iraq at 45 percent.[10]

Despite these weaknesses, the region's social structures continue to be transformed. Increasingly, most Middle Easterners have some education and better access to information about the wider world. As elsewhere, the spread of mass literacy in the Middle East has transformed society. The very large numbers of young people with education pose significant political challenges to the established political order. Rising literacy has contributed to what historians of the region have called the crisis of authority within Islam,[11] which has profound implications for governance.

In a manner reminiscent of the Protestant Reformation in Europe, the spread of mass literacy accelerated markedly during the past generation and has destabilized the religious order. Formerly, only learned, literate religious scholars, the *ulema*, issued religious opinions, or *fetwa*. With the spread of literacy and mechanisms of mass communication, nearly anyone feels entitled to express a religious view and, in many cases, to try to impose it on others. How else to explain, for example, how a business school graduate such as Osama bin Laden can issue repeated *fetawiin*? There is no reason to expect this ferment in the Muslim world to recede any more quickly than similar decentering in early modern Europe. The process takes centuries, not a few years.

Recall that youth politics, and perhaps all politics, includes the search for meaning and justice. The Islamic idiom has always provided the language of protest against tyranny in this part of the world. With huge numbers of young people—many of them unemployed—rapidly spreading literacy, a profound religious crisis of authority, and the widespread use of religious idiom in political life, the stage is fully set for a tumultuous political future. One thing seems certain: attempts by the United States or local elites to exclude the voices of protest against perceived injustice, voiced in Islamic terms, are doomed to fail. At the present time, political Islam dominates discourse in the region and is likely to continue to do so for some time. The politics of youth will not be going away anytime soon.

Alleviating Poverty

Conventional wisdom holds that per capita poverty in the Middle East region is lower than elsewhere in the global South. Since the World Development Report of 1990, the World Bank has used the US$1 per person per day (PPP) or US$2 PPP measure of poverty. World Bank data—World Development Indicators and van Eeghen[12] (1995)—suggest that, at the international poverty line of US$1 PPP, poverty in the Middle East is relatively limited when compared to other regions of the global South.

However, poverty rates are quite sensitive to the choice of a poverty line. Large numbers of people live on incomes close to the line: in Egypt, for example, although 23 percent of the population subsists on less than US$2 per day, another 37 percent lives on less than US$2.60. They are, therefore, highly vulnerable to falling into poverty. Putting these figures in international perspective, even when using the US$2 PPP standard, Middle Eastern countries are faring better than many Latin American countries and far better than India or sub-Saharan Africa. It is notable that the incidence of poverty is typically not significantly greater, and often much lower, in many Middle Eastern countries than in those whose economic development success is often highly touted, such as Thailand and Indonesia.

The trends, however, are disturbing. There is something approaching a consensus on poverty trends (as opposed to headcount levels): most analysts agree that aggregate poverty rates in the Middle East fell during the years of the oil boom from the mid-1970s to the early to mid-1980s, but started to rise after that.[13] Such an observation is compatible with the measured decline in the rate of per capita household consumption and with empirical research on the Middle East, which shows negative growth elasticity of poverty.[14] A growing body of empirical research demonstrates that this relationship holds across most developing countries.[15]

Studies of specific countries[16] are consistent with the results of such regional analysis. A Ford Foundation review of the lively debate over poverty trends in Egypt concludes that there was a large rise in the poverty headcount (from 29.7 to 42.4 percent between 1981 and 1991). Although the rate of poverty increase slowed during the 1990s, by 1995–96 (the last year for which there is data), the poverty headcount stood at 48 percent of households. A study of poverty in Yemen found that the number of families suffering from malnutrition rose from 9 to 27 percent between 1992 and 1999. An International Development Research Centre (IDRC) report concluded, "the proportion of people living in poverty appears to be rising in most of the region's middle and lower income countries." In Jordan, analysts found a reduction in poverty in the late 1990s, but the level remains above that of 1988. Finally, some of the countries for which data are missing—most importantly Iraq and Sudan—have large populations and relatively high poverty rates (although the exact magnitudes are not known).

There are three key factors affecting the rise in poverty.[17] First, unemployment is not only high but still rising in many countries. Second, most job creation has occurred in the low-wage, informal sector, not in the higher-paying, formal one. And finally, real wages in formal sector urban employment are falling. And in some countries, including Egypt, real wages in agriculture have also fallen.

However, the trends in poverty also pose some conundrums. For example, per capita calorie consumption per day has risen in many countries during the past generation.[18] In the absence of strong distribution shifts—a topic about which little is known—this indicates that changes in calorie consumption have occurred across all households, including those that are food insecure. The high level of average calorie consumption suggests that deficiency in this area is not a serious problem. For the period as a whole, the value has increased in all countries except in the United Arab Emirates where it remained at its very high level. Countries with the lowest levels (below 2,500 calories) from 1993 to 1997—Iraq, Sudan, and Yemen—had below-average growth in per capita consumption.

Similarly, Food and Agriculture Organization of the United Nations (FAO) data suggest that the share of undernourished people in the total population has declined over time, from 8.8 percent during 1979–81 to 7.2 percent between 1990 and 1992 to 6.9 percent from 1997 to 1999. However, this decline was not sufficient to reduce the absolute number of undernourished, which grew from 20.9 million in 1979–81 to 26.7 million in 1997–99. The rates of malnourishment were highest in Iraq (13.8 percent), Sudan (21.1 percent), and Yemen (33.7 percent). With only 18 percent of the total population, undernourishment reached a rate of 21 percent and accounted for as much as 56 percent of the entire undernourished population. By contrast, the aggregate undernourishment rate for the other countries was only at 4 percent.[19]

How can an increase in poverty coexist with a reduction in undernourishment and increased per capita calorie consumption? The likely answer is simple: food subsidy programs. These policies have protected the food security of many at-risk households whose poverty levels have increased. Some programs have been modified, but the commitment of Middle Eastern countries to protect the nutritional levels of their substantially disadvantaged populations is striking, particularly when put in the context of an international comparative perspective.

Several political implications follow from this analysis. First, government provisions of both consumer subsidies and public sector employment have prevented poverty from rising further—yet these are among the policies that, according to the Washington consensus perspective, also contribute to sluggish growth, relatively rigid labor market structures, and growing unemployment. The dilemma is clear. Implementing economic reform is likely to be destabilizing. Yet, by contributing to continued stagnation, business as usual is also destabilizing. Either way, the prospects for stability are not good.

Some argue that poverty is politically irrelevant. Because the poor are so busy trying to make a living, they haven't the time or energy for political activities. Moreover, the cadres of Islamic resistance movements are relatively well-educated, middle-class men. Seasoned observers of the region note that large numbers of poor, unemployed, or underemployed young men provide a fertile recruiting pool for political entrepreneurs, particularly Islamist activists. An obvious example is the Mahdi Army of Mustafah al-Sadr in the Shi'i slums of Baghdad.[20] Experts also point out that the growing population of educated young people in the region is not blind, and what they see often engenders disgust and contempt for existing regimes that have failed to provide a decent living to very large numbers of their countrymen. Part of the moral and political strength of Islamists—from Morocco to Egypt to Pakistan—has been their ability to deliver services to the poor, something that the government apparently cannot manage.

Coping with Urbanization

Urbanization has also increased rapidly during the past generation. The number of urban Middle Easterners has increased by about 100 million in the past 35 years. At independence, the population of Karachi was about 1 million, for example, whereas today, it is more than 11 million. Over half (56 percent) of all Arabs live in cities. Only in Egypt, Somalia, Sudan, and Yemen do most people live in rural areas. Furthermore, the number of urban dwellers is expected to rise from its current level of over 140 million to more than 350 million by 2025.

Public services and utilities are already overwhelmed. In Jordan and Morocco, for example, one-third of the urban population lacks adequate sewerage services. Urban water supplies are often erratic at best. Governments attempt to provide services through heavy subsidies, but these usually benefit the relatively better off. Such policies strain government budgets and thwart investments necessary to extend and improve services. Housing problems are severe. Cairo is illustrative with a half-million living on rooftops and well over one million living in and around the tombs of the City of the Dead. New construction has lagged behind new household formation, so that the gap, already vast, is growing.

These problems are both causes and effects of governance deficiencies. Few cities have much independent tax authority, thanks to the typical pattern of fiscal centralization. At the same time, macroeconomic austerity has deprived many municipalities of the funds needed to cope with urban problems. Rapid urbanization and its attendant problems strain budgets, legitimacy, and governance, while swelling the ranks of regime opponents. A recent description of conditions in a Casablanca shantytown could be applied to many other countries:

> Hovels of planks and cardboard boxes found in the streets are heaped in anonymous blocks without formal roads that congregate into districts with no official identity. Inhabitants survive on petty theft and trafficking. These miserable slums, less than half an hour from the centre of Casablanca, have no running water, sewers or electricity. Foul water stagnates in alleyways of packed earth that attract clouds of mosquitoes carrying diseases. The inhabitants call the districts "Chechnyas". . . the state is absent: no schools, no dispensaries, no post office, no savings bank, no public transport.[21]

Islamist parties and organizations have often stepped in to provide the missing clinics, schools, transportation, and welfare services. The abandonment of public space to such forces is quite advanced in many countries and, given fiscal realities, unlikely to be dramatically reversed. This development has helped to further the political agenda of the forces of political Islam.

Consider the Moroccan case. Approximately half a million rural emigrants arrive in Moroccan cities every year. About 10 percent of the urban population lives in shantytowns, called *al-karyan*. In some areas, Islamist movements such as *Al Adl wa'l Ihsan* (Justice and Welfare), led by AbdesalaamYassin, now provide legal aid, night schools, medicines, and subsidies for pilgrimages and funerals. An Islamist leader asserted to a French reporter, "confronted with the neglect of the state, and faced with the brutality of daily life, people discover, thanks to us, solidarity, self-help, fraternity."[22] A former Moroccan leftist confided to Ramonet, "The people of the *bidonvilles* (shantytowns) are entirely cut off from the elites. They see the elites the way they used to see the French."[23]

The alienation is so strong that the poorest and most abandoned areas have become strongholds of Takfiri Salafism, the most extreme form of jihadi Salafism.[24] Salafist dress is prominent in such areas, and there have been attacks on local police stations. Residents of such areas were the perpetrators of the bomb attacks in Casablanca on May 16, 2003. These *takfiris* are considerably more extreme than other Moroccan Islamists such as the Justice and Welfare Party. They are social outcasts. As one author puts it, "The Takfirists are . . . the alienated remnants of disintegrating social groups who have never known anything other than the sordid, brutal world of the slums. In the name of a sectarian idea of Islam, they are now turning the pitiless ferocity that ordinary Moroccans show towards them against the established order."[25]

Saving Water

Although water wars are hardly inevitable, finding mechanisms to cope with increasingly scarce water supplies poses significant challenges to governance, both internally and between countries. Six aspects of the water situation seem particularly relevant.

Water scarcity continues to rise in the region. Annual renewable water resources per capita today, about 1,250 m^3, are less than half of the 3,500 m^3 they were in 1960). By 2025, the number will probably fall to less than 650 m^3. Compare this with a global average of 4,780 m^3 per person per year. Water use in ten countries and Gaza already exceeds 100 percent of renewable supplies.

Water quantity problems are exacerbated by water quality problems. The latter become increasingly serious as nations seek to solve the supply problem through the reuse of water. Technologies exist to do this safely, but they require extensive funds and careful management. Neither is abundant in the region. In the most serious cases, water pollution can generate serious problems. For example, Damietta, Egypt, a city of nearly one million people, has no sewer system. The city depends entirely on the Nile, already heavily polluted. The result is that up to 40 percent of the population in Damietta and neighboring Daqahliyya may be suffering from liver and kidney ailments.

As everywhere in the world, groundwater over-pumping is another serious problem. In Yemen, for example, extraction rates exceed recharge by 130 percent. The region is mining fossil groundwater. As experience in the U.S. Southwest suggests, managing this problem is extremely difficult under almost any set of institutions.

From an economic perspective, the burden of adjusting to an increasing scarcity of water must fall on the agricultural sector because the economic value of water is much lower in farming than for domestic or industrial use. Past government programs to redistribute land, reclaim land, and increase domestic agricultural production have fostered, strengthened, and, in some cases, created powerful interest groups who block reallocation of increasingly scarce water supplies.

Government water management systems suffer not only from lack of money, but also from managerial cultures geared toward a situation of relatively abundant water. Most irrigation ministries are almost entirely staffed by civil engineers, whose training and culture focuses almost exclusively on how to move water from one location to another. Economists, sociologists, and other specialists whose focus is on changing the institutions of water allocation are rare, and their voices are seldom heard.

Most water sources in the region are rivers and aquifers that cross international boundaries. There is a sharp clash between economic/engineering logic, which favors managing a river basin as a unit, and political considerations, often marked by fear and distrust of neighboring countries. Although it is true that international cooperation over shared water resources has been relatively robust, the potential for conflict remains high.

We may draw some implications for stability by simply reflecting on the obvious fact that coping with increased water scarcity implies a shift in the modes of governing access to water. Such changes are certainly likely to provoke conflict since there will be losers as well as winners, and since institutional changes are often difficult to implement for technical reasons. Increasing water scarcity, therefore, implies (once again) significantly enhanced challenges to governance. Consider the options that governments and societies face.

Powerful ideological, bureaucratic, and political reasons ensure that the first response of many countries to increased water scarcity is to try to augment supplies. It is equally likely that such gambits will provide, at best, only short-term palliatives. The continued expansion of public works designed to augment supply will also often exacerbate political controversy and conflict. As always, the manageability of such conflicts is entirely dependent on the specific national and international context within which they occur.

Since expanding the supply of water is necessarily constrained, the only alternative is enhanced conservation or water use efficiency. In the language of economics, if supply cannot be reliably and consistently increased, improved demand management will necessarily loom much larger in the future as a means of coping with scarcity. However, such an approach has formidable hardware requirements of physical infrastructure and software requirements of management systems, configurations of incentives, and modes of cooperating to share increasingly scarce water.

Reallocating water will often require significant investment and new infrastructure. Water is, after all, heavy. Shifting it from farms to cities requires infrastructure—for example, water saved in the Jordan Valley can only help consumers in Amman if it is lifted over 1,300 m. Infrastructure is expensive and will have to compete with other claimants on the public purse for scarce funds. Such projects may also raise important political issues, as is now the norm when new dam construction is considered.

The problems of installing new software may be harder still. After all, the phrase is simply a metaphor for changing the rules of the game by which water is allocated. A change in rules and incentive systems implies that there will be conflicts and crucial questions to be answered. How will conflicts be managed? How will conflicts impinge on other issues of regime legitimacy?

As with other challenges, there is a strong status quo bias in policymaking. The structure of interests and the fact that costs are incurred directly, early, and obviously, whereas benefits accrue indirectly, later, and opaquely make efficiency of water use a slippery term among specialists and the general public. Given the long lead times required for so many necessary changes, status quo bias can make the day of reckoning worse by postponing it until the problems are even more severe.

Coping with rising water scarcity poses the same dilemma as other challenges facing the region's political economies and societies. On the one hand, failure to reform systems, and, therefore, failure to deliver adequate water supplies to increasing numbers of people has destabilizing potential for some governments. On the other hand, the process of decentralizing decision making can itself be destabilizing, depending upon the specific context. The dynamics of reform regarding water allocation policies can add to social and political conflict within increasingly water-scarce societies, but can also present significant opportunities to smooth the transition to more water-efficient allocation systems. Once again, the responsibility for coping with challenges falls to government.[26]

Obtaining Food

The Middle East is the least self-sufficient region in the world when it comes to food. The gap became most notable during the 1970s. Soaring demand, fueled by rapid population growth and rising per capita incomes from the oil boom, far outstripped the sluggish response of relatively neglected agricultural sectors. Alarmed by the dramatic growth of imports and by the fear that the United States might use the food weapon to counteract the oil weapon, many countries paid much closer attention to food production. When declining incomes reduced demand during the 1980s, the supply response accelerated. The downward trend in food self-sufficiency was halted, but not dramatically reversed as regional agriculture continues to require more land, water, fertilizer, machines, and labor just to keep up with population growth.

Regional policymakers have consistently linked food security with food self-sufficiency. Unfortunately, policies designed to achieve the latter have often had disastrous environmental consequences, in particular the overdrawing of groundwater. The Saudi case of heavily subsidizing wheat and alfalfa production may be the most notorious, but other examples abound. By offering farmers prices up to ten times the international market rate, Saudi farmers have dramatically depleted fossil aquifers without any significant long-run improvement in food security.

Geography, with its water constraints, trumps dreams of self-sufficiency, a fact that is becoming increasingly apparent. Consequently, there is no alternative to increased reliance on virtual water and food imports to meet future increased demands for food. The region is already importing an amount of virtual water roughly equal to the annual flow of the Nile River. Sustaining an adequate import level of food over the long term, however, poses daunting challenges.

To put it bluntly, the region must export in order to eat, creating major dilemmas for policymakers and threatening long-term stability. Strategic management requires significant policy changes to ensure robust non-food exports even though food imports fell in most countries during the past decade; serious challenges lie ahead. Most analysts believe that if—and it is a big if—World Trade Organization rules are implemented, the result will be a slight increase in world cereal prices, making it more difficult, not less, to use imports to feed populations. Relying on food imports means that countries of the region are increasingly dependent on the wider health of the global economy, something that they are nearly powerless to influence. Since the 1980s, there has been a strong trend toward greater economic openness and integration. History suggests that such trends might reverse. If, for example, increased rivalry among the world's major economic powers—the United States, the European Union, China, and Japan—increases during the coming decades, then the countries of the Middle East will be relying for food in an increasingly inhospitable international economy.

Halting Environmental Destruction

Long-term stability in the region—indeed, on the planet as a whole—is also threatened by environmental difficulties. Middle Easterners, like the rest of us, are beginning to pay for past and continued environmental neglect and abuse. In the Middle East, the costs of environmental neglect may be about 3 percent of regional GDP. Although the greatest problem is water, other problems are looming. Deforestation and soil erosion are particularly serious in parts of Algeria, Morocco, Tunisia, and Yemen. According to the FAO, over 60 percent of the cultivated lands in Morocco are severely degraded. In the heavily populated cities, air pollution adversely affects the health of approximately 40 percent of the population, or 60 million people. If business-as-usual policies prevail, the World Bank estimates that these numbers will rise to 160 million in the coming decade. Pollution impairs children's learning capacities, reduces labor productivity, and hurts tourism. Countries such as Egypt could be severely impacted by global warming, losing 60 percent of its cultivated area by 2050 as sea levels rise.

As educational levels rise, people around the world have become increasingly sensitive to environmental questions and have become much more demanding of environmental quality. It seems unlikely that Middle East residents will be any different. They will seek to organize NGOs and other modes of expressing their grievances to governments. But, too often, the current governance structures block such activities. Suppression of NGOs and restrictions on press freedoms guarantee the worsening of environmental problems. On the other hand, as the Nobel economist Amartya Sen has amply documented, freedom of the press and freedom of association are a public good.[27] The parallels with the former Soviet Union are obvious: unaccountable, corrupt governance is helping to destroy the region's natural resource base and ambient environmental quality.

Attracting Money for Investment

Improved management of all of these problems will require not only much improved governance, but also large sums of money. Finding and allocating resources present further challenges. World Bank estimates illustrate the sheer magnitude of funds needed:

- To create enough jobs to keep up with the growing labor force over the next 15 years, the following countries will require
  - Algeria: US$25 billion
  - Egypt   US$14 billion
  - Iran   US$31 billion
  - Morocco   US$30 billion
  - Tunisia   US$12 billion
- To meet the increasing demand for education in the region as a whole for the next 15 years may require US$26 billion per year. This means that spending on education needs to increase by about 20 percent.
- To maintain and improve its physical infrastructure, Egypt needs to spend US$2 billion per year, Jordan US$500 million per year.
- To clean up the environment may cost US$58–78 billion over the next 10 years.

So far, money on such a scale is nowhere in sight. Consider both domestic and foreign sources. Domestically, very large sums of money are held offshore by local residents; this is particularly true for the Mashreq and Gulf, less so for Morocco and Tunisia. Estimates are notoriously unreliable, but a reasonable guess is US$100–800 billion; United Nations Development Programme (UNDP) estimates the total sum at approximately US$500 billion. Foreign investors, with the exception of oil companies, shun the region. The Middle East captured less than 1 percent of global FDI during the 1980s and 1990s. In 2000, the share had dropped to 0.4 percent. The actual volume of FDI in 2003 fell to US$4.6 billion from US$5.8 billion the previous year.

The region's relatively closed capital markets provided some insulation from the turmoil of international financial markets during the Asian economic crisis of 1997. Those same closed markets also may have contributed to the observed decline in the efficiency of investment from 1975 to 2000. Poor government plausibly explains all three phenomena—large offshore holdings, the reluctance of foreign firms to invest in Near East South Asia (NESA), and the declining efficiency of investment. Investment, by its very nature, is a gamble on the future. Predictability of government rules reduces risks and, *ceteris paribus*, increases investment. Unaccountable government deters new local and foreign investors. Continual government micromanagement of economic activity reduces the efficiency of any investment that does occur.

Conclusion: Governance and Long-Run Instability

For the past 15 years or so, the conventional remedy to all of these problems has been the policies of the Washington consensus, now supplemented by a call for democracy. Even today, one of the Bush administration's justifications for invading Iraq is the claim that it would pave the way for market-led economies and stable democracies throughout the region. In this view, all good things go together; market economies and democratic politics can cut the Gordian knot from the many challenges sketched here.

It is easy to agree that better governance is a necessary condition for more successfully coping with these challenges. It is also reasonable to assert that better-designed markets could contribute to regional prosperity. And crafting more rules of accountability in the economic game will surely be necessary to stimulate the investment needed to provide jobs, supply exports, buy food, and save water.

However, difficulties bedevil both the older Washington consensus approach and the newer neo-Wilsonian enthusiasm for democracy as panacea. Take the Washington consensus. As a generalization, macroeconomic policy reform has been successful as measured by variables such as government deficits as a percentage of GDP, inflation rates, and real exchange rate overvaluation. By contrast, sectoral and microeconomic policy change has proceeded more slowly. The governance structures created after independence and during the oil boom of the 1970s—state controlled industries, extensive, arbitrary controls, and relative inward-looking trade pictures—remain in place today.

It may be true that more accountable governance—a more level playing field for investors, less intrusive government regulation, and other institutional changes—would greatly facilitate job-enhancing investment. But such institutional changes are precisely those that pose the greatest threats to established regimes. As John Waterbury has persuasively argued,[28] states remain in power precisely by exercising the kind of discretion over resource allocation that orthodox economists deplore. A more level playing field would most likely shift the balance between ruling and alternative, often pro-Islamist, elites.

Furthermore, it is quite unclear whether structural changes would make government better able to cope with the challenges enumerated earlier. Although such changes seem to provide the best management strategy, there is no guarantee of success. For example, investment might be deterred by other factors such as the fear of regional military conflict. As is so often the case with reform, the costs are immediate, visible, and painful, whereas the benefits are distant, putative, and uncertain.

Finally, the institutional changes that would be necessary can only come from within societies because such changes require a strong domestic constituency and legitimacy. It is delusional to think that outside intervention—especially military intervention—can improve the quality of governance. Our historical record has been poor,[29] and it is doubtful that the political economy of the region's countries provides a favorable environment for externally driven reform.

The iron law of unintended consequences has, once again, gripped the United States by the throat. Its actions in Iraq and elsewhere in the region undermine its own stated goals. Ironically, it is less, not more, likely that changes for coping more successfully with these long-run challenges will occur.

Studies of other regions—Latin America, Southern and Eastern Europe—suggest that three features are necessary for a transition to democratic rule.[30] A sufficiently large number of reformers within the existing regime must reach an agreement with moderate opponents of the regime. The reformers must persuade military/security hard-liners within the regime to cooperate with institutional change. And moderates must contain their allies, who are more radical opponents of the regime. If all three conditions are met, it will be possible for a large enough set of social actors to believe that both current power-wielders and their opponents have made a credible commitment to follow rules of the game in which defeat at the polls does not mean annihilation. The literature describes these coalitions and their fruits as "pacted transitions" because a tacit agreement or pact between moderates inside the government and in the opposition is necessary for a transition toward democratic rule.

Unfortunately, current developments discourage such pacts. The continued, increasingly brutal Israeli occupation of the West Bank and Gaza has not only destroyed whatever nascent democracy may have been emerging in Palestine, but has also greatly increased the nervousness of Arab security services and militaries everywhere. The fact that the world's sole superpower refuses to restrain the Israeli government ensures that the conflict will worsen. This situation, in addition to being a grave and ongoing human rights disaster, impedes the development of pacted transitions by encouraging both hard-line authoritarians within governments and extremists in opposition. Furthermore, the American invasion and occupation of Iraq not only alarms Arab military and security elites, but also strengthens the popular appeal of anti-democratic radicals such as al Qaeda.

The American reaction to the events of September 11, 2001, has also provided a poor environment for pacted transitions. From a political economy perspective, the main result of post-9/11 policy shifts is that any authoritarian who resolutely pursues violent enemies of the United States can depend upon

U.S. support. This only bolsters hard-liners within authoritarian regimes, making them less likely to seek accommodation with opposition elements.

Pious public rhetoric notwithstanding, the actions of the world's most powerful democracy block Arab transition to democracy because the United States does not really want it to happen. As Talleyrand famously remarked, "Nations do not have friends, they have interests." American interests in the Arab region have been defined to include: support for Israel, regardless of its occupation policies in the West Bank and Gaza; opposition to any single state having even short-run market power over oil prices; and opposition to any regime that might harbor *jihadi salafi* terrorists. As long as this is the case, U.S. policy actions, as opposed to rhetoric and marginal activities, are destined to undermine pacted transitions.

This is fundamentally the case because the opposition in nearly all Arab countries is dominated by the forces of political Islam. Would the United States really welcome a pacted transition in which moderate Muslim Brothers and reformist, patriotic generals in Egypt agreed to share power? Even assuming that the thorny internal problems of credible commitment to democratic rules of the game had been surmounted, wouldn't the United States oppose such a government—a government that would certainly vociferously oppose American policy in Palestine and Iraq? Given the current balance of forces in the world, wouldn't that opposition endanger the transition?

The situation in the Arab region today resembles that of Latin America during the Cold War. Then, American paranoia about Marxism undermined existing democracies and emerging pacted transitions. Internal and external obstacles to a democratic transition created and reinforced one another. The United States strengthened hard-liners—and, therefore, radicals in opposition—partly because it feared that Marxists would not play by the democratic rules of the game if they won elections. Moderates in opposition were weakened because radicals could argue that winning an election would be meaningless; hard-liners, with U.S. help, would engineer a coup to overthrow an elected opposition government. Substitute Islamist for Marxist, and you have a reasonable picture of the dynamics thwarting a transition to democracy in the Arab region. We live in a looking-glass world in which U.S. policies undermine the very stability it so hopes to promote.

This is hardly to argue that the United States is somehow solely responsible for this tragic situation. This chapter has tried to argue that the roots of long-term instability lie deep in the Middle East's own history. The current crisis of the region, which shows every sign of becoming more severe in the near term, is historically typical of transitions to modernity. The challenges to long-run stability emanating from demographic, economic, social, and natural resource difficulties are profound. Coping more successfully with them will certainly require improved governance. But better governance can only be forged domestically, by local people, using indigenous ideological and organizational resources. Attempts by outsiders to "fix things" only generate the cruel ironies in which Clio, the muse of history, so clearly delights.

NOTES

1. Bernard Lewis, *What Went Wrong? The Clash between Islam and Modernity in the Middle East* (New York: Perennial Press, 2003).
2. Isaiah Berlin, "Notes on Prejudice," *New York Review of Books*, October 18, 2001, 12.
3. Richard Bulliet, *The Case for Islamo-Christian Civilization* (New York: Columbia University Press, 2004).
4. See Karen Armstrong, *The Battle for God* (New York: Knopf, 2000), for a detailed analysis of the role of religious fundamentalism as the "midwife of modernity" for Jews, Christians, and Muslims. For a similar story about the United States, see James A. Morone, *Hellfire Nation: The Politics of Sin in American History* (New Haven: Yale University Press, 2003).
5. The year 2002 was the last year for which full data is available from the World Bank.
6. The region is hardly alone in this. A former president of the Royal Economic Society in the United Kingdom, Partha Dasgupta of Cambridge University, has estimated that accounting for even a portion of "wasting assets" of natural resources turns most Asian growth rates (except for China's) negative. Partha Dasgupta, "Valuing Objects and Evaluating Policies in Imperfect Economies," *Economic Journal*, no. 111 (May 2001), C1–C29.
7. See Kirin Chaudhry, Mick Moore, Paul Collier, and the vast literature on the "Dutch Disease."
8. Gary Hufbauer, "China, the United States and the Global Economy: Trends and Prospects in the Global Economy" (Washington, DC: Institute of International Economics, 1999).
9. John Waterbury and Alan Richards, *A Political Economy of the Middle East*, 2nd ed. (New York: Westview, 1997), chapters 7–11.
10. Primary enrollment completion rates also vary considerably. In 2000, 88% of age groups in the region finished school. In Egypt and Jordan more than 95% did so, whereas between 85 and 94% did in Algeria, Tunisia, Syria, and Iran, between half and three-quarters finished in Oman, UAE, Morocco, Saudi Arabia, Yemen, and Pakistan. Less than half finished in Sudan and Afghanistan. More discouragingly, completion rates in the Middle East and North Africa stagnated in the 1990s.
11. Bulliet, *The Case for Islamo-Christian Civilization*.
12. Willem van Eeghen, "Poverty in the Middle East and North Africa" (Washington, DC: World Bank, 1995).
13. Zafiris Tzannatos, "Social Protection in the Middle East and North Africa: A Review," Paper presented at the Mediterranean Development Forum (March 2000), 5; and Willem van Eeghen, and Kouassi Soman, "Poverty in the Middle East and North Africa," in Ishac Diwan and Karen Sirker, eds, *Voices from Marrakech: Towards Competitive and Caring Societies in the Middle East and North Africa* (1997). Selections from the Mediterranean Development Forum: Knowledge and Skills for Development in the Information Age, Marrakech, Morocco, May 12–17, 1997, at www.worldbank.org/mdf/mdf1/; and George F.Kossaifi, "Poverty in the Arab World: Toward a Critical Approach," Paper presented at the Mediterranean Development Forum, Marrakech, Morocco, September 3–6, 1998, 5.
14. van Eeghen and Soman, "Middle East and North Africa," 19.

15. On the basis of household survey data for 47 countries, Martin Ravallion computes a growth elasticity of poverty of 2.5: for every 1% increase in mean household income, the proportion of the population living on less than US$1 per day (at 1993 PPP value) declines by 2.5%; Ravallion, "Growth, Inequality, and Poverty: Looking Beyond Averages" (Washington DC: World Bank, 2000), 9.

16. Ford Foundation, "Poverty Report," Cairo, 1998, at www.fordfound.org/global/cairo/features.cfm; for Yemen, see Mohamed El-Maitamy, "Poverty and the Labor Market in Yemen," *ERF Forum*, vol. 8, no. 2 (October 2001), at www.erf.org.eg/nletter/oct01_11.asp; see also Max Rodenbeck, "An Emerging Agenda for Development in the Middle East and North Africa," IDRC, 2000, at www.idrc.ca/books/focus/930/ 12rodenb.html. From Jordan, see Radwan Shaban, Dina Abu-Ghaida, and Abdel-Salam Al-Naimat, "Poverty Alleviation in Jordan in the 1990s: Lessons for the Future," *ERF Forum*, vol. 8, no. 2 (October 2001), at www.erf.eg/nletter/ oct01_4.asp.

17. A.G. Ali and Ibrahim A. Elbadawi, "Poverty and the Labor Market in the Arab World: The Role of Inequality and Growth," Paper prepared for the Third Mediterranean Development Forum, Cairo, March 2000.

18. Hans Löfgren and Alan Richards, "Food Security and Economic Policy in the Middle East and North Africa," *Food and Agriculture in the Middle East: Research in Middle East Economics*, vol. 5 (New York: Elsevier Science, 2003), figure 1, 1–32.

19. Ibid., figure 5.

20. For a similar argument for Central Asia, see Ahmed Rashid, *Jihad: The Rise of Militant Islam in Central Asia* (New York: Yale University Press, 2002).

21. Selma Belaala, "Morocco: Slums Breed Jihad," *Le Monde Diplomatique*, English Language Edition (November 2004).

22. Ignacio Aamonet, "Le Maroc Indecis," *Le Monde Diplomatique* (July 2000), 12–13.

23. Ibid.

24. *Takfiris* brand all Muslims who disagree with them as *kufara'*, or infidels and apostates. This includes members of existing governments. Belaala, "Morocco."

25. Ibid.

26. A much more detailed argument along these lines, not limited to the Middle East, may be found in Alan Richards, "Coping with Water Scarcity: The Governance Challenge," Policy Paper #54 (San Diego: Institute on Global Conflict and Cooperation of the University of California, October 2002).

27. Amartya Sen, *Development as Freedom* (New York: Knopf, 1999).

28. John Waterbury, *Exposed to Innumerable Delusions: Public Enterprise and State Power in Egypt, India, Mexico, and Turkey* (New York: Cambridge University Press, 1993).

29. Sara Kasper and Minxin Pei, "Lessons from the Past: The American Record in Nation-Building" (Washington: Carnegie Endowment for International Peace, April 2003).

30. Adam Przeworski, *Democracy and the Market: Political and Economic Reforms in Eastern Europe and Latin America* (Cambridge: Cambridge University Press, 1991).

3

Reforming the Rentier State: The Imperatives for Change in the Gulf

Robert Looney

On a journey through the Kingdom, I heard the word reform everywhere I went, though no one seemed to agree on exactly what it meant.

—Elizabeth Rubin[1]

Introduction

An economic irony that is gaining increasing attention is the "resource curse" effect, whereby many of the poorest and most troubled states in the developing world have paradoxically the highest levels of natural wealth.[2] In fact, a rapidly growing body of literature suggests that resource wealth itself, especially where it accounts for the bulk of government revenues, as in the case of the so-called rentier states,[3] may harm a country's prospects for development. Country growth data bear this out: rentier states, with greater natural resource wealth, tend to grow more slowly than their resource-poor counterparts.[4]

This "rentier state" effect is beginning to manifest itself in what are commonly thought of as some of the wealthiest regions of the world.[5] In the Persian Gulf, for example, relatively stable levels of oil production and flat oil revenues, combined with an unanticipated rapid increase in population, have resulted in declining per capita income in Saudi Arabia. At the height of the oil boom in the 1980s, Saudi Arabia's per capita income was around US$17,000. By 2003 this figure had declined to about US$8,200.

The Saudi Arabian example is not unique. The unfortunate fact is that most oil-rich developing countries are underperformers across a whole spectrum of economic, social, political, and governance standards. Large windfall gains associated with a rapid increase in oil prices have been a particular problem in that they appear to create severe distortions in the working of the economy and the political system with strongly negative sociopolitical consequences. In countries as diverse as Iran, Nigeria, Venezuela, and Indonesia, the combination of state inefficiency and revenue windfalls has proved overwhelming, undermining even the best efforts to develop each country's non-oil economy, eradicate poverty, and improve living standards for broad-based segments of the population.

There is still great controversy over the best way to escape the rentier syndrome. For some analysts, a microeconomic approach stressing increased competition, privatization, and greater incentives for risktaking is key. For others, the establishment of supporting macroeconomic institutions, such as a sound financial system and efficient, equitable tax systems, play a central role. Others focus on the necessity of developing stable and effective macroeconomic policies—the efficient timing and focus of fiscal and monetary policies. In addition, a growing school of thought suggests that governance issues predominate. The failure of the rentier states to eliminate corruption while developing responsive government institutions is the main factor accounting for poor economic performance in the rentier states.

A related controversy surrounds the extent to which useful generalizations can be made about the rentier economies. Although all share a number of common structural conditions, are these similar enough to form an economic environment that responds predictably to a common set of policy initiatives? Or is each rentier economy likely to have unique features to the extent that require a tailor-made economic program for achieving, growth, diversification, and integration into the global economy?

This chapter examines these issues from the perspective of the two largest rentier states in the Gulf—Saudi Arabia and Iran. What do these economies share in common? What are their chief differences? Which has made the most progress to date in transitioning away from the rentier state syndrome? What tasks lay before them in their integration to the world economy? In particular, which area of reforms appear critical for successful transition to a more normal economy capable of generating self-sustained growth independent of conditions in the oil markets? Based on the answers to these questions, a final section examines the implications for Iraq.

RENTIER MALAISE

The recent oil price increases have given both Saudi Arabia and Iran a temporary reprieve from their longer-run economic dilemmas. Both countries are experiencing transitions that are complex and decisive for their futures. Both are facing a dual set of problems: on the one hand, those of a developing country and, on the other, those of a rentier economy. Both possess some of the main characteristics of a developing country: a predominantly young population and an economy mainly focused on the primary sector—oil for both, with Iran having, in addition, a large agricultural sector.

The rentier nature of both economies is no less evident: revenues derived from oil represent the bulk of public and external revenues. In essence, these revenues enable the governments in each country to dominate the private sector and shift resources toward activities not necessarily the most productive economically or desirable from the point of view of the population at large. In short, the collection and subsequent redistribution of oil revenues takes on both an economic and political dimension. Both economies are faced with dual challenges: first, transforming the rentier economy into a diversified economy through encouraging expansion in the non-oil private sector areas of activity and, second, implementing the political reforms necessary for establishing institutions and governance structures capable of creating an environment conducive to enabling non-oil activities to operate on a sustained basis.

Saudi Arabia

Within this context, Saudi Arabia is currently facing a number of challenges. The first problem involves attaining and maintaining economic growth rates that are least sufficient to keep pace with the rise in population. For Saudi Arabia, low economic growth has become a chronic problem (see table 3.1). Gross domestic product (GDP) increased by only 1.6 percent between 1990 and 2000, whereas growth in the country's population grew at an annual rate of 2.7 percent during that period, thus producing a declining trend in per capita income.[6]

This low rate of growth cannot be attributed to a lack of capital formation. In fact, the rate of investment is relatively high in Saudi Arabia. The Sixth Development Plan (1995–2000), for instance, envisaged a total capital of around 472 billion riyals ($125.8 billion), including nearly 212.7 billion riyals ($56.7 billion) from the private sector. It had also targeted an economic growth rate of 3.8 percent over the plan period. By the end of the plan, actual investment increased by around 2 percent to 481 billion riyals ($128.2 billion) including nearly 292 billion riyals ($77.8 billion) from the private sector, an increase of around 37 percent over the projected level.[7]

Thus, even though the plan overachieved in terms of investment, it underachieved in terms of what really counts: real economic growth. The ineffectiveness of investment to sustain growth appears to be structural, stemming in part from a weakening of the linkage between public and private expenditures together with a decline in the ability of public expenditures to stimulate real output.[8] Given the inability of the public sector to directly stimulate real

Table 3.1 Saudi Arabia: GDP growth, 1960–2002 (average annual rate of growth)

GDP measure	1960–2002	1970–2002	1980–2002
Oil	3.8	2.3	−0.9
Private	8.8	8.9	2.0
Public	5.9	5.1	3.0
Total	5.7	4.7	1.0
Non-oil	7.4	7.1	2.3

Note: Compiled from data from the Saudi Arabian Monetary Agency. Raw data are in millions of 1999 Riyals.

non-oil output, all of the pressure to provide expanded employment opportunities, jobs, and output is now placed on the private sector.

Job creation is then the second major problem facing the region. Ironically,
even though the Saudi economy is heavily dependent on foreign workers
(4.6 million or 71 percent of the country's workforce), the unemployment rate
among Saudis is 8.2 percent, reaching 32 percent among younger workers.

The third challenge relates to maintaining the pace of economic reforms.
Here the Saudis have initiated a series of measures designed to attract foreign
investment, deregulate many key industries, and liberalize the economy to qualify
for membership in the World Trade Organization (WTO) as well as to facilitate
further economic integration with the country's fellow GCC members.

If carried out successfully, economic reforms should remove many of the
constraints currently impeding growth and job creation in the private sector.
As discussed below, this is critical, given the current inability of public expenditures to perform this task. The country's three main challenges—restoring
rates of growth above that of the population, expanding job creation, and
implementing a comprehensive reform package—appear to be relatively
compatible. Good progress in the reform area should assure higher rates of
economic growth and, through that, more jobs. But will they be jobs for Saudis?
Apparently, the government is not confident this will be the case because it is
simultaneously broadening and expanding its Saudization program. The
Saudi government appears to feel that if jobs cannot be created through high
rates of investment, then they must be forced through quotas.

Iran

Iran faces a similar set of challenges. Although the country's growth has not
decelerated (see table 3.2) to the extent found in Saudi Arabia, there are several troubling trends.[9] During 1960–76, Iran enjoyed one of the fastest
growth rates in the world. The economy grew at an average rate of 9.8 percent in real terms and real per capita income growth averaged 7 percent.

This growth trend was reversed during 1977–88, reflecting the aftereffects
of the 1979 revolution, the eight-year war with Iraq, sanctions and international isolation, the increased state dominance of the economy, and plummet-
ing oil output and revenue. In 1988, oil production was only 36 percent of its

Table 3.2 Iran: Average sectoral growth, 1960–2002

Period	1960–76	1977–88	1989–2002	1960–2002
Agriculture	4.6	3.9	4.1	4.2
Oil and Gas	10.0	−8.6	2.5	2.4
Industries and Mines	14.0	−1.3	7.3	7.6
Services	11.1	−1.9	4.8	5.4
Non-oil GDP growth	10.1	−0.5	5.0	5.5
GDP	9.8	−2.4	4.7	4.6

Source: Islamic Republic of Iran—Selected Issues (Washington: JMF, September 2004), 1.

level in 1976 and oil prices were 40 percent lower in real terms. This resulted in a negative real GDP growth of 2.4 percent per annum. Excluding oil output, non-oil GDP also declined, averaging a fall of 0.5 percent per annum.

With the reconstruction effort and partial recovery in oil output, real economic growth recovered during 1989–2002, averaging 4.7 percent per annum. This period, however, was marked by sharp fluctuations in the growth pattern as the postwar economic boom (1989–2002) was followed by the stagnation of 1993–94 when the economy was hit by lower oil prices, lack of external financing, and economic sanctions. The ensuing severe debt crisis, together with inappropriate macroeconomic policies, had an adverse impact on growth, which hovered around 3.6 percent during 1995–2000.

In the more recent period (2000–03), real GDP growth has increased to 6 percent due to significance progress in economic reforms: exchange rate unification, trade liberalization, opening up to foreign direct investment (FDI), and financial sector liberalization. Higher oil prices and expansionary monetary and fiscal policies have also contributed to the country's recent economic recovery.

As is the case with Saudi Arabia, growing unemployment is becoming a major social and political problem. During the 1996–2000 period, 693,000 new workers entered the labor market whereas only 296,000 jobs were created. The result is a current rate of unemployment of over 20 percent of the active population. This unemployment mainly affects the young urban population. According to the World Bank, the creation of between 700,000 to 800,000 new jobs each year (thereby achieving unemployment rate stability) would require an annual growth of the economy of at least 6 percent per annum.

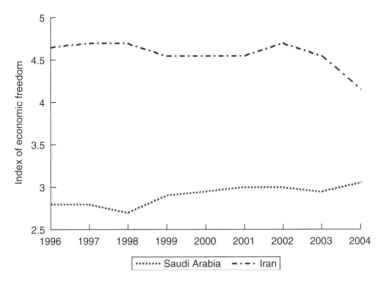

Figure 3.1   Economic freedom in Saudi Arabia and Iran.

Iran is attempting to put more flexibility and job creating capacity into its economy through a series of reforms. Although some progress has occurred in the last several years, the country still lags considerably behind Saudi Arabia in many critical areas. Using the aggregate economic freedom index discussed below (where higher numbers signify lower levels of freedom), it is interesting to note a general backsliding in Saudi reform efforts, whereas those in Iran appear to be cautiously moving ahead (see figure 3.1).

Although notable differences exist, Saudi Arabia and Iran appear to share a number of common economic characteristics and face a set of similar challenges. In recent years many of these problems seem to have intensified, perhaps because the pace of population growth, globalization, and technological change are outpacing the ability of the rentier system to effectively resolve new challenges as they arise.

COMMONALITIES ASSOCIATED WITH OIL

In attempting to explain the inability of rentier economies to sustain steady expansions in their economies, most researchers have focused on their most apparent defining features: the manner in which oil revenues accrue to the government and the subsequent impacts the utilization of these revenues have on economic activity. In this regard, a large literature has spawned in recent years attempting to clarify some of the complex and negative transmission mechanisms associated with oil revenues, especially those that occur during periods of rapidly rising petroleum prices.[10] There are many competing explanations, but they are not necessarily mutually exclusive.[11] They may reinforce each other, resulting in a slowing of economic growth and productivity. In extreme cases, the non-oil sector of the economy even begins to contract.

One way to understand the uniqueness of the rentier state is to contrast its dynamics to that of a normal economy, known as the production state (see table 3.3). Because the rentier state is not based on broad-based production, its main dynamic stems from the forces set in motion by the distribution of revenues. Several mechanisms associated with this expenditure help define the rentier state's rather unique development pattern.

Table 3.3 Rentier or allocative versus non-rentier or production states

Production states	Rentier states
State based on extractive capability and economic growth	State based on rent
Representational pressures and political conflict over economic policy	Economic policies do not create same degrees of political conflict or representational pressures Spends without taxing
Unequal distribution of wealth leads to pressures for redistribution of change in status quo	Distribution of rent-generated wealth creates less pressure to change status quo

The Dutch Disease Effect

The mechanism that has probably gained the most attention in academic circles is the so-called Dutch Disease. This phenomenon has two effects both of which should concern postwar Iraq. The first focuses narrowly on the exchange rate. In technical terms, the Dutch Disease refers to the potentially adverse effects of a booming export sector on the performance of other exports and of industries competing against imports. These effects work through a strengthening (appreciation) of the exporting country's exchange rate. In the 1960s, the Netherlands experienced a vast increase in its wealth after discovering large natural gas deposits in the North Sea. Unexpectedly, this seemingly positive development had serious repercussions on important segments of the country's economy, as the Dutch guilder became stronger (a 30 percent appreciation), making Dutch non-oil exports less competitive. The exchange rate appreciation resulting from a ramp-up of oil exports is likely to reduce the profitability and competitiveness of traditional agricultural exports. It would also encourage imports of food and raw materials, which may compete with domestic production. It is also likely to discourage the emergence of new manufacturing exports, essential for the successful diversification of the economy. The expansion of Iranian oil export earnings in the 1970s provides a good example of these effects.[12]

The second effect of concern is that, during the modernization and expansion of the oil sector, the rest of the economy may be crowded out from access to key factor inputs. That is, the oil sector, with its financial resources, would preempt these resources, weakening the ability of the private sector to invest and diversify.

The Dutch Disease also tends to result in increased poverty, but here the links are more difficult to establish.[13] The price distortions created by the appreciating exchange rate can be seen as a tax on exports, and, if the country has a trade pattern based on comparative advantage, this would likely involve labor-intensive activities. Rates of economic growth in these areas would decline, inhibiting any tendency for benefits of oil-based expenditures to "trickle down." Under these circumstances, the economy would likely become more vulnerable to external shocks from which the poor cannot protect themselves. Finally, the inflation stemming from expanded oil-financed expenditures would, again, likely harm the poor disproportionately.

Although the disease is generally associated with a natural resource discovery, it can occur from any development that results in a large inflow of foreign currency, including a sharp surge in natural resource prices, foreign assistance, and FDI, all of which are distinct future possibilities for a country such as Iraq.

The Rentier Society/Authoritarian Effect

The second dimension of negative oil-related effects has to do with governmental decision-making. The relatively easy availability of foreign exchange arising from large-scale oil exports is likely to take the pressure off necessary institutional and other policy changes. It also can lead to the development of a rentier society where there is often a disconnect between effort and reward. A common result is the creation of a dualistic economy where a vibrant oil and gas sector coexists with a weak, poorly performing non-oil economy.

Along these lines, Halliday has noted that

> the uniqueness of oil resides . . . in the peculiar form of payment resulting from it, a rent to producer states that does not entail the forward and backward linkages within the local economy that are characteristic of other primary production in the third world. The collection of this "rent" enables the producer state, and those controlling it, to amass enormous sums of money without engaging in any form of production; it is this which has generated such major social tensions within the producer states. These tensions include growing income inequality, rampant corruption in the state, grandiose development projects, and the neglect of productive activity and skills, especially in agriculture.[14]

Because oil infrastructure can be controlled easily by a few, it leads to a concentration of political power. Thus, rentier states tend to be authoritarian (as shown in table 3.4). There are several reasons for the political system to evolve in this direction.[15] First, an oil-rich government can provide vast social services without taxing the public. Because there's no taxation, there's less demand for representation. Rentier governments also tend to buy off the opposition and amass large internal security forces capable of crushing dissent. Second, the skewed development of oil-dependent states means that they lack the working- and middle-class citizens, who historically have been a force pushing for democracy. In short, whereas oil exporters fall into a number of political categories, lack of accountability and transparency is a common characteristic of the group. Again, these patterns are readily apparent when, as noted earlier, comparisons are made with so-called production economies (table 3.2). The net effect of these factors has led (to one degree or another) to corruption, mismanagement, and a colossal waste of resources.

Table 3.4 Political classification of oil exporters

Factional democracy
  Political features
    Government and parties often unstable relative to interest groups
    Political support gained through clientelistic ties and patronage
    Wide social disparities, lack of consensus
    Politicized bureaucracy and judicial system

  Institutional implications
    Short policy horizon
    Policy instability, nontransparency, high transaction costs
    Strong state role in production
    Strong interests attached directly to state expenditures

  Economic implications
    Saving very difficult
    Pro-cyclical expenditure—instability

Continued

Table 3.4 Continued

Rents transferred to different interests and public through subsidies,
   policy distortions, and public employment

Main Examples
   Ecuador, Venezuela, Colombia

Paternalistic autocracy
   Political features
      Stable government, legitimacy originally from traditional role,
         maintained through rent distribution
      Strong cultural elements of consensus, clientelistic and nationalistic
      Bureaucracy provides both services and public employment

   Institutional implications
      Long horizon
      Policy stability, nontransparency
      Low Competitiveness, high transaction costs
      Strong state role in reduction
      Strong interests attached directly to state expenditures
      Weak private sector

   Economic implications
      Procyclical expenditure, mixed success with stabilization
      Risk of unsustainable long-term spending trajectory leading to
         political crisis
      Little economic diversification

   Main examples
      Saudi Arabia, Kuwait, Qatar, UAE, Oman

Political classification of oil exporters
   Political features
      Stable government, legitimized by development
      Social range of consensus toward development
      Constituency in non-oil traded sectors
      Insulated technocracy

   Institutional Implications
      Long horizon
      Policy stability, nontransparency
      Drive for competitiveness, low transaction costs
      Strong constituency for stabilization and fiscal restraining

   Economic implications
      Expenditure smoothing stabilization
      State investment complementary to competitive private sector
      Active exchange rate management to limit Dutch Disease

   Main examples
      Nigeria (elected governments), Indonesia

Predatory autocracy
   Political features
      Unstable government, legitimized by military force
      Lack of consensus-building mechanisms
      Bureaucracy exists as mechanism of rent capture and distribution
      Corrupt judicial system
      Little or no civic counterweight

   Institutional implications
      Short horizon

Continued

Table 3.4 Continued

Policy instability, no transparency
Low competitiveness, high transaction costs
Spending interests strong vis-à-vis private interests or prostabilization interests
Economic implications
No saving
High procyclical expenditure
Very high government consumption, rate absorption by elites through petty corruption and patronage, capital flight
Main examples
Nigeria (military governments), Iraq

Source: Eifert, Gelb, and Tallroth, 2003.

Whereas Saudi Arabia's political system clearly falls in the "paternalistic autocracy" group, Iran's is rather unique and hence more difficult to characterize. The Iranian state appears to be guided by a "benevolent neutrality" in its relations with citizens where any modification (in the form of decreases in subsidies, for example) or reduction in living standards has a major political impact. These forces are offset to a certain degree by an additional element ensuring the cohesion of the system: a strong ideological system (Shi'ite Islam) encompassing all economic and political spheres, both at the public and private level.[16]

The Fiscal Uncertainty Effect

The final dimension of oil-related problems stems from the fiscal implications of fluctuating and uncertain revenues. Although one cannot say that oil revenues create a certain political system, it is a fact that, for the most part, the political systems adopted by most of the oil-exporting countries are short-sighted and pursue a pro-cyclical stabilization policy. The net effect is to intensify the detrimental impact that fluctuations in oil prices have on the domestic economy.

Oil-exporting countries' budgetary patterns tend to be an extreme version of the fiscal rules used in many developing countries facing fluctuating revenues. Many of these countries initiate expanded capital expenditures during periods of rising revenues on the assumption that these revenues are sustainable. When revenues decline, budgetary cuts occur, but in a fairly predictable manner.[17] In general, social sectors are less vulnerable to cuts than defense and administration, which, in turn, are considerably less vulnerable than production and infrastructure.[18] Of course, these patterns can be affected by the willingness of countries to assume increased governmental debt in an attempt to maintain programs during periods of declining revenues. Another complicating factor, especially for Middle Eastern oil exporters, is their large budgetary commitment to defense expenditures. These factors combine to produce a budgetary pattern typified by Saudi Arabia, a country that consistently allocates over 30 percent of its budget to defense.

Budgetary Patterns in Saudi Arabia

As is well known, Saudi Arabia has experienced ongoing budget difficulties since the mid-1980s. Growing deficits have been the norm with non-oil revenues unable to pick up the slack during periods of falling oil revenues. What is less well known is that the composition of public expenditures has been undergoing some profound changes during this period. Of particular significance is the fact that economic expenditures (economic services, transport and communications, and infrastructure) have declined steadily since 1980, from around 25 percent of the budget at that time to a little over 7 percent by 2003.[19] Social expenditures (human resource development and health) have been the major beneficiaries of the decline in economic allocations more than doubling their share of the budget over the period 1979–2003 (from 13 percent to nearly 32 percent of total expenditures). As noted, defense remains the largest budgetary item, fluctuating in the 35–40 percent range in the period after 1988 (figure 3.2).

Public expenditures (administration, loans, and subsidies) have shown the most erratic pattern. After fluctuating at around 35 percent of the budget between 1979 and 1994, they fell sharply to less than 20 percent in 1999 only to increase to about 27 percent in 2003. The sharp decline in public expenditures in the early-to-mid-1990s stemmed, in part, from a sharp cutback in the government's loan programs.

The patterns described are suggestive of an environment in which the public sector is contracting in many areas. This is especially the case with regard to economic expenditures and other activities directly supportive of the private sector. Budgetary shifts away from economic categories are the

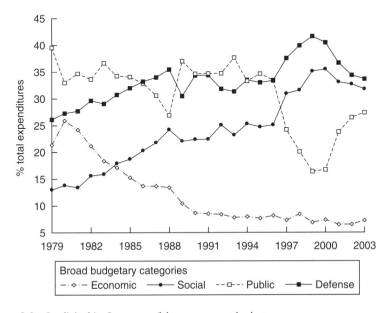

Figure 3.2   Saudi Arabia: Structure of the government budget.

most obvious manifestation of this phenomenon. Falling shares of investment relative to non-oil output are also indicative of Saudi Arabia's capital
stock and productive expenditures playing much less of a stimulating role as
in the unbalanced growth strategy implicit in the early oil-boom years.[20]

More subtle shifts in policy or policy effectiveness can only be inferred
from a more detailed analysis of budgetary patterns and their impacts. Of particular importance are the linkages between public and private sector expenditures (output) on non-oil production and investment. In this regard, a
common theme in the development literature is that economic processes in
oil-based countries become more complex as these economies mature and
begin to diversify away from a complete reliance on oil revenues and associated public sector expenditures. There is clear evidence that this process is well
advanced in Saudi Arabia.[21] With regard to the economy's leading productive
sectors, several patterns stand out:[22]

(1) Growth in the agricultural and mining sectors became more dependent
    on private expenditures and less dependent on public expenditures, espe-
    cially during the 1975–2001 period.
(2) The non-oil manufacturing sector has become almost completely
    dependent on private sector expenditures, with strong linkages to these
    expenditures in both the short and longer term. In contrast, public sec-
    tor expenditures now have little stimulating effects on the sector.
(3) Traditionally the wholesale and retail trade sectors have been dependent
    on both public and private sector expenditures. Whereas this remains the
    case for private sector expenditures, public sector expenditures currently
    have only a short-run transitory effect on the sector's output.
(4) In a major change from earlier periods, output in the construction sector
    is no longer dependent on public expenditures. Instead, output in this
    sector now depends primarily on the long-term pattern of private sector
    expenditures.
(5) Private expenditures have strengthened their linkages to the housing sec-
    tor as well as to transport, storage, and communications sectors.
    Although output in this sector is still responsive to public sector expen-
    ditures, this linkage has weakened over time.
(6) Other financial activities are dependent on private expenditures.
    However with regard to public expenditures, this effect is confined to
    the longer-term effects of governmental expenditures.
(7) Finally, linkages between private expenditures and the service sector
    (community, social, and personal services) have strengthened consider-
    ably in recent years. This sector's links to public sector expenditures have
    also weakened.

In sum, the pattern found here is one of strengthening linkages between
private sector expenditures and sectoral output. At the same time, the ability
of public sector expenditures to provide a positive stimulus to output has
weakened considerably. In fact, in several key sectors, including non-oil

manufacturing and construction, public sector expenditures no longer play a role in affecting output growth. In other areas, such as agriculture, mining, trade, and services, public expenditures may only play a minor role in the overall growth of these areas of activity.

The question that immediately arises concerns the factors responsible for the deterioration in links between government expenditures and, for all practical purposes, the rest of the economy. Given the fall in the relative share of government expenditures in such areas as non-oil GDP, diminishing returns can no doubt be ruled out. The major changes in the composition of the government's budget noted above would appear to be a more likely source of the decline in the strength of public sector linkages.

Again, in aggregating the various sections of the government's budget into four main categories (social expenditures, economic expenditures, public expenditures, and defense), several interesting statistical patterns emerge that may help to explain the effect of public expenditures on the non-oil private sector. First, looking at the links between government revenues and expenditures, economic expenditures, public expenditures, and defense spending reveals a similar pattern: each expands in the short run with increased government revenues (of course, they would also contract with falling revenues). This pattern carries over into the longer term with each category of expenditure maintaining a stable relationship with revenues.[23]

On the other hand, there do not appear to be any links, either short or long term, between revenues and social expenditures. As noted, this category has been the fastest growing category of expenditures. More importantly, it, along with defense, now dominates the government budget. The fact that the expansion in social expenditures appears to be independent of the government's revenue position suggests that either these allocations receive a much higher priority over other expenditures and/or that the government is willing to incur large deficits to fund these programs. No doubt their rather steady increase until the last several years means that they have played a rather limited role in fiscal macroeconomic stabilization.

A closer look at social expenditures reveals that their budgetary share has grown largely at the expense of several economic sections of the budget, namely transport, communications, and direct economic allocations. Short run increases in social expenditures had a negligible impact on their budgetary shares. However, the more fundamental long-term impact was clearly negative. The only economic category not adversely affected was infrastructure, where social expenditures did not appear to affect this categories' budgetary share in either the short or longer term. The dramatic decline in the budgetary share of subsidies may be attributed in part to the growth of social expenditures. Both the short- and long-term impacts of expanded social expenditures reduced the proportion of the budget allocated to subsidies.

Interestingly, defense allocations did not suffer at the hands of social expenditures.[24] Short-run increases in the budgetary share going to social categories actually increased the share of the budget controlled by defense. The same was true for allocations to the municipalities. Governmental loans were the only budgetary subcategory unaffected by the expansion of social expenditures. The contraction of this category apparently was due, in part, to a shift in governmental priorities rather than a direct allocation conflict with social expenditures.

In short, the high priority given to social expenditures, followed by defense together with limited oil revenues during most of this period, resulted in a tremendous contraction in the public sector's allocation to economic services of various types.

Patterns of Productivity and Growth

The three dimensions of the "Paradox of Plenty"—Dutch Disease, rentier state, and fiscal uncertainty—have combined to produce, in part, the dismal performance of rentier states noted earlier. This pattern has been confirmed in a recent study examining the sources of economic growth in various parts of the world.[25] At issue is how much of the growth in output per worker is associated with growth in physical and human capital per worker and how it can be attributed to other factors, such as technological change. This latter category is often referred to in the literature as total factor productivity (TFP).[26]

The importance of TFP stems from the fact that, in its absence, economic growth eventually slows and stagnates due to diminishing returns to capital formation. Within this context, there are striking differences in the manner in which oil and non-oil economies grow (see table 3.5):

(1) Looking at the Middle East as a whole, oil exporters have sustained an average output growth of 0.83 percent. Associated with this expansion has been a growth in physical capital of 2.24 percent and in human capital of 1.96 percent.

(2) These growth rates occurred in an environment characterized by negative growth in total factor productivity per worker of 1.22 percent.

(3) The high negative rates of growth of TFP for the major oil exporters is particularly telling: Iraq (-1.92), Oman (-2.28), Saudi Arabia (-2.99), Iran (-0.95), and UAE (-2.89).

(4) In contrast, non-oil exporters in the Middle East grew about twice as fast (1.59 versus 0.83) and invested at a rate about twice that of the oil exporters (4.94 versus 2.24). And, if Yemen, an oil producer, is omitted, they had less of a decline in TFP (-0.47 versus -1.22). Noteworthy here are the positive TFPs achieved by the major economies: Egypt (0.19), Israel (0.10), Morocco (0.02), and Tunisia (0.15).

(5) Oil exporters allocated a proportionate amount of resources to human capital (1.96 percent versus 1.86 percent for the non-oil producers).

(6) Other oil exporters experienced similar patterns with stagnant growth (0.07 percent) and total factor productivity per worker declining by 1.74 percent per annum. This is in sharp contrast to an average growth in TFP per worker of 0.84 in Southern Europe.

Table 3.5 Average growth of output and input by country

	First year	Output	Capital	Growth rate per worker Human capital	TFP
Middle East					
Oil exporters					
Algeria	1948	3.00	3.04	1.85	0.76
Iran	1956	1.56	3.02	2.26	−0.95
Iraq	1950	1.14	5.51	1.86	−1.92
Kuwait	1980	−0.35	−4.58	1.55	0.12
Libya	1960	3.68	4.99	2.47	0.38
Oman	1970	0.67	4.63	2.11	−2.28
Saudi Arabia	1960	0.70	7.73	1.70	−2.99
UAE	1980	−3.74	−6.42	1.89	−2.89
Average		0.83	2.24	1.96	−1.22
Non-oil exporters					
Egypt	1917	2.00	2.63	1.14	0.19
Israel	1948	3.10	4.64	2.20	0.10
Jordan	1960	1.36	4.16	1.61	−1.09
Morocco	1951	1.77	2.54	1.36	0.02
Syria	1953	0.76	4.37	2.25	−2.19
Tunisia	1956	2.61	2.99	2.20	0.15
Yemen	1970	−0.44	13.24	2.27	−6.33
Average		1.59	4.94	1.86	−1.31
Other oil exporters					
Norway	1855	2.05	2.68	0.89	0.57
Nigeria	1952	0.08	3.76	1.12	−1.91
Venezuela	1936	0.55	2.41	1.46	−1.22
Ecuador	1950	1.15	3.32	2.13	−1.36
Indonesia	1951	1.76	4.21	1.72	−0.78
Russia	1917	1.98	3.72	1.74	−0.41
Azerbaijan	1990	−6.40	−4.41	2.92	−6.90
Kazakhstan	1990	−0.65	−1.24	2.47	−1.89
Average		0.07	1.81	1.81	−1.74
Southern european					
Cyprus	1950	6.03	6.66	1.81	2.62
Greece	1910	2.85	3.41	1.24	0.89
Italy	1861	1.79	2.57	0.96	0.30
Portugal	1849	1.97	2.46	0.75	0.65
Spain	1857	1.34	1.77	0.82	0.21
Turkey	1935	1.99	2.12	1.36	0.38
Average		2.66	3.17	1.16	0.84

Source: Adapted from Scott L. Baier, Gerald Dwyer, and Robert Tamura, "How Important Are Capital and Total Factor Productivity for Growth, April 2002, at www.vanderbilt.edu/Econ/faculty/Crucini/tamura.pdf

Total Factor Productivity in Iran

A more detailed examination of TFP in Iran sheds further light on possible TFP patterns over time.[27] Also illustrated are several measurement problems often encountered in exercises of this type. Specifically, depending on the manner in which increased schooling is allocated, one gets two estimates of TFP in Iran, each with a particular bias. The noninclusion of the effect of increased schooling on the productivity of the labor force results (as shown in table 3.6) in appositive contribution of TFP to growth during the 1969–2002 period (because changes in the quality of the labor force are implicitly included in TFP). Using an alternative specification assuming human capital increases linearly with the average years of schooling, the contribution of TFP to growth becomes negative (-1.2 percent on average during the 1960–2002 period).

Under both accounting exercises, the contribution of TFP to growth is positive during the high growth subperiod of 1960–76 and becomes negative during the political turmoil and war period of 1977–78. This result points to the critical importance of political and external developments for Iran's economic growth. The results differ in the growth accounting for 1989–2002. Under the first specification, in which human capital equals raw labor, the contribution of TFP to growth is positive. On the other hand, if we assume a linear effect of education to human capital, the contribution of TFP becomes negative. As the IMF notes,[28] a more realistic TFP estimate may lie between these two extreme cases. In particular, it is likely there was a very small (or even negative) contribution of TFP to growth during the 1989–2002 subperiod due to slow progress in structural reforms and increased macroeconomic instability.

If Iran, Saudi Arabia, and the other rentier states want to achieve better economic performance, their governments will have to create an environment that encourages and forces sustained levels of positive TFP. Again, it is unlikely this has happened on a sustained basis in the oil economies outside of Norway.

Table 3.6 Iran: Sources of economic growth, 1960–2002

Period	Average growth rate	Contribution of		
		Capital	Raw labor	TFP
1960–76	9.8	3.9	1.2	4.7
1977–88	−2.4	1.7	1.4	−5.5
1989–2002	4.7	2.3	1.5	1.0
1960–2002	4.6	2.1	1.4	1.1
		Capital	Human capital	TFP
1960–76	9.8	3.9	2.7	3.2
1977–88	−2.4	1.7	5.5	−9.6
1989–2002	4.7	2.3	4.3	−1.8
1960–2002	4.6	2.1	3.7	−1.2

Source: *Islamic Republic of Iran—Selected Issues* (Washington: International Monetary Fund, September 2004), 13–14.

COMMONALITY IN REFORM EFFORTS

There is still great controversy over the best way to stimulate TFP. For some analysts, increased competition, privatization, and greater incentives for risk-taking are key.[29] For others, the establishment of supporting institutions (i.e., an independent central bank, a sound financial system, and efficient, equitable tax systems) play a central role.[30] Both of these strategies are critically dependent on the progress made in economic reforms (economic freedom) and improved governance.

Economic Freedom

Both the Heritage Foundation/Wall Street Journal's *Index of Economic Freedom*,[31] and the Fraser Institute's *Economic Freedom of the World*[32] provide good measures of the relative progress made by countries in moving to a deregulated, limited government, free-market environment. Because the Heritage Foundation data set included more of the Middle Eastern countries, it was used for the analysis that follows. The Heritage Index reflects the absence of government constraint or coercion on the production, distribution, or consumption of goods and services. Stripped to its essentials, economic freedom is concerned with property rights and choice. To measure economic freedom the Heritage Foundation/Wall Street Journal index takes ten different factors into account:

- Trade policy
- Fiscal burden of government
- Government intervention in the economy
- Monetary policy
- Banking and finance
- Capital flows and foreign investment
- Wages and prices
- Property rights
- Regulation
- Informal market.

Implied in these measures is the notion that economic freedom also requires governments to refrain from many activities. They must refrain from actions that interfere with personal choice, voluntary exchange, and the freedom to enter and compete in labor and product markets. Economic freedom is reduced when taxes, government expenditures, and regulations are substituted for personal choice, voluntary exchange, and market coordination. Restrictions that limit entry into occupations and business activities also retard economic freedom.

The index provides a framework for assessing progress toward a modern market economy integrated into the global economy: how open countries are to competition, the degree of state intervention in the economy (whether through taxation, spending, or overregulation), and the strength and independence of a country's judiciary to enforce rules and protect private property. Some countries may have freedom in all factors; others may have freedom in just a few. One of the most important findings of research carried out using the index is that economic freedom is required in all aspects of economic life. Countries must score well in all ten of the factors in order to improve their economic efficiency and consequently the living standards of their people.[33]

As noted earlier, Saudi Arabia's progress in attaining economic freedom has been rather slow, suggesting that despite the fact that a number of reforms have been enacted in recent years, their impact has been somewhat limited. According to the Heritage/Wall Street Journal index, economic freedom by 2004 was a bit lower than in the mid-1990s (figure 5.1). In 1996, Saudi Arabia was classified as mostly free (index = 2.95). Starting in 1999, however, Saudi Arabia's economic freedom index moved into a range characterized as mostly un-free, reaching its lowest point in 2002.[34]

Saudi Arabia's relative lack of economic freedom is illustrated by particularly low scores (table 3.7) in several of the ten categories noted above: trade policy; government intervention; foreign investment; and banking and finance. In fact, the country consistently received a "free" score in only one area—monetary policy. Wages and prices and fiscal burden were the only areas consistently receiving a "mostly free" score, whereas trade policy, government intervention, foreign investment, and banking and finance consistently received scores of "repressed." Clearly, these are the areas that need the most immediate attention.

In contrast to Saudi Arabia, Iran's economy has been in the "repressed" range as defined by the economic freedom index. Hopes for broad-based economic reform were raised under President Mohammed Khatami, who was reelected in June 2001. But, Khatami's reform efforts were largely thwarted by opposition from entrenched interests, government bureaucrats who

Table 3.7   Saudi Arabia and Iran: Progress in economic freedom, 2004

	Saudi Arabia	Iran
Overall score	3.1	4.3
Trade policy	4.0	2.0
Fiscal burden	2.0	3.6
Government intervention in the economy	4.5	5.0
Monetary policy	1.0	4.0
Capital flows and foreign investment	4.0	4.0
Banking and finance	4.0	5.0
Wages and prices	2.0	4.0
Property rights	3.0	5.0
Regulation	3.0	5.0
Black market	3.0	5.0

Source: Based on the *2004 Index of Economic Freedom*. See note 31 in this chapter.

manage many of the state enterprises, and Islamic hardliners in the judiciary and other state institutions who value ideological purity over economic progress. As a result, Khatami made little progress in reforming the economy.

Iran's economic freedom lags behind that of Saudi Arabia in all areas with the exception of trade policy. The country receives the lowest score possible (5.0) in a number of areas including, (a) government intervention, (b) banking and finance, (c) property rights, (d) regulation, and (e) informal (black) markets.

Looking at the specific areas of economic freedom, several distinctive patterns stand out between the two countries.

Trade Policy. Saudi Arabia receives consistently low scores in this area largely because of a wide range of nontariff barriers. Saudi Arabia also has a number of preferences for Gulf Cooperation Council (GCC) countries as well as a vast government program that favors domestic producers. Hopefully, the phasing out of these restrictions will also pave the way for Saudi Arabia's entry into the World Trade Organization.

Iran's trade policy score in the 2004 index was 2.0, signifying a relatively open economy. The country's weighted average tariff rate in the 2004 index was 3.1 percent, down from the 6.1 percent rate in the 2003 index. In contrast, Saudi Arabia's average tariff is approximately 10.0 percent. Traditionally the main instruments used by Iran to restrict trade were nontariff barriers and the system of multiple exchange rates. However, with the unification of the exchange rate, the country has taken a major stride toward freer trade.

Government Intervention. Saudi Arabia was considered to have a low degree of economic freedom in this area because of the high level of government consumption (27 percent of GDP in 2001). A gradual shift in budget priorities toward investment and away from government salaries/welfare state should assist Saudi Arabia's movement to a higher degree of economic freedom without disrupting the economy or risking higher levels of unemployment.

Iran received the lowest score possible (5.0) in this area, largely because of its inefficient state-owned enterprises (SOEs) and politically powerful individuals and institutions such as the *bonyad* (Islamic charities that control large business conglomerates). The *bonyad* have established a tight grip on much of the non-oil economy, utilizing their preferential access to domestic credit, foreign exchange, licenses, and public contracts to protect their positions. These advantages have made it difficult for the private sector to compete and, as a result, it remains small and incapable of playing a major role in creating new employment opportunities.

Capital Flows and Foreign Investment. Although Saudi Arabia receives a relatively low score in this area, the country appears to be actively working to eliminate many of the existing restrictions. However, much work remains to be done. Outside observers also note a wide gap between reform rhetoric and actual practice.[35] Commonly noted problems for foreign investors include: the existence of many disincentives to invest (including the absence of accurate data); a government requirement that companies hire Saudi nationals; slow payment of government contracts; a restrictive visa policy for all workers; and enforced segregation of the sexes in most businesses.

Iran received a similar score for reforms in this area. However, in 2002 the government updated its foreign investment code for the first time in over 50 years with the enactment of the Law on the Attraction and Protection of Foreign Investment. Certain limitations on foreign investment were incorporated into this law including the prohibition of a market share of greater than 25 percent in one sector or 35 percent in individual industries. The statute also guaranteed market-rate compensation for assets that are nationalized. Most importantly, the country now allows for international arbitration in legal disputes, addressing a key concern of foreign investors. By late 2004, however, hard-liners were advancing a legislative agenda in the Iranian parliament that would effectively hamper foreign investment, make it more difficult for the government to negotiate deals with foreign companies, and roll back privatization plans.[36]

Banking and Finance. The Saudi Arabian Monetary Authority, the country's central bank, maintains tight control over the country's banking system. Saudi domestic commercial banks are heavily exposed to the government and to contractors dependent on government payments. As a result, the country receives a fairly low score in this area. A major complaint is that credit institutions such as the Saudi Industrial Development Fund (SIDF) allocate credit based largely on government-set criteria rather than on market conditions.

Iran's banking and finance system received the lowest score possible. A number of factors contributed to the sector's dismal state of affairs, including the fact that the ability of banks to charge interest is restricted under Iran's interpretation of Islamic law, and much of the country's commercial bank loan portfolio is tied up in low return loans to state-owned enterprises and politically connected individuals and businesses. However, in 2000 the government began permitting private banks for the first time since the revolution. Several private banks have opened, but they are not expected to have a major impact on the country's financial system because their operations are tightly regulated. Their ability to attract funds is also limited by the central bank's policy that limits the interest rate they set to within 2 percentage points of those offered by the state-owned commercial banks.

Wages and Prices. The Saudi Arabian domestic market for private goods and services is fairly free of wage and price controls. Religious leaders in the country consider market interferences as contrary to Islamic law. Hence, the country received a relatively high score in this area. However, in the past, public sector goods and services such as water and power have often been heavily subsidized. Although revenue shortfalls in the1990s forced the authorities to cut back many subsidies, some remain, especially for basic food commodities, utilities, medicines, and cement.

Iran has made some progress in this area in recent years with the deregulation and abolishment of the "price enforcement courts." Still, the country received a fairly low score largely because of massive subsidies and price controls on "essential" items such as fuel, power, and basic foodstuffs. The total cost of these subsidies is currently in the range of US$8–10 billion annually. In addition, the government sets minimum wages for each sector and region.

Property Rights. The Saudi judiciary is not perceived as independent, but as influenced by other branches of government. In addition, many businessmen complain that the enforcement of contracts is slow and often arbitrary. A recurring complaint is that the Saudi courts more often than not side with local partners when disputes involve foreign firms or individuals. This is especially true in the case of well-connected Saudis.

Property rights are even more tenuous in Iran. The country again received a 5.0 or the lowest score possible due to the widely held view that property rights are not protected. A common complaint is that the rule of law in Iran is inconsistent or unsatisfactory. The courts are unwieldy and rarely arrive at a swift resolution. Many firms will not deal with Iran because the court system is perceived to be under government or religious influence. At best the judicial system is opaque. At worst it is corrupt and arbitrary.

Regulation. There is considerable regulation in Saudi Arabia, but for the most part, it is not transparent or oriented toward serving the consumer. There are also many inconsistencies in the country's regulatory process. "Saudization" or the mandated quotas of Saudi nationals on payrolls, changes often and unexpectedly. The regulatory system also facilitates a high level of corruption. Bribes often disguised as "commissions" are common in many industries. This situation may change, however, as Crown Prince Abdullah has made anticorruption one of his major priorities.

Again, Iran comes in with the lowest score possible. Many firms find dealing with the government a long, tedious process. The government effectively discourages the establishment of new businesses. Contract negotiations are often lengthy, excessively detailed, and painfully slow to finalize. The whole process appears riddled with corruption. President Khatami's efforts at reform have been thwarted by the bureaucracy and various religious leaders.

In sum, there has been little movement toward increased economic freedom in Saudi Arabia during the last several years. In fact, during 1996–2004 there was a slight deterioration in the country's overall index. Future movements are difficult to predict simply because they appear to depend in large part on the state of the government's finances. When oil revenues are low and the government needs more employment generation in the private sector, there is usually increased resolve to undertake a new round of reforms. In 2004, with oil prices high and revenues abundant, official discussions of reform subsided.[37]

To some extent, official resolve in Iran to push ahead with reforms may also be driven by public finances. However, the failure of the reformers to make significant changes in the last few years despite the seriousness of the country's unemployment suggests that the entrenched bureaucracy and Islamic hard-liners will remain a formidable obstacle to change in that country. Even more ominous, a new Iranian neoconservative movement hostile to reform of any sort and comprising mostly young and fervent advocates of Islamic republican ideals is making a bid to seize control of Iran's political agenda.[38]

Governance

In addition to economic freedom, democracy and governance are increasingly seen as essential for long-run economic growth and prosperity. In fact, some dimensions of governance now sit at the center of academic and policy discussions of economic development.[39] Although the ranking of countries on the basis of their relative progress in attaining improved governance is inherently subjective, a recent World Bank study provides a set of rankings incorporating the full extent of our knowledge about this phenomenon.[40] More precisely, the World Bank data set presents a set of estimates of six dimensions of governance covering 199 countries and territories for 1996, 1998, 2000, and 2002: voice and accountability, political stability and absence of violence, government effectiveness, regulatory quality, rule of law, and control of corruption.

REFORM GAPS AND CATCHING-UP

As expected, the overall quality of governance in Saudi Arabia and Iran lies below the norm (as shown in table 3.8). Of the two countries, Saudi Arabia has made considerably more progress in several areas, with governance levels actually above the norm in political stability, rule of law, and control of corruption. Saudi Arabia is also near the norm in the areas of government effectiveness and regulatory quality. The country's big governance deficit is in voice and accountability. There is considerable room for improving its governance structures, but Saudi Arabia appears to have a good initial start in laying a fairly solid foundation for sustained economic growth.

Iran's governance paints a stark contrast to that of Saudi Arabia, with the country consistently below the norm. Also, many of Iran's largest governance deficits fall in areas with direct economic ramifications: regulatory quality, control of corruption, and the rule of law. However, although the country did achieve some improvements over the 1996–2002 period in many of the governance subcategories, the country's overall average governance deteriorated due to a fairly sharp deterioration in political stability.

As a whole, both Middle East rentier and non-rentier economies have lagged considerably behind other major groupings of countries (see table 3.9).[41] The high-growth (so-called catching-up) developing countries[42]—Malaysia,

Table 3.8 Governance attainment in Iran and Saudi Arabia

Country	Iran	Saudi Arabia
Voice accountability		
1996–98	−0.962	−1.263
2000–02	−0.862	−1.333
Average	−0.912	−1.298
Political stability		
1996–98	−0.191	0.028
2000–02	−0.392	0.281
Average	−0.292	0.154
Government effectiveness		
1996–98	−0.314	−0.221
2000–02	−0.307	0.010
Average	−0.310	−0.106
Regulatory quality		
1996–98	−1.515	−0.068
2000–02	−1.273	−0.010
Average	−1.394	−0.039
Rule of law		
1996–98	−0.610	0.804
2000–02	−0.507	0.537
Average	−0.558	0.670
Control of corruption		
1996–98	−0.702	0.022
2000–02	−0.497	0.326
Average	−0.599	0.174
Overall governance		
1996–98	−0.640	−0.032
2000–02	−0.678	−0.074
Average	−0.716	−0.053

Thailand, Mexico, and so on—have made considerably more progress in nearly all of the major areas of reform. In turn, there is a comparable, but generally smaller, gap between the various reform measures of the catching-up and advanced, endogenous growth countries.[43]

The reform gap between the Middle East rentier and non-rentier economies varies considerably with the rentier states attaining lower levels in voice and accountability, but higher scores in the other major categories. In the economic area, the rentier states are much more interventionist than their non-rentier counterparts. Rentier states also lag in creating an environment conducive to foreign investors and in domestic price and wage reform. On the other hand, the rentier states lag considerably behind the more successful (catching-up) developing countries, especially in the area of governance. Monetary policy and the fiscal burden are the only areas where the rentier states have made more progress than their catching-up counterparts.

Table 3.9 Middle East rentier/non-rentier advanced countries governance—economic freedom group comparisons

	Voice	Political stability	Government effectiveness	Regulatory quality	Rule of law	Control of corruption	Trade policy	Fiscal burden	Government intervention	Monetary policy	Foreign investment	Banking and finance	Wages and prices	Property rights	Regulation	Informal market
Middle East non-rentier countries (11 countries)																
Mean	−0.93503	−0.72547	−0.31767	−0.43910	−0.38383	−0.43424	4.28000	3.82600	2.90000	2.28000	2.94000	3.30000	2.86000	3.44000	3.58000	3.95000
Middle East rentier (10 countries)																
Mean	−1.00535	−0.01978	−0.01233	−0.37366	0.19158	0.12086	3.50000	3.10200	3.93000	2.06000	3.62000	3.64000	3.40000	3.22000	3.43333	2.94000
Catching-up countries (21 countries)																
Mean	0.87424	0.77986	0.66561	0.77078	0.63895	0.54852	2.70952	3.60595	2.36429	2.23810	2.35238	2.48571	2.39762	2.38571	2.83095	2.94048
Endogenous growth countries (23 countries)																
Mean	1.21215	1.09461	1.66271	1.41013	1.67973	1.75939	1.96522	3.90174	2.47391	1.14783	1.88696	1.93043	2.03478	1.20870	2.45217	1.44348

Note: Average values for 2000–02. Values are derived from an index for each measure. The index has a mean of zero so negative values indicate inferior governance.

Source: Compiled from *Governance Matters III: Governance Indicators for 1996–2000* and *Index of Economic Freedom Rankings.*

Although it would not necessarily guarantee the economic successes enjoyed by the catching-up countries, progress in a number of areas of reform is no doubt a necessary first step in transitioning into an environment capable of encouraging those economic forces necessary for achieving self-sustained growth. Statistically, the Middle East rentier states and the catching-up countries fall into two unique groupings based on their progress in (1) voice and accountability, and (2) reducing corruption.[44] In other words, knowing the progress made in just these two areas would allow one to predict which grouping a country belonged with a 96.8 percent chance of success. In all of the areas needing increased reform efforts, these two, especially voice and accountability, should have the highest priority.

A further statistical[45] analysis (see figure 3.3) of the dimension[46] leading from rentier to catching-up status suggests the Middle East rentier states fall into three groupings of relative progress based on the level of voice and accountability reform: (1) a low group comprising of Iraq, Libya, and Saudi Arabia; (2) an intermediate group consisting of Algeria, Bahrain, Iran, Oman, Qatar, and the UAE; and (3) the top group consisting only of Kuwait. Once progress in voice and accountability enables the threshold to catching-up status to be reached, improvement in regulatory quality would become a top priority for further advancement.

As a basis of comparison, in their quest to become high performing developing countries, the non-rentier economies in the Middle East must first achieve significant progress in reforming three key areas (in declining order of importance): (1) voice and accountability; (2) foreign investment; and (3) fiscal burden. For this group, the dimension leading to catching-up status is dominated by voice and accountability (as shown in figure 3.4).

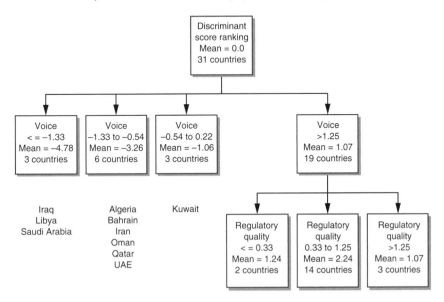

Figure 3.3   Steps in Middle East rentier, catching-up country progression.

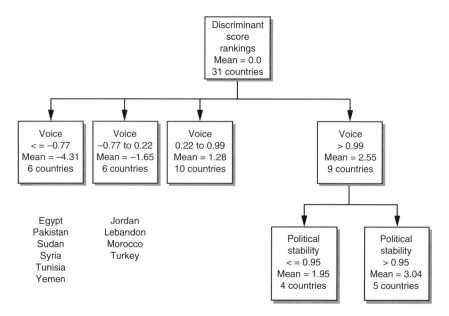

Figure 3.4   Steps in Middle East non-rentier, catching-up country progression.

Although Jordan, Lebanon, Morocco, and Turkey have made the most progress in moving toward an environment more conducive for economic success, it is clear that they have a considerable distance to go before reaching that goal. Of the three main clusters of pre–catching-up countries, none has reached the third stage.

Although these findings provide interesting insights as to the challenges confronting the Middle Eastern countries, the question remains as to whether this is the best perspective for examining the two key rentier states in the region, Saudi Arabia and Iran. Clearly these two countries are considerably larger, both economically and demographically, than the other Gulf rentier states. Does this size factor systematically define a reform strategy unique to their needs?

To test whether a meaningful delineation of rentier states exists, several larger non-Middle Eastern rentier economies—Angola, Nigeria, and Venezuela—were added to the analysis. As before, using the five governance and ten economic freedom variables as the basis of profiling unique policy environments shows (in table 3.10) considerable differences between them. The states fall into two groups: one with relatively large rentier states composed of Algeria, Angola, Iran, Iraq, Libya, Nigeria, Saudi Arabia, and Venezuela, and the other with smaller rentier states—Bahrain, Kuwait, Oman, Qatar, and the UAE.

In particular, the larger rentier states have lagged considerably behind the smaller states in all areas of governance. Although the gaps are not as large, the larger rentier economies have also not made nearly the same progress as the smaller rentier states in achieving higher levels of economic freedom.

Somewhat surprisingly, the key reform area separating the two groups of countries is trade policy with the larger rentier countries lagging considerably behind their smaller counterparts. Just knowing the relative attainment of reforms in this area would have been sufficient to have correctly classified, with a high degree of probability, each country as a large or small retainer economy.

The progression from largest (Angola, Iraq, Libya, Nigeria) to smallest (UAE) rentier state is defined by the progress made in the governance area of regulatory quality (figure 3.5) with the smaller rentier states defined as a cluster of high regulatory quality environments. A middle cluster of countries consists of Saudi Arabia and Venezuela with moderate attainment in this area. The remaining large rentier economies, including Iran, are in a cluster of extremely low regulatory quality. These findings are consistent with the fact that the large rentier economies have pursued considerably different development strategies than their smaller counterparts. Because of their larger populations and domestic markets, industrialization made a certain amount of economic sense for this group. This industrialization has been achieved in large part through an inward-oriented import substitution strategy as evidenced, in part, by the group's lack of progress (openness) in trade policy.

The findings are also consistent with the patterns of declining effectiveness of government expenditures in Saudi Arabia and Iran, as well as the observed negative TFP in both countries. Lack of good regulation (together with other reform deficiencies) in both countries has limited the potentially positive economic role of governments in both countries. Negative TFP is also found in many developing countries attempting to industrialize through relatively inward-oriented import substitution development strategies.[47]

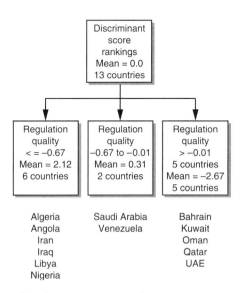

Figure 3.5 Large–small rentier economy progression.

Table 3.10 Large–small rentier governance—economic freedom group comparisons

	Voice	Political stability	Government effectiveness	Regulatory quality	Rule of law	Control of corruption	Trade policy	Fiscal burden	Government intervention	Monetary policy	Foreign investment	Banking and finance	Wages and prices	Property rights	Regulation	Informal market
Small rentiers (5 countries)																
Mean	−0.59191	0.76373	0.68647	0.56745	1.01083	0.84929	2.48000	2.39600	3.62000	1.00000	3.16000	2.84000	2.88000	2.08000	2.84000	1.80000
Std. deviation	0.248959	0.430938	0.279736	0.355327	0.121150	0.122204	0.363318	0.601232	0.383406	0.000000	0.753658	0.942338	0.178885	0.889944	0.753658	0.374166
Large rentiers (8 countries)																
Mean	−1.19190	−1.04153	−0.87597	−1.19469	−0.84223	−0.78901	4.55000	3.62500	3.97500	3.65000	3.82500	4.17500	3.70000	4.20000	4.11667	4.23750
Std. deviation	0.556134	0.808771	0.528483	0.887352	0.670689	0.539870	0.531843	0.761333	0.922342	1.488048	0.958794	0.736304	0.997139	0.732900	0.817856	1.019716

Note: Average values, 2000–02.

Source: Compiled from *Governance Matters III: Governance Indicators for 1996–2002* and *Index of Economic Freedom Rankings*.

If higher oil revenues over the next few years are not sufficient to begin reducing both countries' unemployment problems, increased reforms will have to be given a much higher priority than at present. This is especially the case in many key governance areas such as voice and accountability and regulatory reform. Government expenditures will have to be refocused on activities that directly support private sector investment. In Saudi Arabia's case (and to a lesser extent Iran's), the welfare state will have to be scaled back and a higher priority given to economic allocations. More emphasis must be placed on efficiency and productivity in government activities. There is also tremendous waste in government ministries that will have to be dealt with. In short, an environment will have to be created that encourages investment and provides better incentives for risktaking and job creation. Without these efforts, growing unemployment, rising poverty, and unfulfilled expectations will produce a volatile situation, perhaps beyond the control of either government.

TRANSITION STRATEGIES

Interestingly, nearly all of the patterns of governance, economic reform, and transition out of the rentier state described here are consistent with the assumptions underlying a model of growth and terrorism developed by Bremer and Kasarda.[48] Bremer and Kasarda see countries moving through three distinct stages as their economies evolve and become more sophisticated and market driven. By their criterion, Saudi Arabia and Iran fall in the first stage (along with countries such as Egypt and Pakistan) (see figure 3.6). This group of economies has failed to move forward to the middle stage largely because of growth-limiting policies (captured by the various measures of economic freedom) and institutional rigidities (depicted by the various areas of governance).

To this basic economic/governance framework, Bremer and Kasarda add the dimensions of disillusionment and resentment. In effect, these countries have had a "failed take-off" in Rostow's terms.[49] Expectations of rapidly improved standards of living have been raised only to be left unfulfilled by the inability of the economy to sustain growth. Following Hirschman's observations on income disparity in developing countries, the tolerance of lower-income groups for large-income inequalities also wears thin as they see their dreams of a better life fade, especially if they perceive the country's elites are a source of the country's economic stagnation or decline.[50]

The key feature of Bremer and Kasarda's model is the historical record: "History suggests that failure to make steady progress through the New Second World transition's early phase to the middle period is extremely dangerous. If the transition stalls here—as it did in post–World War I Russia, and as it has now in much of the Middle East—failure can lead to revolution and al Qaeda–style international violence."[51] The one thing that the nations stuck in the early phase have in common is slowness in adopting choice-based systems. Bremer and Kasarda define "choice-based" systems as encompassing both market-based economies and democratic political institutions and

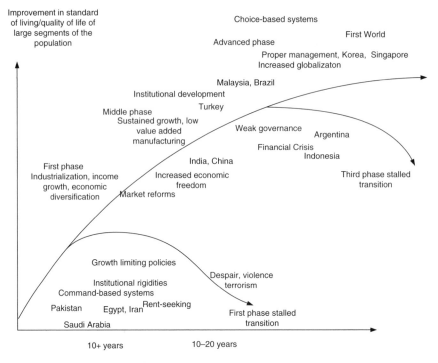

Figure 3.6   New Second World transitions.

Source: Based on the description of transition provided in Jennifer Bremer and John Kasarda, "The origins of Terror: Implications for U.S. Foreign Policy," *The Milker Institute Review* (Fourth Quarter, 2002).

organizations—basically the economic freedom and governance measures noted earlier.

The large rentier states appear particularly susceptible to the failed processes noted by Bremer and Kasarda. By any standard, the economic freedom and governance indicators of the first group (table 3.11) lie well below that of the second group. Deficiencies are seen nearly across the board, but are particularly evident in regulatory quality and government intervention, areas where Bremer and Kasarda stress lack of reforms are likely to retard progress to higher stages.

To further assess the relevance of the Bremer and Kasarda model for the large rentier economies, our set of six governance and ten economic freedom variables were examined statistically to see if they were capable of classifying groups of countries in a manner similar to those described by Bremer and Kasarda. The analysis was successful in identifying Stage 1 and Stage 3 as unique groupings based on their relative progress made in reforms. Significantly, all of the large rentier economies fell in the first stage with a high degree of correct placement in this category. In addition, a group of eight countries (Albania, Russia, Brazil, China, Egypt, Indonesia, Turkey, and India) fell into an intermediate or transition stage.

Table 3.11   New Second World/advanced country governance—economic freedom group comparisons, 2000–02

	Voice	Political stability	Government effectiveness	Regulatory quality	Rule of law	Control of corruption	Trade policy	Fiscal burden	Government intervention	Monetary policy	Foreign investment	Banking and finance	Wages and prices	Property rights	Regulation	Informal market
First Stage—failed take-off countries																
Mean	−.86315	−.71912	−.78036	−.85507	−.76866	−.79876	3.90000	3.46875	3.39375	3.26250	3.52500	3.76379	3.46766	3.77639	3.88740	4.34444
Second stage countries																
Mean	−.44289	−.47498	−.04219	−.09212	−.17796	−.43235	3.73333	3.70000	2.88333	2.96667	3.10000	3.33333	3.00000	3.11667	3.81667	3.92500
Third stage countries																
Mean	.76082	.69934	.74122	.82972	.70999	.61611	2.58750	3.45021	2.46042	2.11667	2.24167	2.52800	2.41944	2.11833	2.54278	2.71800
Advanced countries																
Mean	1.40122	1.27231	1.75752	1.45466	1.77718	1.88875	2.00000	4.09455	2.37727	1.14545	1.91818	1.99545	2.08725	1.22778	2.55720	1.30505

Note: Average values, 2000–02. Variables significant in the 4 group discriminant analysis in order of importance: government effectiveness, voice regulation, corruption. Correct placement: failed take-off 87.5% (14 of 16), second stage countries, 100.0% (6 of 6), third stage countries, 87.5 (21 of 24), advanced countries, 90.9% (20 of 22).

Source: Compiled from *Governance Matters III: Governance Indicators for 1996–2002* and *Index of Economic Freedom Rankings.*

The variables critical for profiling the countries in these groups were (in declining order of importance): government efficiency, voice and accountability, and corruption. These are all areas consistent with the Bremer and Kasarda contention that deficiencies cause growth in the first stage to fall to levels incapable of creating adequate jobs and sustaining economic growth.

As noted earlier, another area stressed by Bremer and Kasarda, improved regulatory quality, seems to be critical in moving countries along the New Second World dimension to higher stages (figure 3.7). In the progression to the second stage, Iran is in a group of countries with very low regulatory quality. Through their modest efforts at improving government effectiveness, the Iranians have passed Libya and Algeria. The country clearly lags behind Saudi Arabia (and Egypt and Turkey) in moving up the ladder to the second stage of Bremer and Kasarda's New Second World of development. However, compared with the progress made by a country such as Israel, it is apparent the Saudis have a very long reform road ahead of them.

None of this bodes particularly well for the Saudis or the Iranians. Both countries appear to be going down the road to disaster projected for Bremer and Kasarda's stage one countries. In Saudi Arabia's case, it is clear that ten or fifteen years ago, when many of the economy's problems were becoming clearly apparent, the government had time on its side.[52] A well thought-out neoliberal reform program stressing free markets, access to capital, integration into the world economy, and major efforts in the various areas of governance, especially regulation and corruption, could have been undertaken at a safe pace, laying the foundation for the transition to a higher growth path and Bremer and Kasarda's middle stage of development.

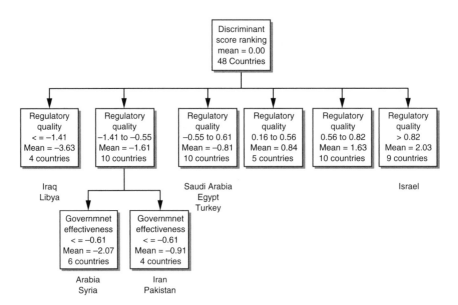

Figure 3.7   Steps in the New Second World progression.

Instead, the government postponed hard decisions, hoping that a new oil boom would solve all of its problems. None was forthcoming, nor will one likely appear in the foreseeable future after the current oil boom subsides. As a result, the Saudi authorities find an economy still mired in Bremer and Kasarda's first stage and facing an unemployment rate that is approaching 30 percent.[53] Poverty is definitely on the rise and, even more ominously, an increasing number of Saudis complain that their national wealth is being plundered by corrupt members of the royal family.[54] Increasingly, one hears:

> there's a lot of frustration and anxiety among young Saudi men. Almost half of them have lost hope for the future. And they are ripe for recruitment by Islamic extremists . . . Adding to the frustration are the lack of outlets for discussion and debate. Trade unions are barred as are all other professional associations . . . Saudi society has few political tools to counter the extremism that has taken root here and the results are actions like the recent bombings in Riyadh.[55]

Domestic terrorism does not plague Iran nearly to the extent found in Saudi Arabia, nevertheless the picture in many ways is gloomier because Iran lags considerably behind Saudi Arabia in nearly all areas of reform. Vested interests in the existing system have greatly limited reform. Because many opposed to reform have religious legitimacy, there are only modest prospects for dramatic reforms in the near future. In turn, the reform gap has limited the private sector's ability to create jobs. At the same time rapid demographics are overwhelming the public sector's ability to expand hiring. The result is a progressive breakdown of the link uniting the population to the state through the rentier distribution system. Given the government's low tolerance for direct protest, the population's growing dissatisfaction and frustration is likely to manifest itself in the form of increased political and economic instability.

Implications for Iraq

Iraq certainly has a lot to learn from the experiences of Saudi Arabia and Iran. With the fall of Saddam, the country had the golden opportunity of starting with a clean slate. Perhaps because of the difficulties in moving ahead with reform, once entrenched interests were strengthened by the rentier state redistributive mechanisms. The Coalition Provisional Authority (CPA) was quick to install a package of reforms reminiscent of the shock therapy programs carried out in the early to mid-1990s in many of the Transition Economies of Central and Eastern Europe. Overnight, Iraq became the most open economy in the Arab world.[56]

The reforms clearly incorporated much of the agenda originally laid out in the now somewhat discredited Washington Consensus.[57] The main thrust of the Washington Consensus was a set of actions that, if taken at an early stage of transition, should have facilitated a smooth evolution into the world economy. It consisted of many elements of the economic freedom measures noted here. In addition, it incorporated elements of macroeconomic reform (liberalization, stabilization, and fiscal austerity), stressing the importance of bringing down inflation and establishing economic growth. It also incorporated a number of elements of microeconomic reform (e.g., privatization, promoting FDI), as well as structural/administrative reforms (e.g., property rights, replacement of quantitative restrictions). Specifically, these included:

- Fiscal discipline: limits to budget deficits
- Public expenditure priorities: redirect expenditure toward building human capital and infrastructure
- Tax reform: broaden tax base and cut marginal tax rates
- Financial liberalization: abolish interest rate controls
- Exchange rates: introduce unified and competitive exchange rates
- Trade liberalization: replace quantitative restrictions by tariffs and then reduce the tariffs over time
- Foreign direct investment: encourage increased international capital inflows
- Privatization: privatize state enterprises
- Deregulation: regulate only safety, environment, and financial sectors (i.e., prudential supervision)
- Property rights: introduce secure enforcement at low cost

Progress of reform design and implementation varies considerably by categories; the September 2003 CPA reforms have little to say about fiscal discipline or public expenditure priorities, no doubt due to the great uncertainty surrounding oil revenues, the external debt situation, and foreign assistance. Surprisingly, however, property rights, a key element of the neoliberal reforms, has received less attention than one might have expected. It is also clear that, by any measure, Iraq world score very high on an economic freedom index. On the other hand, very little has been implemented or even discussed in the important areas of complementary governance: corporate governance, anticorruption, flexible labor markets, World Trade Organization agreements, financial codes and standards, prudent capital account opening, nonintermediate exchange rate regimes, independent central banks/inflation targeting, social safety nets, and targeted poverty reduction. Of these, only some initial, albeit limited, progress has occurred in the areas of financial standards and central banking.

Perhaps the intent of the CPA and the current provisional government is to simply defer many of the specifics in these areas to an elected Iraqi government. However, as the cases of Iran and Saudi Arabia illustrate, governance reform may be a more critical element in assuring Iraq is able to progress along the path to a stable modern economy. Without significant improvement in these areas in the near future, the country is likely to have only the disadvantages of the free market to show for its reform efforts. The great danger is the fact that lack of economic progress early on will no doubt give legitimacy to the dormant Baathist movement's efforts to revert the economy back to its prewar status as a predatory rentier state.[58]

Notes

1. Elizabeth Rubin, "The Opening of the Wahhabist Mind," *New York Times Magazine*, March 7, 2004, 38.

2. A more detailed account is given in Robert Looney, "Iraqi Oil: A Gift from God or the Devil's Excrement?" *Strategic Insights*, vol. 2, no. 7 (July 2003), at www.ccc.nps.navy.mil/si/july03/middleEast2.asp.

3. A loose definition of a rentier state is one where significant amounts of oil/mineral royalties (rents) accrue directly to the state and where only a few are engaged in the generation of this rent (wealth), the majority being only involved in the distribution or utilization of it. Cf. Michael Ross, "Does Oil Hinder Democracy," *World Politics*, vol. 53 (April 2001), 329.

4. Jeffrey Sachs, "Globalization and Patterns of Economic Development," *Weltwirtschaftliches Archiv*, vol. 136, no. 4 (2000), 584.

5. An assessment of the rentier state dynamics as they pertain to Saudi Arabia are given in Robert Looney, "Saudi Arabia: Measures of Transition from a Rentier State," in Joseph A. Kechichian, ed., *Iran, Iraq and the Arab Gulf States* (New York: Palgrave, 2001), 131–160.

6. Unless otherwise indicated, all economic data are from the Saudi Arabian Monetary Agency Annual Report, various issues.

7. Nadim Kawach, "Saudis Need to Adopt More Reforms to Spur Growth," *Gulf News*, August 17, 2003.

8. Robert Looney, "Can Saudi Arabia Reform Its Economy in Time to Head off Disaster?" *Strategic Insights*, vol. III, no. 1 (January 2004), at www.ccc.nps. navy.mil/si/2004/jan/looneyJan04.asp.

9. This description of Iran's recent growth patterns draws heavily on IMF information. Cf. *Islamic Republic of Iran—Selected Issues* (Washington: International Monetary Fund, September 2004), 7–9.

10. Alan Gelb, *Oil Windfalls: Blessing or Curse* (Washington: World Bank, 1988); see also Robert Looney, "Diminishing Returns and Policy Options in a Rentier State: Economic Reform and Regime Legitimacy in Saudi Arabia," *Political Crossroads*, vol. 5, nos. 1 and 2 (1997), 31–50.

11. Paul Stevens, "Resource Curse and Investment in Oil and Gas Projects: The New Challenge," *Internet Journal*, June 2002.

12. Robert Looney, *The Economic Origins of the Iranian Revolution* (New York: Pergamon Press, 1982).

13. Stevens, "Resource Curse."

14. Fred Halliday, *Islam and the Myth of Confrontation* (London: I.B. Tauris, 1995), 40.

15. Michael Ross, "Does Oil Hinder Democracy," *World Politics*, vol. 53, no. 3 (2001), 325–361.

16. "Iran: the Future of the Rentier System in Question," *Banque Paribas Conjoncture*, October 30, 2003, 12.

17. Norman Hicks and Ann Kubisch, "Cutting Government Expenditure in LDC's," *Finance & Development*, vol. 2, no. 3 (September 1984), 37–39.

18. Robert Looney, "The Budgetary Impact of Defense Expenditures in the Middle East," *The Middle East Business and Economic Review*, vol. 5, no. 2 (1993), 38–49.

19. Unless otherwise indicated, all data on Saudi Arabia is from the Saudi Arabian Monetary Agency (SAMA) Annual Report, various issues.

20. Robert Looney, "A Post-Keynesian Assessment of Alternative Austerity Strategies," *Kuwait University Journal of the Social Sciences*, vol. 23, no. 3 (Autumn 1995), 239–273.

21. Robert Looney, "Saudi Arabia: Measures of Transition from a Rentier State," Kechichian, *Iran, Iraq and the Arab Gulf States*, 131–160.

22. Robert Looney, The Saudi Arabian Quandary: The Economy's Inability to Sustain Growth," *METU Studies in Development*, vol. 31, no. 1 (June 2004), 71–92.

23. Ibid.

24. Using different statistical techniques, a similar result was previously found in Robert Looney, "Deducing Budgetary Priorities in Saudi Arabia: The Impact of Defense Expenditures on Allocations to Socio-Economic Programs," *Public Budgeting and Financial Management*, vol. 4, no. 2 (1992), 311–326; and Robert Looney, "Budgetary Priorities in Saudi Arabia: The Impact of Relative Austerity on Measures of Human Capital Formation," *OPEC Review*, vol. 25, no. 2 (Summer 1991), 133–152.

25. Scott Baier, Gerald Dwyer, and Robert Tamura, "How Important Are Capital and Total Factor Productivity for Growth?" 2002, at www.vanderbilt.edu/Econ/faculty/Crucini/tamura.pdf.

26. Blair et al. calculate TFP in the standard manner. Details can be found at www.vanderbilt. edn/Econ/faculty/crucini/tamura.pdf.

27. The following draws heavily on *Islamic Republic of Iran—Selected Issues* (Washington: International Monetary Fund, September 2004), 11–14.

28. Ibid.

29. Jeffrey Sachs, "Globalization and Patterns of Economic Development," *Weltwirtschaftliches Archiv*, vol. 136, no. 4 (2001), 579–600.

30. Dani Rodrik and Arvind Subramanian, "The Primacy of Institutions," *Finance & Development*, vol. 40, no. 2 (June 2002).

31. See, for example, Marc Miles, Edwin Feulner, Mary Anastasia O'Grady, and Ana Eiras, *2004 Index of Economic Freedom* (Washington: Heritage Foundation, 2004).

32. Available from Global Economic Software, Ltd, at www.globaleconomicsoftware.com. Robert Looney, "Iraq's Economic Transition: The Neoliberal Model and Its Role," *The Middle East Journal*, vol. 57, no. 4 (Autumn 2003), 568–587, for an application of this data set to the Middle East.

33. Ana Isabel Eiras, *Ethics, Corruption and Economic Freedom* (Washington: Heritage Foundation, December 9, 2003).

34. Miles et al., *2004 Index of Economic Freedom*.

35. Miles et al., *2004 Index of Economic Freedom*.

36. Kamal Yasin, "Iranian Neo-Cons Make Power Play in Tehran," *Iran Press Service.com*, October 6, 2004.

37. Mohamad Bazzi, "Fledgling Saudi Arabia Reforms Don't Fly," *San Francisco Chronicle*, October 31, 2004.

38. Yasin, "Iranian Neo-Cons."

39. Herbert Kitschelt, "A Review of the Political Economy of Governance," *World Bank Policy Research Working Paper 3315*, May 2004, 1.

40. Daniel Kaufman, Aart Kraay, and Massimo Mastruzzi, *Governance Matters III: Governance Indicators for 1996–2002* (Washington: World Bank, June 30, 2003).

41. Higher governance scores indicate greater progress in these areas whereas lower economic freedom scores signify greater progress in the economic area.

42. As defined in Sachs, "Globalization and Patterns of Economic Development," 581. Sachs considers these countries to be narrowing the income gap with the higher technology and richer countries through a process of technological diffusion and capital flows from the leader to follower.

43. Defined by Sachs as countries that in residents in 1995 were able to register at least ten U.S. patients per million inhabitants of the country.

44. The procedure used was discriminant analysis. For a description of this technique see *SPSS Base 10.0 Guide* (Chicago: SPSS Inc., 1999), 243–292. A full set of results are available from the author upon request at relooney@nps.edu.

45. See *AnswerTree 3.0 User's Guide* (Chicago: SPSS Inc., 2001) for a description of the technique.

46. As depicted by the discriminant function (table 5.4) with rentier countries characterized by large negative scores and catching up countries, positive scores.

47. The classic study in this regard is Henry Bruton, "Productivity Growth in Latin America," *American Economic Review*, December 1967.

48. Jennifer Bremer and John Kasarda, "The Origins of Terror: Implications for U.S. Foreign Policy," *The Milken Institute Review*, Fourth Quarter 2002. For an application of this model to Pakistan, see Robert Looney "Failed Economic Take-Offs and Terrorism: Conceptualizing a Proper Role for U.S. Assistance to Pakistan," Center for Contemporary Conflict, February 1, 2003.

49. W.W. Rostow, *The Stages of Economic Growth* (Cambridge: Cambridge University Press, 1960).

50. Albert Hirschman, "The Changing Tolerance for Income Inequality," Quarterly Journal of Economics, vol. 87, no. 4 (November 1973), 544–566.

51. Bremer and Kasarda, "The Origins of Terror," 36.

52. Robert Looney, "Saudi Arabia's Development Strategy: Comparative Advantage vs. Sustainable Growth," *Orient*, vol. 30, no. 1 (1989), 75–96, at http://web.nps.navy.mil/~relooney/RelOrient_2.pdf.

53. "Saudi Arabia's Unemployment Reaches 30 Percent," *Arabic News.Com*, March 5, 2003, at www.arabicnews.com/ansub/Daily/Day/030305/2003030513.html.

54. "Analysts Warn of Needed Reforms in Saudi Arabia to Stem Extremist Movements," *NPR Morning Edition*, May 26, 2003.

55. Ibid.

56. Samson Mulugeta, "Reform Concerns: Changes Have Iraqi Workers Nervous," *Newsday*, December 14, 2003.

57. Comprehensive surveys and critiques of the Washington Consensus can be found in: Kaushik Basu, "Globalization and the Politics of International Finance: The Stiglitz Verdict," *Journal of Economic Literature LLI* (September 2003), 885–899; and Dani Rodrik, "Understanding Policy Reform," *Journal of Economic Literature*, (March 1996).

58. Robert Looney, "A Return to Ba'thist Economics?" *Orient*, vol. 45, no. 3 (September 2004), 385–400.

Emerging Political Dynamics

4

Oslo's Success, a Militarized Resistance: Changing Opposition Tactics in the Palestinian Territories

Anne Marie Baylouny

Introduction

As the United States embarks on an ongoing relationship with Iraq and the resistance movements there, it would do well to learn from other experiences in dealing with opposition groups. The case of Israel in the Palestinian territories provides a powerful lesson in which seemingly sound military tactics led to an increase in radicalization, not pacification, of the resistance.

A recurring obstacle in policy formation is the persistence in viewing resistance actions, including Islamist ones, as centrally directed and hierarchically organized. Whereas some may fall into this category, most movements are highly decentralized. Policymakers are surprised when, after assassinating the organization's leaders, the movement not only persists but fights back harder. Equating the opposition with, and attributing all responsibility to, its elite leaders has led to an incorrect evaluation of the causes and dynamics of the resistance itself, and yielded flawed policies to moderate these movements.

The trajectory of resistance movements in Palestine in the 1990s demonstrates that militarization becoming a fundamental characteristic and strategy of the conflict was not a foregone conclusion. Continued collective repression, combined with divide-and-conquer population control policies, which are embodied in Oslo, has made both the Palestinian territories and Israel less secure. In this chapter, I advance theories of repression and underground movements using social movement theory, and use the experience of Palestinian opposition groups since the 1993 Oslo accords to demonstrate factors promoting its militarization. Promoting the decentralization and fragmentation of a domestically based movement will not lead to the dismantling of the movement as long as the underlying issues remain. Instead, fragmentation may create a situation of continuing military insecurity and an increase in violence.

It is generally acknowledged that the Oslo peace accords between Palestine and Israel have failed, and this failure is often viewed as causing the radicalization of opposition groups. I argue the opposite. The very implementation of Oslo's provisions constituted one major cause for the militarization of the resistance. Oslo entailed the repression of dissent, the removal of the masses from the organized opposition, the targeting of Islamist and secular leaders, and the extreme fragmentation of the resistance. Fundamental to the Oslo process is the fragmentation of the territories and continued Israeli control of exit points. These policies, perhaps premised on a false conception of security for Israel through disarming the Palestinian opposition, have resulted in the opposite: the decentralization and fragmentation of resistance created competition, as local resistance groups were cut-off from both their leadership and a larger public constituency. Therefore, their actions were unhindered by any source of accountability as the struggle for movement leader raised the bar for activists.

My theoretical conclusions regarding the dynamics of decentralization in resistance movements are tested on two groups of the Palestinian resistance. The case of the Palestinian group Fatah, in particular, accords with my expectations. The more fragmented and leader-less the resistance group, the higher the level of anarchy, independent decision-making, abrogation of agreed-upon truces, and internal battles for dominance. Often, such battles are characterized by the use of bold military maneuvers in order to establish and institutionalize a new leadership. In decreasing order of fragmentation, the groups are Fatah's al-Aqsa Martyrs Brigade, Islamic Jihad, and Hamas. Hamas is currently the most disciplined and hierarchical of the movements. Fatah's al-Aqsa Brigades was relieved of its middle leadership in approximately 2002, from which time autonomous tendencies increased substantially. If the current wave of assassination of Hamas leadership continues, the future of that group will likely resemble the current anarchy in Fatah.

On a proactive note, this study yields policy prescriptions designed to moderate domestic-based conflicts.[1] An analysis of the causes for growing militancy in the Palestinian resistance provides insight into movement dynamics in other locations, which will hopefully lead to policies effectively deterring further militarization. Instead of treading the bloody path of Israel, the United States has the ability to learn from those mistakes. I argue that the hierarchical leadership of resistance movements should be left in place, and popular nonviolent social movements encouraged. Population control policies designed to fragment the opposition are counterproductive, as they lead to an exit of much of the general population from the movement. It is this popular involvement that can moderate resistance actions, provided nonviolent protest and organizing is allowed.

I start by analyzing the provisions of the Declaration of Principles, more commonly known as the Oslo accords, and the Israeli perspective of obtaining security in the occupied Palestinian territories.[2] Next, I develop theories of the dynamics of terrorism and underground movements in the context of policies of repression and decentralization, policies contained in the accords and part of Israel's security concept. Finally, I trace the timeline of the Palestinian resistance from the first Intifada through the militarization of the opposition in Oslo, analyzing how policies intended to increase security for Israel worked in the opposite direction. I conclude with policy implications that arise from this study for reducing the violent wings of grassroots opposition movements.

The Israeli Perspective on the Accords: Security as Control

The Declaration of Principles was negotiated in Oslo, Norway, and was signed in September 1993 in Washington, D.C., by Yasser Arafat and Yitzhak Rabin, with President Bill Clinton presiding.[3] Initially, many hailed the Oslo accords as a solution to the long-standing Israeli–Palestinian conflict. Over a decade later, however, Oslo's timetable has not been met. It is this failure that is generally held responsible for the increased violence by opposition groups in the West Bank and Gaza strip. The common interpretation is that Hamas and other militarized Islamist groups emerged out of "frustration" with the lack of progress in negotiations. The assumption is that if Oslo had been fully implemented, societal opposition and violent rebellion would not occur.

If Oslo was meant to bring peace to Israel via the creation of a Palestinian state, it has indeed failed. However, those goals were not in the Oslo accords. The aim was an open-ended process whose main and concrete provision was the establishment of a Palestinian Interim Self-Government Authority. Oslo entailed a piecemeal process by which a Palestinian authority would gain partial control over increasingly more land. The substance of this land transfer was to be negotiated in interim agreements, none of which dealt with "final status" issues or the ultimate fate of the territories: water control, borders, and refugees, amidst others. The end game was left undecided.

Much has been made of the ambiguity of the Oslo treaties, the power discrepancy embodied in the agreements, and the many subjects they leave unresolved. Nonetheless, from an objective perspective, to a large extent, Oslo has been enacted. Intermediate transfers of authority to the Palestinian Authority (PA) have certainly gone beyond the stated timetable. The result is a drastically, radically altered landscape of the West Bank and Gaza.[4]

Palestinians hoped that Oslo would lead to an independent state, but Israel's primary goal was security. That security was obtained through the accords in two ways: first, through military policing policies, and second through population control policies such as checkpoints. Through these means, twin goals were achieved that the Israelis presumed would thwart violent resistance. Formal opposition organizing of all types, including peaceful forms, was officially prevented and repressed, and existing opposition groups were fragmented and forced underground, effectively inhibiting the functioning of group hierarchies.

Military policing functions are clear in Oslo. The Palestinians agreed to bear responsibility for the suppression of Islamist groups and all dissent, and Israeli withdrawals were conditional on Palestinian ability to meet Israel's security needs. Indeed, one of Oslo's few clear stipulations is the creation of a Palestinian police force to enforce internal order.[5] A "strong Palestinian police force" for this purpose is repeatedly mentioned in the accords. That force now numbers about 40,000. Even so, Israel retained the right to

Oslo II, 1995

Map 4.1: Oslo II plan for the west Bank, 1995

Source: Palestinian Academic Society for the Study of International Affairs, www.passia.org.

intervene in areas under the authority of the Palestinians (areas "A") when security justified it. This notion of security included protection of Israeli settlers in the occupied territories.

Oslo expanded and legitimized Israel's supervision of population movements, resulting in a "matrix of control."[6] The tiny West Bank, smaller than Delaware, is currently fragmented into 300 separate areas as shown in map 4.1.[7] Measures designed to exercise control over population movements were variously coded in the accords as economic, bureaucratic, or demographic. The accords increased the number of borders, checkpoints, and the use of closure or refusing Palestinian workers entry to Israel. As per Oslo II, the responsibility for the security of all Palestinian borders would rest with Israel.[8] "Borders" became internal borders, including exit or entry from any areas transferred to the PA. In effect, the occupied territories became a patchwork of small areas under the control of the PA, surrounded by borders that Israel had the right to police.

Oslo involved planned, partial withdrawals from land in the West Bank and Gaza, which would then come under the PA's rule. These were termed areas "A." The Israeli military would be redeployed from these areas and be stationed outside them. Areas B and C would remain in Israeli hands during the initial phases of Oslo. By the end of 1999, the PA was in control of over 200 small areas—most of them smaller than one square mile.[9] Passage to or from them was controlled by Israeli military checkpoints. Border controls and physical barriers, such as trenches, electric fences, and barricades of sand, rock, or concrete, lie outside each of these areas. Additionally, roads in the territories are policed by numerous standing and mobile checkpoints, the latter termed "flying checkpoints" due to their lack of a permanent location. In the last four years, over 500 new military checkpoints have been established.[10] A Palestinian going from one area of the PA in the north, Jenin, to another in the south, Hebron, would have to pass through 50 such border crossings.[11]

Further bisecting the territories is a grid of bypass roads, linking the settlements to Israel but insulating them from the surrounding Palestinian population. Unlike the Palestinian traveler mentioned above, Israelis travel freely throughout the territories, via bypass roads, without ever changing zones or being held up at a checkpoint. According to a member of the Knesset, settlements were purposely located in the midst of densely populated Palestinian areas in order to prevent territorial integrity for the PA and thus any possibility of a Palestinian state.[12] The confiscation of land to build these roads was approved by Oslo II,[13] and the Hebron protocol served as an exemplar to justify positioning Israeli settlements in the middle of Palestinian population centers.[14]

The wall that Israel is currently constructing is another means of segregating Israel from the Palestinians. Like the bypass roads and settlements, it incorporates Palestinian land, de facto, into Israeli control and cuts villages off from each other and from their agricultural lands. Sixteen Palestinian villages are caught between the wall and the official Israeli border, isolated not only from Israel but from the rest of the West Bank as well.[15]

Closure is a further element of population control in Oslo. Closure is defined as limitations imposed by Israel on the movement of the Palestinian population and its goods. Closure can be internal, within the West Bank and Gaza strip; external; or between those territories and Israel. It can be partial or total.[16] Whereas closure predates Oslo and the advent of suicide bombings inside Israel, it was institutionalized by the accords and presented as an antiterrorism measure.[17] Internal closure is effectively a curfew, preventing movement between villages. Closure combines with the pass or permit system, whereby even when restrictions are lifted the population needs permission to move from place to place.[18]

Curfews are closely linked to closure, and serve as yet one more method for controlling population movement. In those areas remaining under Israeli control (B and C), curfews were enacted throughout the Oslo process. Further, if Israel deems that the PA fails to meet Israel's security concerns, area A could come under curfew also. This last provision was used as a rationale for the al-Aqsa or second Intifada.[19]

These measures accord with the Israeli military's basic premise for interacting with the Palestinian population. Indeed, the military had a hand in Oslo, one that was more pronounced in Oslo II, and it viewed the agreements as fulfilling Israel's security requirements.[20] For Israel, security consists of preventing attacks or deterrence. Deterrence is achieved through the demonstration of military superiority, communicating the futility of resistance. Disproportionate military responses to real or alleged security threats are an integral part of this deterrence. Retaliating with overwhelming force was termed "escalation dominance," as stated by Moshe Dayan; it was believed to deter future attacks by raising the cost of Israeli blood to a level untenable for the Palestinians or enemy populations.[21] In the beginning of the second Intifada, the Israeli military acted with disproportionate force, since they believed their mistake in the first Intifada was initially responding without enough strength, thus not communicating sufficient resolve and force.[22] This policy has remained central to Israeli military philosophy and relations with the Palestinians.[23]

Oslo embodied the Israeli military solution for insurgent populations: demonstrating military superiority and deterring resistance activities. The Oslo regime provides a daily display of Israel's overwhelming military power through population control. Closures, permits, checkpoints, and curfews serve as an ongoing "shock and awe" program. These policies are meant to increase frustration among the Palestinian population, convincing them of the futility of defeating the Israeli military.[24] The population, in turn, would theoretically compel the fighters to cease their attacks. The population must have the will and capacity to force the insurgents or protesters to stop.[25] However, Oslo prevents the populace from being able to play such a role.

The separation of the population into fragmented and separate territories is believed to enhance deterrence. Thus the parcellization of territory accords with Israeli security doctrine, which aims to prevent actions by others, rather than work toward direct military conquest.[26] The location of Israeli settlements has both political and military goals. In addition to the political goal of preventing a contiguous Palestinian state, placing settlements in densely populated Palestinian areas also increases the presence of the Israeli Defense Forces. This provides more opportunities to thwart military advances or even the organizing of Palestinian forces, preventing insurgency. In addition, it creates new borders to police, red lines whose crossing signals international (primarily American) justification for retaliation. This is particularly important since securing international legitimacy for military actions ranks high in Israeli calculations, more so than domestic considerations.[27]

Decentralized Mobilizing and Competition

Israeli policy rests on collective punishment, popular frustration, and physical separation to impede the organizing capability of the populace. Ultimately, so the theory goes, the Palestinians should realize that opposition cannot succeed, and give up.

Clearly, the pacification expected by the Israelis has not occurred. Instead, Oslo has resulted in the radicalization and militarization of the opposition, an increase in insurgency, and more attacks on Israelis. Why? Is it because, as Israel maintains, the opposition is part of a well-organized and directed challenge, which neither Arafat nor his successors acted to prevent, or indeed, has encouraged and led? If that were the case, increased enforcement of the above measures would be called for: more separation between Israelis and Palestinians and collective punishments.

The evidence from cases worldwide demonstrates that the tactics employed by Israel should be expected to increase, rather than end, the political violence of the resistance.[28] The radicalization of the opposition during the Oslo period and the second Intifada is due, in part, to policies pushing groups into increasingly decentralized organizing, while at the same time exacerbating the underlying grievances and causes of opposition.[29]

Numerous Israeli–Oslo policies caused the decline of mass popular participation, including the inability to move freely or gather together. Oslo's provisions inhibited organization and freedom of association, which removed the popular character of the opposition and forced the remaining activists to work underground in decentralized cells. Prohibitions, harsh penalties for organizing, and increased difficulties of convening meetings caused the exodus of most classes from organized resistance. Closure has almost completely hindered all forms of involvement and community participation and, in many cases, even the ability to work. Increased economic hardship, repression, and the lack of public space created by Oslo's fragmentation of the territory all decreased the ability and willingness of the populace to become involved in the opposition. These same mechanisms diminished the levers of political control and hierarchy within opposition groups. Further, the nature of the PA itself added to the dissociation of the community from formal organizing. Coming from outside the territories, the PA wanted to establish a governing base independent of the indigenous leaders developed in the Intifada. It did so by drawing on old traditional elites and its own street cadres. The middle class and popular leadership, which organized democratically, were marginalized.

Economic hardship, caused by closure, has exacerbated these tendencies by reducing the number of individuals available for protest actions. The increase in poverty which resulted from closure is not directly responsible for the radicalization of the opposition.[30] The poor are not the mainstay of organized oppositions, even in suicide actions, and are, in any case, too busy trying to survive to participate in such organizations.[31]

Theories of Popular Mobilization

Policies to inhibit mobilizing are based on the premise that these movements are hierarchical, controlled by a leader who commands his followers. Without the leader, the reasoning goes, the masses would be either unable or unwilling to act. One theorist calls this the "microwave" theory of political violence. The leader pushes a button, and militancy is turned on or off.[32] However, the difficulty of formal organizing more often leads to decentralized and underground activities, not to the disappearance of the organization as top–down theories of opposition suggest.

What happens when a movement becomes exclusive and fragmented? Accountability and moderation suffer, and violence increases. The remaining small groups of activists move underground to survive, becoming isolated from the influence of the community and immune to external factors. Without a social base to consider, the movement is liberated from the constraint of maintaining the good will of the masses.[33] Cut off from outside contacts, they become trapped within underground "spirals of encapsulation," which diminish the potential of outside ideologies, ideas, and individuals to alter activists' views.[34] Such isolation, or segregation from the object of their resistance, is key to the creation of oppositional consciousness. For this, autonomous spaces where the movement can develop without ties of affection, friendship, or business are necessary to promote more radical views.[35] Integration spoils this oppositional consciousness. Insulation from alternative opinions or practices has been instrumental in creating loyal members for cults.[36] In the extreme, as is the case in exclusive and underground organizing, separation promotes "anti-system" ideologies, a process that has led to violence against civilians in Algeria.[37]

Violence is most prominent when the majority of the movement has either integrated into the establishment or disbanded. The relationship between numbers and the use of violence in protest activities is inverse: the more people, the less violence is necessary to demonstrate commitment to the goals of the movement. The majority, in any movement, is unwilling to engage in violence, and this logic is behind the democratic regulation of social movements. Once danger exists, most participants exit, leaving behind only those most committed.

As numbers dwindle, the need to make a big statement remains. During Italy's period of social activism and terrorism, it was the groups that lacked resources and the ability to engage in organized movement politics that specialized in violence, a cheap and available resource not requiring much coordination. Without the necessary numbers to communicate such a message, more violent methods are used to achieve the desired result. Violence indirectly aids the cause through publicity, demonstrating the credibility and commitment of the protesters, which adds legitimacy to their cause, recruiting members by being the most active organization in the field, keeping members in line and committed, and provoking a response that polarizes the sides, forcing previously neutral individuals to take a stand.[38]

Organization and bureaucratization tend to moderate movements, both by subjecting members to a hierarchy of authority and through the constraining influences of the majority. Arguably, this pushes formal organizations toward greater acceptance of the status quo. Theorists of the poor bemoan the co-optation and pacification of social movements through the establishment of formal organizations. In particular, the use of disruptive actions decreases, since the organization incorporates various classes: the middle, which has an aversion to violence; and the leadership, with an interest in becoming part of the "reputable" establishment.

What if the community itself approves of the use of violence? Currently a majority of Palestinians condone continuing military operations within Israel.[39] In this case, too, formal organizing moderates the movement. The community may condone the actions of the few who take violent action, but it is unwilling to engage in or take responsibility for those acts. In addition, organizational dynamics themselves mitigate against violence.

Violence is problematic for the stability of organizations. The practical organizational need for resources and money limits the amount of anti-establishment and disruptive activities.[40] Organizations are fragile and resource dependent. In order to survive, they must incorporate various classes with access to necessary resources, including money, networks, access to elites and influential individuals, and meeting locations. The middle professional and business classes are usually involved—classes with concrete, tangible interests, which can easily be threatened by negative repercussions from the authorities. Organizations institutionalize decision-making processes, spreading responsibility for the organization's actions among the membership. Formal organizations incorporate hierarchical control and adherence to the decisions of the leadership, factors that moderate group activities.

Leaderships not only authorize but also constrain resistance activities. In Hamas, as in most Islamist movements, political wings are separate from military branches, and political approval is required before operations are authorized. Leaders not only authorize but also prohibit operations. Subjecting the military to political constraints has the potential to moderate the movement with practical considerations. Numerous cease-fires have been enacted by Hamas leaders. Only leaders popularly recognized as authorities are able to pledge their movement's commitment to a deal. Since the organization is not formal, leadership depends on accepted authority. In Lebanon, the use of suicide bombing by Hizballah was subject to the approval of the clerical leadership. After the Israeli withdrawal in 1985, leaders proclaimed an end to the use of the tactic, with rare exceptions.[41]

Further, leaderships are subject to the requisites of public opinion in their constituency, which can act as a brake on violent movement activities. The community was able to perform this function in Egypt, for example. Popular outrage against the killing of tourists in November 1997 by al-Gama'a al-Islamiyya convinced the leadership of that group to amend its ideological stance and strategy, effectively ending the violence.[42] Israeli policies of collective punishment rely on the community to rein in the activists. To do this, the populace must have the will and capacity to deter the insurgents or protesters. By severing the link between the community and the activists, decentralization prohibits the community from performing this moderating function.

The absence of leaders able to command the respect and adherence of movement followers means that community influence is not felt on activists. An extreme example is the international Islamist group al Qaeda, which is divorced from any domestic or community connections, and therefore accountability. Similarly, externally based leaderships are less moderating, since they too lack the consideration of a social base in constraining their decisions. Domestic-based leaderships are the most moderating and accommodating to political opportunities. This is clear in Hamas. The external leadership in Jordan and the decentralized cells are both more radical and willing to use violence than the domestic leadership.

Israeli policy is expanding on Oslo's decentralizing tendencies by systematically eliminating the resistance leadership. This opens the field for potential leadership battles, characterized by a competition of one-upmanship. Competition is an important factor in violent protest actions. Competition within a social movement among various groups with similar goals, for example, led to high amounts of violence during Italy's experience with terrorism. Violent acts are advertisements that distinguish one group from the rest. Increased use of violence occurs when numerous groups with like goals exist, all vying for prominence and social support.[43] In the extreme, would-be leaders attempt to outdo each other through demonstrating their ability to implement ever more daring acts.

The dynamics outlined here hold when the underlying issues remain unaddressed, or indeed those problems are exacerbated, as is the case in the West Bank and Gaza strip. Grassroots support will continue to feed the opposition in such a case. In the Palestinian territories, ongoing collective repression and general punishment have effectively renewed and strengthened the commitment to the fight. The opposition in the West Bank and Gaza has more volunteers for suicide operations than it can handle.[44] It is they who seek out the organizations. Recruitment plays a marginal role.[45]

Repression, particularly indiscriminate repression applied to all without regard to whether they participated in opposition activities or not, is by itself powerfully linked to the militarization of opposition movements and the formation of broad revolutionary coalitions against the reigning authorities. Removing nonviolent options to change and influence, or even to voice protest, increases the likelihood of violent protest. Violence is legitimized as the only "way out."[46] By contrast, nonviolent options are dependent upon the response of the authorities: if the authority is not bound by "universalistic moral principles," then such action is worthless. The government remains unlimited in the range of its responses, and can merely eliminate the protesters.[47]

In a democracy, repression of unlawful activities will channel most of the group into lawful pursuits. In contexts where no mobilizing is allowed, repression will, over time, create more violent actions on the part of the group. Whereas Israel is a democracy, the occupied territories are not. Freedom of peaceful association is not a right in either the territories under Israeli or PA control.

Despite the predominance of militarized protest and substantial public support for it, nonviolent possibilities are not dead. Clearly nonviolent demonstrations are logistically more difficult than previously, as less public space is available to mobilize, network, and stage protests. Still, nonviolent actions are discussed, debated, and undertaken. Generally, however, they are neither reported by the media nor do their participants escape (Israeli) military or (Palestinian) police action. There is a widespread opinion that nonviolent protest, although desirable in theory, will only result in slaughter for the participants, effectively removing the masses from such participation.[48] This opinion is backed by experience, as nonviolent demonstrations have been met with lethal force by both the PA and Israel.[49] Advocates and organizers of nonviolent activities end up in jail alongside those engaging in violence, even members of organizations uniting Israeli Jews and Palestinians. For example, a leader of such a demonstration was placed under administrative detention since, according to authorities, he was embarking on an "unhappy" path.[50] Thousands of Palestinian political prisoners on a hunger strike, similarly, found their effort did not seem to warrant media coverage or draw attention to the conditions they were protesting. An Israeli official likened the hunger strike to terror, saying he would not give in to their demands.[51] Explicitly in reference to the lack of attention to this nonviolent action, armed groups declared their desire to kidnap soldiers and settlers to promote the prisoners' demands.[52] A demonstration in which Americans and Israeli Jews participated was greeted by live fire.[53] Another nonviolent demonstration, declared free of weapons by Amnesty International, held to draw attention to the plight of the Rafah refugee camp under curfew, was attacked by four tank shells, killing eight.[54]

Populations do rebel against more powerful authorities. Jeff Goodwin states that political exclusion and repression, not economic exploitation or poverty, explain the revolutionary movements that took place throughout the Cold War.[55] It is only states that were particularly closed politically, and excessively repressive, that faced broad revolutionary movements. Insurgencies will be popularly supported where the authorities have abused civilians in a random fashion. Continuing and increasing repression and political exclusion, Goodwin concludes, will most likely give rise to revolutionary movements.

Oslo's policies achieved the end desired in Israeli security doctrines. The cumulative effect has been to increase frustration, humiliation, and feelings of injustice among the Palestinians. However, they have not led to surrender or pacification. Nor should they be expected to. In other contexts, such effects have been crucial in creating a broad base of community support for rebellion. Senses of injustice and victimization provide tacit community approval for militarization by creating oppositional consciousness, a mental state that facilitates protest actions against a more powerful opponent. Frustration and "righteous" anger fuel this mental state.[56]

Although Israeli doctrine presumes that frustration should result in a cold calculation that insurgency is pointless and should therefore cease, only riots and crowd violence have been associated with frustration in the social analysis of protest.[57] In older crowd analyses, rational thought and action were believed to be inhibited by an increase in frustration among the populace. Whether frustration is in fact behind such events is questionable, but the emotions involved have not been linked with passivity or surrender.[58]

Failure to grasp the essential grassroots nature of the opposition and the broad support for its activities has been the mistake of many governments. Within a context of general support for opposition activities, decentralization of a movement will not end it, but only exacerbate the characteristics found in underground and exclusive organizations. If, in fact, the underlying rationale is addressed, or when the populace is provided a political opportunity to participate in formal institutions, pushing the few remaining holdouts underground can terminate the violent movement itself.

THE PALESTINIAN OPPOSITION: FROM MASSES TO MILITARIZATION

This section tests the theory outlined above against the chronology of opposition organizing from the first through second Intifada. It concentrates on two groups, Hamas (Harakat al-Muqawima al-Islamiyya—the Islamic Resistance Movement) and Fatah (Harakat al-Tahrir al-Wataniyya al-Falastiniyya—Movement for the National Liberation of Palestine), the main religious and secular opposition groups, respectively. During the first Intifada, the popular character of organizing, incorporating multiple classes of society, was directly responsible for the (relatively) nonviolent character of that uprising.[59] The progressive fragmentation of hierarchical authority in Fatah, and the increasing anarchy in that movement, resulted in less security for people in both Israel and Palestine. Fatah's lack of organizational control was partially caused by the territorial fragmentation and anti-leadership policies of Oslo. The predicament of Fatah demonstrates the future we can expect for Hamas, should these policies continue. To a large degree, and Hamas has to date maintained discipline in its ranks. Such hierarchical control should be recognized as a situation to be encouraged; fragmentation in a resistance movement with widespread support will increase its violence and inhibit a conclusion to the conflict.

The First Intifada

The first Intifada, beginning at the end of 1987, was a time of massive popular organizing involving all sectors of society. Particularly evident was the participation of women and children. A new mobilizing infrastructure emerged, revolving around democratic local committees and a rotating leadership comprising all the political factions. Strictly speaking, the Intifada was not nonviolent; however, its violence was limited to the throwing of stones against the Israeli military, not civilians. The main weapons were economic: the boycotting of Israeli commodities and taxes, and commercial strikes. Stores closed as merchants joined the Intifada, refusing to open or to sell Israeli goods.

This was not the first time the population protested. It had been doing so for years. But previous demonstrations, protests, and strikes had ended. In the period from 1977 to 1982, an average of 500 such protest events took place per year. From 1982 to the start of the uprising, the average was between 3,000 and 4,000 per year.[60] The first Intifada saw popular organizing reach a new stage by daily strikes encompassing all areas of the territories.

The self-perpetuating nature of this uprising was possible due to the development of a new organizational infrastructure. A new middle class and professional leadership, including merchants, created a network of committees that provided support for everything from education to health care. Committees ran and decided all types of actions, from strike days to the provision of education, since schools were closed by Israel. Estimates suggest that tens of thousands of committees were established, including those focused on food storage, security, health and medical relief, and agriculture.

The first Intifada had created a new leadership infrastructure in the territories. The Intifada itself came as a surprise to the Palestinian Liberation Organization (PLO) leadership outside the territories: they were politely "informed" of UNLU (United National Leadership of the Uprising) decisions; their permission was requested for demonstration events usually after the fact. Instead, up-and-coming personalities took control, subjecting their decisions to popular consent. The democratic and popular character of the Intifada demonstrated this, with prominent roles played by women, children, and even the elderly.

The leadership of the uprising was organized through the UNLU. UNLU members were young, educated, lower and middle social strata. The leadership was rotating, providing a steady flow of new leaders. They mediated quarrels, made binding decisions and imposed fines, announced demonstrations and strikes, and issued communiqués on behalf of the uprising.[61]

Hamas participated in the first Intifada along with other groups, and gained popularity due to its nationalist activities.[62] Hamas began as an off-shoot of the Muslim Brotherhood in the Palestinian territories, an organization that had been conciliatory or passive toward the Israeli occupation until the first Intifada began in December 1987. Hamas was created in order to not lose the public, which was fast demanding active opposition to the occupation.[63] At this point, the group's military wing conducted occasional operations against Israeli soldiers and military targets, but not against civilians.[64]

Repression by the Israeli authorities merely increased the level of protest.[65] The Israeli military government's attempt to keep stores open by force backfired, solidifying the merchants' support for the Intifada. Defense Minister Rabin later admitted that trying to force commercial stores to open was the biggest mistake made at that time.[66] The merchants added needed credibility and organizational and financial resources to the uprising.

The Peace Process and Arafat's Return

The Intifada led to the Madrid conference, a negotiating process involving all parties to the conflict, sponsored by President George H.W. Bush after Gulf War I. The Palestinian parties to the conference were unaware, as was everyone else, of Arafat's intermediaries negotiating directly in Oslo, Norway. The premise of the Madrid conference was that negotiations to solve the Palestinian–Israeli conflict needed to involve the countries neighboring Israel and those that hosted Palestinian refugees. This process was abruptly halted when it was announced that Arafat and Rabin had reached an agreement. The news took the Palestinian negotiators in Washington, DC, by surprise. Within days, Arafat arrived in the capital, shook Rabin's hand on the White House lawn, and they agreed to recognize each other.

The Declaration of Principles between the two sides effectively ended the Intifada. The Palestinian community was split on the merits of the agreement: those in the West Bank and Gaza were mainly in favor, those in the diaspora in the Arab countries were against. The Palestinian leaders found it hard to object to being upstaged by such a revered leader, whose name became equated with the Palestinian cause internationally and who had publicized the little-known cause until it had become widely recognized. Some leaders did express disapproval. As time went by, more moved into the critical opposition against the PLO, which by this time had become the PA. However, for the first few years, even Hamas could not remain opposed to the new situation, or again risk being out of step with its public support and losing its constituency.

Arafat could not enter and rule over this existing indigenous infrastructure: the new leadership created by the first Intifada would not acquiesce to be ruled in the style of a dictator. Their resistance, after all, had established the most democratic institutions in the Arab world during the uprising. They earned street credentials, popular legitimacy based on their own personal suffering for the cause, time spent in prison, and leadership abilities. But to build a centrally controlled state, Arafat had to dominate these internal leaders.[67] Coming from the diaspora, Arafat needed some basis for his leadership, and he found this in the same social base as the Jordanian monarchy: the old landed elite families or notables who had been marginalized by the democratic Intifada.[68] Arafat's entourage were viewed as outsiders. Coming from

Tunisia, they were termed the "Tunisians." The decision to base his rule on the old upper class was consequential, since the lack of social mobility has been a frequent complaint of the Islamists. Indeed, the main Islamist social base is among those rising stars, would-be leaders butting up against the lack of meritocracy.

Further opposed to the Intifada's democratic and meritocratic structure was the revival of the influence of extended families, tribal law, and notables in support of Arafat's administration. As is true of resurrections in general, the newly revived family was not the same as the older version, but its place in the social structure and social role was the same.[69] As Mona Younis demonstrated in her comparison of the revolutionary nationalist movements in South Africa and the Palestinian territories, the passage from elite to mass movement is necessary for the resistance's overall goals to be met.[70] In this case, the mass movement phase was the first Intifada. Arafat's homecoming signaled a reversal of the process to a conservative, status-quo social base. In one of the least clannish and tribal societies in the Arab world, tribalism made a comeback in the 1990s.

Arafat managed to create a system personally dependent on him, in which the power brokers and networks of influence and jobs were those closest to him. The new president's signature was necessary for everything. Beneath the formal structures of democracy lay informal control and patronage networks. Control over job provision, increasingly important with the closure imposed by Israel, was in the hands of Arafat loyalists. A large portion of employment was with the PA: 17 percent of all employment in the West Bank, upward of 30 percent in the Gaza strip. The new political elite allied with and in many cases became part of the economic elite. Holders of VIP cards were able to pass Israeli checkpoints during closure, providing them a comparative advantage economically.[71]

In order for the PA to fulfill its side of the Oslo bargain, a large security force was needed. As mentioned earlier, the Palestinian police forces were one of the only concrete institutions stipulated by Oslo. Shortly after Oslo, 40,000 police and intelligence officers operated among the small West Bank and Gaza strip population of around three million people. These forces were heavily staffed by foreign-based Palestinians, in addition to Fatah loyalists or the Tanzim (the Organization). The latter were internal PLO activists, somewhat hesitantly embraced by Arafat. They proved difficult to control and of dubious loyalty to the PA. They became active during the second Intifada, against the wishes of the PA, fighting Israeli military forces during their incursions into the West Bank and targeting military posts.[72]

Arafat attempted to maintain control of these forces by borrowing a page from Machiavellian and colonialist tactics. He created numerous security and intelligence forces (from between seven and nine in 1995 to eleven security services during the second Intifada), intentionally fragmented, with overlapping and vaguely specified boundaries.[73] Some groups monitored others, but ultimately, they were all supposed to be directly responsible to Arafat.[74]

Meanwhile, the indigenous Intifada-era leadership was bypassed. Faced with the reality of their marginalization and increasing power in the hands of Arafat loyalists, the domestic-based leadership was divided between several forms of retreat from the new PA system. Some accommodated themselves and attempted to integrate into the system, particularly Fatah members. Many were co-opted, often in the logical pursuit of employment. Other leaders of civil society organizations, unions, women's organizations, committees, and professional associations were integrated into the PA's governing structure.[75]

Much of the nonreligious opposition, the left, democrats and intellectuals who were unwilling to participate in the nondemocratic PA, retreated into nongovernmental organizations (NGOs). They were easily marginalized through threats of imprisonment, harassment, and threats to their funding. Desiring to do good works, and dependent on external financing from the West channeled through the PA's Ministry of the Interior, the secular opposition was effectively removed from politics and fragmented among multiple NGOs. The perceived elite character of these NGOs further divided this leadership from the grass roots of the first Intifada. Arafat's government had control over all the aid money coming into the territories, from government to the PA.[76] These associations, far from the hopes put upon them by the West as emerging centers of resistance to the state and watchdogs for democracy, have been unable to accomplish any of these goals. They did not even try, apart from mobilization to resist imposition of laws based on Egypt's version of NGO control.

By contrast to the incapacity of the secular opposition, religious opposition was independent of Western and PA financing. Their funds were from alternative sources, such as almsgiving and charitable donations. Vacated by the secular groups, the field of protest and activism became dominated by the religious groups. The PA dealt with these through alternative means. PA–Islamist relations deteriorated, progressively, from an understanding to avoid conflict, to imprisonments and raids on Islamist organizations. Originally hopeful that it could participate in the PA's government, Hamas became aware that the PA intended to stick by its agreement in Oslo, stipulating that all forms of dissent be stamped out.[77] In fact, progress in Oslo's planned redeployments was conditional upon Israel's security concerns. Since the PA's legitimacy was based on Oslo and continued progress toward Oslo's goals, the PA was obligated (and Arafat had agreed) to enforce Israel's version of security. Even if it had desired to allow participation of the Islamist groups in the government, Oslo would prevent it.

As part of the Oslo accords, the PA was charged with stamping out Hamas and all voices of protest. It did so. Waves of arrests took place of suspected opposition members. Within a few years, there were 17 PA prisons in Gaza.[78] PA clashes with Hamas resulted in deaths of the latter. After each attack, the PA conducted roundups of suspected militants. In 1996, it raided social service and educational institutions, and even mosques.[79] In 1997, after hundreds of arrests, the PA closed 16 religious-run charities and commandeered almsgiving committees.[80]

Hamas and the PA came to an agreement at the start of Oslo.[81] Realizing the popularity of the Oslo accords, Hamas had to align itself with public opinion and agreed not to fight the PA or do anything to hinder Oslo. The group desired to be part of the governing process, and contemplated forming a separate political party for that purpose, a development parallel to that of the Sinn Fein and IRA that led to the eventual end of the conflict there.[82]

Numerous analyses of Hamas have detailed the movement's pragmatism over idealism, its doctrinal flexibility, and the essential retaliatory logic of military attacks.[83] The movement is nationalistic, and only marginally concerned with religious edicts, unlike Islamist movements in other countries.[84] Leaders repeatedly proclaimed their desire to be part of the political process. The use of violence was "controlled" in order to prevent jeopardizing the continued existence of its social service organizations, initiate direct confrontation with the PA, or lose the support of popular opinion.[85] What Hamas is fundamentally after is an alteration of the terms of Oslo and a larger role in the political process within the PA itself.

What is crucial is the relationship between Hamas' leadership and the actions of its following. The structure of Hamas has, essentially, been decentralized, but with a legitimate and authoritative leadership able to speak for the membership and obtain their allegiance to central decisions. Due to the decentralized nature of the organization, and the lack of direct communication between the branches, the decisions are announced publicly.[86] The political leadership of the Islamic resistance issued decrees to either halt or initiate action, which were then enacted by the military wing. Waves of military actions by Hamas against civilians, occurred in response to specific events, such as the Hebron massacre of Palestinian worshippers in February 1994, and mass arrests or repression by the PA and Israel periodically through the Oslo years.[87] Truces or "hudna" have been called at different points in time, ceasing military actions. This first occurred after Oslo, from September 1994 to February 1996, as per the Islamist resistance's agreement with the PA.[88] This ended with Israel's assassination of Yahya Ayyash in January 1996, triggering a number of suicide bombings. Arrests and roundups of suspected activists by the PA and harsh repression of the organization followed.

As the Oslo regime wore on, the Palestinian population lost progressively more public space and rights, due both to enforcements by Israel and the PA. Israeli settlements and land confiscations of West Bank territory continued and the economic isolation of the Palestinian territories and their dependence on Israel increased. Oslo provided for the increasing isolation into small cantons and the PA denied them a political voice. The public spaces that did open up were ones of confrontation: checkpoints and border crossings, from one zone to another.[89] The time consumed in these activities, along with the humiliation they entailed, fueled existing claims of injustice. As one observer noted, a major consequence has been the "theft of time" and the inability to make plans, even for work.[90] Criticism of the PA began even from within, from Fatah and the Tanzim. Marwan Barghouti is the face of this democratic criticism. Further, the international political process of negotiations was seriously stalled.

Second Intifada

Seven years after the handshake on the White House lawn inaugurating the Oslo accords, the condition of the Palestinians had worsened and laid the groundwork for a violent movement by small numbers of activists. Paradoxically, although control of some areas had passed from Israeli to Palestinian hands, Oslo created sweeping changes in the geography of the West Bank and Gaza, parceling the territories with crisscrossed checkpoints of control. Israeli settlements increased by over 50 percent during those seven years, and the settler population almost doubled.[91]

The second Intifada began the day after Ariel Sharon's visit to the Dome of the Rock or al-Aqsa mosque in late September 2000. Palestinian demonstrators and worshipers were fired upon, sparking an uprising. In contrast to conditions during the first Intifada, the masses were now marginalized, leaving the field of resistance to small groups of activists.

Fatah and the Tanzim were at the forefront of this uprising. They made up the internal leadership, those who had lived through the first Intifada. From the start of Oslo, their adherence to PA authority had been conditional. This made the disintegration of movement authority in the absence of its leadership more pronounced. Although Arafat did not order the al-Aqsa uprising, he did not act forcefully to halt it in the initial period. His low approval rating, scoring only about one-quarter of the population at that time, led analysts to conclude that any decision to counter the Intifada on his part would have been ignored and his leadership jeopardized.[92]

During the first two years of this Intifada, Israel assassinated over 100 political activists, both religious and secular.[93] During the reoccupation of West Bank towns in spring 2002, much of Fatah's mid-level leadership was eliminated. The leadership vacuum was filled by young men increasingly autonomous of any hierarchy or control. Loosely, they are collectively known as al-Aqsa Martyrs Brigade, but other names have been coined for some, including Battalions of the Return and Jenin Martyr's Brigade. When the phenomenon first developed, it was interpreted through an elite bias. These new "splinter" groups were assumed to be taking orders from leaders abroad.[94] Later it became clear that groups were acting on their own. The PA leadership increasingly complained about them, calling them gangs, "armed men," thugs, or mafias.[95]

The rise of localized and independent power centers, divorced from national authorities, is clear from the events of the last few years, particularly in the northern area, including Nablus, Jenin, Qalquiliyya, and Tulkaram. Truces accepted by other opposition groups, including the Islamists, have been ignored and violated by the Brigade.[96] Decisions by the Fatah Revolutionary Council could not be enforced. The popular resistance committees refused Arafat's order for them to dissolve.[97] Independent military actions were conducted, including the assassination of collaborators and recruiting children for suicide bombings, without the approval or knowledge of the Brigade leader.[98] Against PA orders for calm before the hearing at the International Court of

Justice, in The Hague, on the legitimacy of the separation wall, one of these groups carried out a bombing.[99]

PA officials have become targets of these groups. For example, the PA's interior minister was threatened in Nablus.[100] Further, that town's governor's cars were set on fire and his brother kidnapped.[101] The Gaza police chief was kidnapped. In Jenin, the governor was kidnapped and beaten publicly, accused of corruption, and his successor's office raided. The home of a PA police officer was set on fire, while 100 other policemen were across the street.[102] Individuals close to Arafat have been attacked, killed, or kidnapped.[103] Offices and journalists have also been attacked. Most recently, Mahmud Abbas was fired upon in Arafat's mourning tent by individuals calling themselves the Abu Ammar (Arafat's *nom de guerre*) brigades.[104] In Gaza, the rift between Arafat's nephew and choice for governor (Musa Arafat) and Muhammad Dahlan has seen much of Fatah siding with the latter, explicitly attacking President Arafat and his orders.[105] The motive, according to PA observers, is to solidify the leadership positions of the actors, and force changes in the PA leadership and policies.[106]

This dynamic of fragmentation is illustrated in the Brigade leader of Jenin, Zakariya Zubeidi. Although he began as a peace activist, he is now known as the unofficial mayor of Jenin.[107] He is independent of PA authority, and his group has attacked and kidnapped PA officials and their offices on numerous occasions. One governor was given a public beating for his alleged corruption.[108] The use of violence in consolidating the chain of leadership is clear. Two days after assuming the reigns of authority, he authorized a suicide bombing in Israel. Since then, he has not authorized any suicide bombings.[109] Other groups tried to join his, exemplifying the stakes of these power struggles. The leader of Fatah in Jenin decided to join his group to Zubeidi's, which won him the ire of Arafat and landed him in prison.[110]

Whereas Islamist actions get all the press, the Israelis held the secular Tanzim and Fatah branches as responsible for half of all attacks on Israelis in 2002.[111] Previously, it had followed the PA's orders, battling against the Islamists and suppressing them. Now many branches of (nominally) Fatah members join the Islamic opposition. In fact, as of 2004, Israeli press reported that these groups were a larger security threat than Hamas.[112] Nablus, in particular, is seen as a prime source of suicide bombers. Hamas and Islamic Jihad, for the most part, are viewed as disciplined and trustworthy by comparison, remaining aloof from the "turf wars" going on around them.[113] It is Hamas that is heading the electoral registration drive, attempting to convince the populace to exercise their democratic rights.[114]

Particularly since the assassination of the Hamas leader Shaykh Yasin and then Abd al-Aziz Rantisi, fragmentation has been observed in Hamas in the West Bank, but still less than that in Fatah or Islamic Jihad. In Gaza, Hamas is the most centralized. Although the leadership assassinations were meant to deter the formation of a "Hamasland" in Gaza, Hamas is more solidified there than previously.[115]

CONCLUSION AND POLICY IMPLICATIONS

What causes movements to use violence, and under what circumstances can they be induced to abandon such methods? What tactics should be used to battle a violent nationalist insurgency with grass roots support? In many cases, an inaccurate appraisal of the phenomenon has resulted in policy prescriptions that have exacerbated, not solved, the problem. One of the most violent, ongoing, national-based conflicts with Islamism today is in the occupied Palestinian territories. The Oslo process expressly provided the elements for the future militarization of the opposition to the PA. Oslo exacerbated the underlying issues in the Palestinian conflict, while at the same time pushing the decentralization of the resistance.

Oslo embodies Israel's tactical strategies for battling the opposition movement. Identical strategies are being utilized in the current U.S. battle with Iraqi insurgents. If intended to moderate violent opposition, the premises of Israeli interaction have proven inaccurate. The intent of the Oslo accords is a secondary and less pressing conclusion arising from this study. The more important implication of this analysis is the effect of increasing the decentralization of a movement and fragmenting it, the use of collective punishment, prevention of any political role, and eliminating the movement's leadership.

This study showed that resistance movements cannot be characterized by a broad brush, as either violent or not. The use of violence can be calculated or the result of internal organizational factors, such as the quest to establish leadership or compete with other factions of the movement. Collective punishment or indiscriminate repression provides increased support for opposition activities and justifies the use of violence against an unjust oppressor. When any individual, guilty or not, young or elderly, can be the object of military or police reprisals, a backlash occurs and creates more resistance.

Just as violent actions can be the result of tactical and organizational concerns, rather than essential ideologies of the movement, so too can seemingly neutral processes of institutionalization moderate the movement. Movements do pay attention to their public's opinion. Formal organization and hierarchy create structures of accountability to the community and multiple classes, which approve the use of violence much less than underground, exclusive groups.

The repeated insistence on seeing insurgencies as coordinated, hierarchical movements has clouded the policy options for both the United States and Israel, and has enflamed the militarization of the conflicts. Leaving the leadership in place provides a negotiating partner with the ability to command allegiance to whatever deal that leader negotiates. Removing the leader does not increase the chances of peace, but merely transfers the resistance to uncontrollable underground and uncoordinated groups. When the underlying causes of the movement still exist, such as collective punishment, lack of political voice, population control, and humiliation, a violent spiral will be created. Both history and social science have shown that to formulate policy options for an insurgency, one must first identify the movement's character.

Too often, the fundamental reality of an insurgency with grass roots appeal, not hierarchically controlled, has not been acknowledged. Eliminating leaders in this situation will prolong and deepen the conflict.

Notes

The views expressed here are the author's alone, and do not represent the Naval Postgraduate School or any institutional affiliation. I would like to thank Glenn Robinson for his help and constructive suggestions. A version of this study, entitled "Oslo and Militarized Islam: Implementing Disaster in Palestine," was given at the Middle East Studies Conference, San Francisco, November 22, 2004.

1. Internationally based movements without a domestic constituency behave differently.
2. I concentrate here on Israeli security perspectives; this should not be construed as neglecting the very real Palestinian security concerns. However, this chapter focuses on the effect of counterterrorist techniques used by the Israelis.
3. The Declaration of Principles (1993), and the Israeli–Palestinian Interim Agreement on the West Bank and the Gaza Strip (1995), Oslo I and II respectively, can be found at the Israeli Ministry of Foreign Affairs website, www.mfa.gov.il, accessed May 27, 2005; and on MidEast Web, *www.mideastweb. org*, accessed May 27, 2005.
4. I take no position here on the justice of the accords, but analyze their implications for opposition tactics.
5. See Oslo II, especially Annex I.
6. The goal of this control, according to Halper, is not defeating but paralyzing the enemy. He likens this strategy to that of the Viet Cong, who used it successfully to defeat an army of superior numbers. Jeff Halper, "The 94 Percent Solution: A Matrix of Control," *Middle East Report*, no. 216 (2000), 15.
7. Sara Roy, "The Palestinian State: Division and Despair," *Current History*, January 2004, 33.
8. Oslo II (1995) established three zones of jurisdiction within the West Bank. The PA now ruled over Area A, Area B was controlled by both the PA and Israel, and Area C was Israel's sole responsibility. This patchwork of differential territorial control resulted in exit and entry checkpoints for passage between areas. See also Rabin's speech to the Knesset on the Interim Agreement, October 5,1995, printed in "The Peace Process," *Journal of Palestine Studies* vol. 25, no. 2 (1996), 137–139.
9. Sara Roy, "Why Peace Failed: An Oslo Autopsy," *Current History*, January 2002, 9.
10. Roy, "The Palestinian State."
11. Camille Mansour, "Israel's Colonial Impasse (Essay)," *Journal of Palestine Studies*, vol. 30, no. 4 (2001), 85.
12. Quoted in Cheryl A. Rubenberg, *The Palestinians: In Search of a Just Peace* (Boulder: Lynne Rienner, 2003), 118.
13. Roy, "Why Peace Failed," 10.
14. The Hebron protocol (1997) split the city internally into areas of Israeli and Palestinian control, effectively placing a Jewish population center or enclave in the middle of a densely populated Palestinian area. Ibid., 12.
15. Lucy Mair and Robyn Long, "Backs to the Wall: Israel's Stranglehold on the Palestinian Economy Is Consolidated by a Massive Wall," *Dollars & Sense*, November/December 2003.

16. Leila Farsakh, "Under Siege: Closure, Separation and the Palestinian Economy," *Middle East Report*, no. 217 (2000); Sara Roy, "Ending the Palestinian Economy," *Middle East Policy*, vol. 9, no. 4 (2002), 124. Closure is provided for in the Economic Protocol of Oslo II, Article VII.1.

17. Amira Hass, "Israel's Closure Policy: An Ineffective Strategy of Containment and Repression," *Journal of Palestine Studies*, vol. 31, no. 3 (2002).

18. The pass system is included in Oslo II, Annex III, Article 11.

19. Rubenberg, *The Palestinians*, 115.

20. Eva Etzioni-Halevy, "Civil Military Relations and Democracy: The Case of the Military-Political Elites' Connection in Israel," *Armed Forces & Society*, vol. 22, no. 3 (1996), 407; also Yoram Peri, "The Israeli Military and Israel's Palestinian Policy: From Oslo to the Al Aqsa Intifada" (Washington, DC: United States Institute of Peace, 2002), 27.

21. Quoted in Uri Bar-Joseph, "Variations on a Theme: The Conceptualization of Deterrence in Israeli Strategic Thinking," *Security Studies*, vol. 7, no. 3 (1998), 152. On retaliation in Israeli military practice, see Ranan D. Kuperman, "Rules of Military Retaliation and the Practice by the State of Israel," *International Interactions*, vol. 27, no. 3 (2001).

22. Peri, "The Israeli Military and Israel's Palestinian Policy," 31.

23. Zeev Maoz, "The Unlimited Use of the Limited Use of Force: Israel and Low-Intensity Warfare, 1949–2004," Paper presented at the International Studies Association, Montreal, March 17–20, 2004.

24. Israel Tal, *National Security: The Israeli Experience*, trans. Martin Kett (Westport, CT: Praeger, 2000), 52.

25. Maoz, "The Unlimited Use of the Limited Use of Force."

26. Tal, *National Security*, 47.

27. Bar-Joseph, "Variations on a Theme," 155; Ranan D. Kuperman, "The Effect of Domestic and Foreign Pressure on Israeli Decisions to Use Limited Military Force," *Journal of Peace Research*, vol. 40, no. 6 (2003).

28. Political violence can be defined as activities by individuals or collectives aimed at creating social or political change through public protest. Donatella Della Porta, *Social Movements, Political Violence, and the State: A Comparative Analysis of Italy and Germany* (New York: Cambridge University Press, 1995), 3.

29. Radicalization is the process of increasingly stringent and uncompromising views among a group; militarization refers to the group's turn to political violence as the mainstay of its tactics.

30. See, for example, Alan B. Krueger and Jitka Maleckova, "Education, Poverty and Terrorism: Is There a Causal Connection?" *Journal of Economic Perspectives*, vol. 17, no. 4 (2003).

31. Economic hardship does increase the legitimacy of protest, since poverty demonstrates the injustice of the authority's policies. This merely adds to the pile of current complaints, and is neither necessary nor sufficient for large-scale protest to occur. In fact, the countries that experienced revolutions were not the most poor, but were those with closed political systems and political repression. Jeff Goodwin, *No Other Way Out: States and Revolutionary Movements, 1945–1991* (New York: Cambridge University Press, 2001).

32. Glenn E. Robinson, "The Peace of the Powerful," in Roane Carey, ed., *The New Intifada: Resisting Israel's Apartheid* (New York: Verso, 2001), 111.

33. Marc Sageman, *Understanding Terror Networks* (Philadelphia: University of Pennsylvania Press, 2004), 149.

34. Della Porta, *Social Movements, Political Violence, and the State*, 12.

35. Aldon Morris and Naomi Braine, "Social Movements and Oppositional Consciousness," in Jane Mansbridge and Aldon Morris, eds., *Oppositional Consciousness: The Subjective Roots of Social Protest* (Chicago: University of Chicago Press, 2001).

36. Charles Tilly, *From Mobilization to Revolution* (New York: McGraw-Hill, 1978), 72–73.

37. Mohammed M. Hafez, "From Marginalization to Massacres: A Political Process Explanation of Gia Violence in Algeria," in Quintan Wiktorowicz, ed., *Islamic Activism: A Social Movement Theory Approach* (Bloomington: Indiana University Press, 2004).

38. Richard E. Rubenstein, "The Psycho-Political Sources of Terrorism," in Charles W. Kegley Jr., ed., *The New Global Terrorism: Characteristics, Causes, Controls* (Upper Saddle River, NJ: Prentice Hall, 2003), 140.

39. Jerusalem Media & Communication Center, Public Opinion Poll Unit, Poll no. 51, June 2004, at www.jmcc.org/publicpoll/results/2004/no51.pdf, accessed May 26, 2005.

40. Frances Fox Piven and Richard A. Cloward, "Normalizing Collective Protest," in Aldon D. Morris and Carol McClurg Mueller, eds., *Frontiers in Social Movement Theory* (New Haven: Yale University Press, 1992); and Frances Fox Piven and Richard A. Cloward, *Poor People's Movements: Why They Succeed, How They Fail* (New York: Pantheon Books, 1977).

41. Ehud Sprinzak, "Rational Fanatics," *Foreign Policy*, September/October 2000, 70.

42. Mohammed M. Hafez and Quintan Wiktorowicz, "Violence as Contention in the Egyptian Islamic Movement," Quintan Wiktorowicz, ed., in *Islamic Activism: A Social Movement Theory Approach* (Bloomington: Indiana University Press, 2004), 62.

43. Donatella Della Porta and Sidney Tarrow, "Unwanted Children: Political Violence and the Cycle of Protest in Italy, 1966–1973," *European Journal of Political Research*, vol. 14 (1986), 626, 29; Sidney Tarrow, *Democracy and Disorder: Protest and Politics in Italy 1965–1975* (New York: Clarendon Press, 1989).

44. United States Institute of Peace, "Islamic Extremists: How Do They Mobilize Support?," (Washington, DC: USIP, 2002).

45. Even in international terrorism, recent data shows that members are not recruited, but it is they who actively seek to join the organization. Sageman, *Understanding Terror Networks*.

46. Goodwin, *No Other Way Out*.

47. Gay W. Seidman, "Blurred Lines: Nonviolence in South Africa," *PS: Political Science & Politics*, vol. 33, no. 2 (2000).

48. Lori A. Allen, "Palestinians Debate 'Polite' Resistance to Occupation," *Middle East Report*, no. 225 (2002).

49. This is in addition to many technically nonlethal methods, which in fact often result in critical injuries.

50. Amira Hass, "Non-Violence Frightens the Army," *Ha'aretz*, November 10, 2004.

51. *Middle East International*, August 27, 2004, 13–14.

52. Khaled Abu Toameh, "Frustrated Fatah Threatens Kidnappings," *Jerusalem Post*, August 27, 2004.

53. Graham Usher, "The End of the Road?" *Middle East International*, January 9, 2004, 15.

54. Graham Usher, "Rafah: The End of the Rainbow," *Middle East International*, May 28, 2004, 5.
55. Goodwin, *No Other Way Out.*
56. Jane Mansbridge, "The Making of Oppositional Consciousness," in Mansbridge and Morris, eds. *Oppositional Consciousness.*
57. Historical and social scientific analysis reveals that frustration and feelings of injustice from indiscriminate repression merely increase the potential for developing a broad revolutionary coalition. See Goodwin, *No Other Way Out*; Mohammed M. Hafez, *Why Muslims Rebel: Repression and Resistance in the Islamic World* (Boulder: Lynne Rienner, 2003).
58. Recently, the IDF have become aware of the dangers of humiliation, and instituted seminars to attempt to train soldiers on proper checkpoint behavior. However, the inherent power discrepancy embodied in the border crossing, with Israeli soldiers in charge, will effectively prevent humiliation from being erased from the situation. Amira Hass, "Checkpoint Behavior," *Ha'aretz*, September 2, 2004.
59. Throwing stones at armed soldiers and tanks is relatively nonviolent. Certainly, unarmed civilians were not targets. The context here can be compared to other insurgencies against heavily armed authorities that do not obey universalistic principles. See Seidman, "Blurred Lines."
60. Lisa Hajjar, Mouin Rabbani, and Joel Beinin, "Palestine and the Arab–Israeli Conflict for Beginners," in Zachary Lockman and Joel Beinin, eds., *Intifada: The Palestinian Uprising against Israeli Occupation* (Boston: South End Press, 1989).
61. Ghassan Andoni, "A Comparative Study of Intifada 1987 and Intifada 2000," in Carey, ed., *The New Intifada*; also see Joost R. Hiltermann, *Behind the Intifada: Labor and Women's Movements in the Occupied Territories* (Princeton: Princeton University Press, 1991).
62. See Graham Usher, "What Kind of Nation? The Rise of Hamas in the Occupied Territories," in Joel Beinin and Joe Stork, eds., *Political Islam: Essays from Middle East Report* (Berkeley: University of California Press, 1997). Census data shows that even now, at the height of Hamas' popularity, its own adherents do not share the Islamist goals of the organization, but support it due to its nationalist actions. See Jerusalem Media & Communication Center, at www.jmcc.org, accessed May 26, 2005.
63. Glenn E. Robinson, "Hamas as Social Movement," in Wiktorowicz, ed., *Islamic Activism*, 121.
64. The exception to this was in 1990, after Palestinian civilians were killed at the al-Aqsa mosque by the IDF. The method was knife stabbings.
65. Marwan Khawaja, "Resource Mobilization, Hardship, and Popular Collective Action in the West Bank," *Social Forces*, vol. 73, no. 1 (September 1994).
66. Salim Tamari, "The Revolt of the Petite Bourgeoisie: Urban Merchants and the Palestinian Uprising," in Jamal R. Nassar and Roger Heacock, eds., *Intifada: Palestine at the Crossroads* (New York: Praeger, 1990), 159.
67. Glenn E. Robinson, *Building a Palestinian State: The Incomplete Revolution* (Indianapolis: Indiana University Press, 1997), 175.
68. Ibid., chapter 7.
69. Hillel Frisch, "Modern Absolutist or Neopatriarchal State Building? Customary Law, Extended Families, and the Palestinian Authority," *International Journal of Middle East Studies*, no. 29 (1997).
70. Mona N. Younis, *Liberation and Democratization: The South African and Palestinian National Movements*, ed. Bert Klandermans, vol. 11, *Social Movements, Protest, and Contention* (Minneapolis: University of Minnesota Press, 2000).

71. Hans-Joachim Rabe, "Palestinian Territories: From State Building to Crisis Management," in Volker Perthes, ed., *Arab Elites: Negotiating the Politics of Change* (Boulder: Lynne Rienner, 2004), 274, 278.
72. Graham Usher, "Fatah's Tanzim: Origins and Politics," *Middle East Report*, no. 217 (2000).
73. Graham Usher, "The Politics of Internal Security: The Palestinian Authority's New Security Services," in George Giacaman and Dag Jørund Lønning, eds., *After Oslo: New Realities, Old Problems* (Chicago: Pluto Press, 1998).
74. Robinson, *Building a Palestinian State*.
75. Jamil Hilal, "The Effect of the Oslo Agreement," in Giacaman and Lønning, eds., *After Oslo*.
76. Rema Hammami, "Palestinian NGOs since Oslo: From NGO Politics to Social Movements?" *Middle East Report*, vol. 30, no. 214 (2000).
77. Oslo II, Annex 1, Article 2. See Usher, "The Politics of Internal Security."
78. Ibid., 158.
79. Graham Usher, "Closures, Cantons and the Palestinian Covenant," *Middle East Report*, no. 199 (1996), 33.
80. Rabe, "Palestinian Territories."
81. Naomi Weinberger, "The Palestinian National Security Debate," *Journal of Palestine Studies*, vol. 24, no. 3 (1995).
82. Shaul Mishal and Avraham Sela, "Participation without Presence: Hamas, the Palestinian Authority and the Politics of Negotiated Coexistence," *Middle Eastern Studies*, vol. 38, no. 3 (July 2002).
83. Shaul Mishal and Avraham Sela, *The Palestinian Hamas: Vision, Violence, and Coexistence* (New York: Columbia University Press, 2000), chapter. 3.
84. United States Institute of Peace, "Islamic Extremists."
85. Mishal and Sela, *The Palestinian Hamas*.
86. Ziad Abu-Amr and Haider Abdel Shafi, "Interviews from Gaza: Palestinian Options under Siege," *Middle East Policy*, vol. IX, no. 4 (2002); and Abd al-Aziz Rantisi et al., "Interviews from Gaza: What Hamas Wants," *Middle East Policy*, vol. IX, no. 4 (2002).
87. For a concise list of specific terrorist campaigns, see Robert A. Pape, "The Strategic Logic of Suicide Terrorism," *American Political Science Review*, vol. 97, no. 3 (2003).
88. Wendy Kristiansen, "Challenge and Counterchallenge: Hamas's Response to Oslo," *Journal of Palestine Studies*, vol. 28, no. 3 (1999).
89. Rema Hammami, "On the Importance of Thugs: The Moral Economy of a Checkpoint," *Middle East Report*, no. 231 (2004).
90. Hass, "Israel's Closure Policy."
91. Graham Usher, "Facing Defeat: The Intifada Two Years On," *Journal of Palestine Studies*, vol. 32, no. 2 (2003), 22.
92. Rubenberg, *The Palestinians*, 243.
93. Ibid., 138.
94. Khaled Abu Toameh, "New Fatah Groups Controlled by PLO Dissident in Lebanon," *Jerusalem Post*, August 26, 2002.
95. Mouin Rabbani, "A Smorgasbord of Failure: Oslo and the Al-Aqsa Intifada," in Carey, ed., *The New Intifada*; and Usher, "Facing Defeat."
96. Khaled Abu Toameh, "Fatah Heads Worried about Renegades," *Jerusalem Post*, July 1, 2003.
97. Usher, "Facing Defeat."
98. Amira Hass, "Palestinian Parents' Nightmare in Nablus," *Ha'aretz*, August 1, 2004.

99. Khalid Amayreh, "The Killings Go On," *Middle East International*, March 5, 2004, 13.

100. Khaled Abu Toameh, "Aksa Martyrs Brigades Threatens PA minister," *Jerusalem Post*, February 9, 2003, 2.

101. Khaled Abu Toameh, "Losing Authority," *Jerusalem Post*, March 5, 2004.

102. Graham Usher, "Facing Defeat," *Middle East International*, September 24, 2004, 17.

103. "Fatah in Disarray," *Middle East International*, March 5, 2004, 12.

104. Arnon Regular and Jack Khoury, "Dozens of Fatah Gunmen Open Fire on Abu Mazen," *Ha'aretz*, November 15, 2004.

105. Graham Usher, "Waving and Drowning," *Middle East International*, August 6, 2004, 12; Amira Hass, "Demonstrations in Gaza For and Against Mousa Arafat—Sometimes Called Moshe," *Ha'aretz*, July 20, 2004.

106. Usher, "Waving and Drowning."

107. Ibid.

108. Molly Moore, "Refuge Is Prison for Hunted Palestinian," *Washington Post*, August 23, 2004.

109. Ibid.

110. Matthew Gutman, "Al-Aksa's Wild Card Continues to Trump Arafat," *Jerusalem Post*, August 4, 2003.

111. "Marwan Barghouti, Fatah-Tanzim, and the Escalation of the Intifada," Jerusalem Issue Brief, Jerusalem Center for Public Affairs, vol. 1, no. 16 (January 24, 2002), at www.jcpa.org.

112. Ellis Shuman, "Arafat's Fatah militias responsible for most of the terror," *Israelinsider*, March 19, 2004, at http://web.israelinsider.com/home.htm. In fact, Hamas was quiet by comparison during the end of 2003. Graham Usher, "The End of the Road?" *Middle East International*, January 9, 2004, 15.

113. Usher, "Facing defeat."

114. *Middle East International*, September 24, 2004, 18.

115. *Middle East International*, April 2, 2004, 4.

5

ISLAMIZATION AND
AMERICAN POLICY

Barak A. Salmoni

At the end of the twentieth century, observers of the Middle East worked to define the parameters, reach, and trajectory of Islamization. Particularly after 9/11, policymakers and analysts redoubled efforts to gauge the extent of Islamization's current and future progress and to grasp its implications for American interests. The American political–military policy community has also publicly and analytically worked to disaggregate the seemingly monolithic Islamist threat into two camps: those whose interests are inimical to American interests and those whose attitudes toward the United States do not go beyond mild antipathy or ambivalence.[1]

These are no doubt important matters. The nature of religious debate, and its impact on mass ideological proclivities and state policies of interest to America, are of deep concern to the United States. Although an internal matter, American power and diplomacy cannot forego engagement with trends possessing transnational potential in favor of an abstract, sterile notion of nonintervention in other countries' affairs. It is important to grasp the differential meanings of Islamization in various geographical environments and among diverse economic and intellectual strata.[2] No less important is the debate over whether moderate Islamists are moderate in fact—whether they are auto-reforming—or whether moderate tactics and democratic rhetoric conceal goals no less authoritarian and sociopolitically intrusive as those of the Middle East's current authoritarian, aging, and decidedly secular regimes.[3]

This chapter begins with a broader reflection on Islamization in the twenty-first century Middle East. For purposes of this discussion, the term re-Islamization is preferable to Islamization. Such semantic modification signals a substantive conviction. Rather than identifying the sociopolitical, cultural, and discursive prominence of Islam as breaking a pattern or presenting a new, divergent phenomenon within the natural teleology of modernity, it has been secularism that has presented the break. This interruption is best viewed as a slight course correction within a larger, historically authentic Islamic trajectory of Middle Eastern history.

SECULARISM, NATIONALISM, AND ISLAMISM

This is not to say that secularism, and its adjunct nationalism, have not had an impact on state formation, identity, and socioeconomic practices from North Africa to South Asia. Their impact, however, has been colored by Islam, the region's most enduring legitimacy resource. Islam has been appropriately referred to as the handmaiden of nationalism in the region.[4]

Aside from the Christian Levantines—whose contribution to the spread of Arab nationalism remains questionable—Arabism has been expressed in Islamic terms from its very origin. Kawakibi (and in their own ways Tahtawi and later 'Abduh), for example, criticized the Ottoman-Turkish yoke for suffocating the Islamic vibrancy of Arab peoples.[5] The Syrian-turned-Iraqi Sati'al-Husri, one of the chief interwar ideologues of Fertile Crescent secular Arabism, Egyptian 'Abd al-Rahman al-Bazzaz, Palestinian Christian Qustantin Zurayq, and Lebanese Christian Edmond Rabbath—all appealed to fellow Arabs to eschew religious obscurity and celebrate the life of Muhammad and early Islam as specifically Arab nationalist accomplishments.[6] The Christian Syrian Michel Aflaq, founder of the Ba'th party, was also prepared to look to Islam as proof of metahistorical Arab nationalist continuity and accomplishment.[7]

Some aspects of today's re-Islamization are indebted to forms, mechanisms, and assumptions associated with Western secular modernity. In effect, secularism and nationalism have been incorporated into—though they have not diluted—the Islamic trajectories in the Middle East, adding new, preservative components to its metahistoric repertoire. It appears that in every Middle Eastern area of concern to the United States, Islam—from rhetoric to discursive code to implicit system of meaning—has defined the quality and parameters of secularism and nationalism. At the same time, Islam has been processed according to a variety of ethno-national, local, regional, and lineage-based identities.

As a corollary, pronouncing secular Middle Eastern nationalism dead in the post-1990s era overlooks the movement's Islamic role in Islamic history as a contemporary vehicle to recommunicate indigenous Islamic authenticity. It also disregards the variegated understandings of nationalism among Middle Easterners themselves. For example, Egyptian opposition to the British in 1882 and 1919 was as much Islamic as it was nationalist.[8] Likewise, Turkish resistance to European occupation after World War I was seen by most Anatolians as an Islamic defense against Christian encroachment.[9] Shi'i community leaders cast opposition to the British in the same terms in 1920.[10] Similar impulses motivated much of the Algerian opposition to the French after World War II and were portrayed as such by secularist Front de Libération Nationale (FLN) leaders.[11] Finally, there is no doubt that the content and idiom of Pakistani nationalism has always been overwhelmingly Islamic,[12] as has been Palestinian resistance to Zionism and Israel.[13] In 1956, Egyptian President Gamal 'Abd al-Nasser proclaimed that he was nationalizing the Suez Canal *bism-il-umma*—in the name of the nation. Of which *umma* (nation) did Egyptians and other Arabs hear him speaking—Islamic or Arab?

To claim that the Muslim Middle East is fundamentally Islamic does not imply that a Muslim from the region is monolithically, genetically programmed to think in ideological Islamic terms divergent from those of non-Muslim Westerners.[14] It is high time to abandon the sterile, academic hesitancy to say that people have a tendency to think and act in terms of the societies and cultures that formed them. Intellectual assaults on the notion of culturally influenced proclivities focus on Aristotelian accidents and are articulated by expatriate Muslims, non-Muslim Arabs acculturated to non-Muslim environments,[15] or by Westerners who know little of the Muslim Middle East.[16]

Though every Muslim is a unique human being with particular approaches to his or her religious and historic legacies, Muslim Middle Easterners today are Muslims. This is even truer than claiming that Christian Americans are Christians. The latter are the postindustrial products of a half-millennium-long process of declericalization, scientization, individualization, and recalibration of communal identity to focus on territory, ethnicity, profession, or socio-economic stratum. Even authoritarian Western polities espouse the idea that people living in an area are citizens who can mobilize or participate in politics.

Without attaching a normative value to such Western processes, note that during the same period Muslims were subjected to equally powerful social and cultural formative processes. These include the longevity of self-defined, popularly legitimate Islamic polities in the Ottoman, Safavid-Qajar, and Mughal states. These states and their subjects painfully tried to stave off political, economic, military, and cultural penetration by foreign, self-identified Christian powers that located indigenous non-Muslims as points of contact and levers of influence. Later, leaders and thinkers attempted to modernize both polity and religion, often in order to preserve and energize the religion's relevance. In the twentieth century, new states emerged whose leaders' most authentic idiom was one of Islamic loyalty and whose legitimacy was based on the ability to eject the reality and traces of foreign—Christian—presence.[17] Though Muslim religious observance may have declined in the mid-twentieth century, the social vitality of the Islamic lens and ambience endured.

Significantly, in those Middle Eastern areas most associated with secularization, such as Turkey, Egypt, and Iran, the geographic diffusion of secularization was quite limited. In each case, to differing degrees, the urban bias of regime-allied modernizers combined with fiscal restraints and technological limitations to prevent the spread of secular norms, convictions, and approaches beyond the urban area.[18] At the same time, in Muslim states committed to elements of secularization, the continued use of terms and idioms associated with Islam, particularly in modernist and nationalist contexts—for example, *umma, watan/vatan, muqaddas, kutsal, jihad, fida'i/fedakar, shahid/sehit, munawwar/munevver/ziyai,* and *rehber*—had a preservative effect on the sociocultural relevance and meaning of Islam.[19]

THE CYCLE OF RENEWAL AND REFORM

Several aspects associated with Islamization can be viewed as continuations of dynamics integral to Islamic historical patterns. If Islamic activism is defined as new types of people calling for what they consider a more authentic approach to Islam in an effort to purify and reinvigorate it, it is important to remember that the ideas of renewal and reform, *tajdid* and *islah*, are integral to traditional, canonical Islam. In fact, sacred Islamic tradition asserts that every generation witnesses a renewer or reformer—a *mujaddid* or *muslih.* The Prophet Muhammad is reputed to have said, "God will send to this umma at the head of each century those who will renew its faith for it."[20] The legal schools (*madhahib*) emerging from the eighth century that determined the concepts of traditional Islamic jurisprudence were agents of reform; they began to cut away at caliphal religious power and established orthodox jurisprudence principles. This was a relatively revolutionary idea that was perpetuated by a clerical class that arose in the tenth century—henceforth known as *'ulama*—who convincingly ejected temporal rulers from spiritual matters. They also elected to withdraw from temporal matters themselves.[21] Al-Shafi'i (d. 820 C.E.), a *mujaddid* with a legacy lasting nearly a millennium, reconciled contending approaches to jurisprudence, thereby providing the basis for an enduring consensus on the principles of Islamic jurisprudence—*usul al-fiqh.*

Throughout history there has been a largely unbroken cycle of renewal and reform. At the turn of the eleventh century, Abu Hamid al-Ghazali's *Revivification of the Sciences of Religion (Ihya 'Ulum al-Din)* was a revolutionary synthesis. It articulated Islamic mysticism (Sufism) in terms legally and theologically more acceptable to orthodox *'ulama*, while invigorating orthodox Muslim practice and belief with greater spirituality. Breaking with past tensions, Sufism was able to "gain total legitimacy as being an essential part of the Islamic way of life."[22] By the time Ghazali died at the beginning of the sixth Islamic century, he was already known as a renewer.

Also conceptually congruent with *tajdid* and *islah* was the emergence of an invigorated *madrasa* culture based on the union of sultan and *'alim* in the Seljuk and post-Seljuk Turkic sultanates. In the sixteenth and seventeenth centuries, the senior Ottoman *'ulama* worked to reconcile state law with *shari'a*, while standing against innovations such as the coffeehouse.[23] The Wahhabi phenomenon of the late eighteenth century epitomizes efforts to renew and purify Islamic practice.[24]

Outside what are generally considered the central Islamic lands, Islamization and re-Islamization was also a continuous process. Imam Shamil was a militant, anticolonial Islamist in the mid-nineteenth-century Russian Empire and a spiritual precursor of Chechen nationalism. Major impulses for him included a combination of sufi aspirant guide (*murid-murshid*) mysticism and a bolstered Islamic orthodoxy.[25] A similar spirit motivated the African jihadist movements of the same era. 'Uthman Don Fodio (1754–1817), explicitly inspired by the idea of the mujaddid, denounced the tolerance of non-Muslim practices in the name of Islam among the elites and leaders of West African Muslim society. Rallying adherents in the Hausaland, 'Uthman don Fodio battled against religious synchronism. He established the Sokoto Caliphate, which engaged in mosque construction, sponsorship of schools, and the invigoration of an *'ulama* culture. In this way, a vitalized Islam spread throughout the Lake Chad region, western Sudan, Senegambia, and Nigeria, spawning conversion and Central African Islamic statelets into the 1870s.[26]

The educational and literary efforts of what Western academic historiography conventionally calls Islamic Modernism during the nineteenth century—beginning with Tahtawi in Egypt, the Jadidists in Central Asia, and soon thereafter touching every part of the *umma* including the Far East—should be viewed as links in the chain of *tajdid* and *islah*.[27] The nineteenth century seems to mark the beginning of the reform era. That history begs the question of what is new about the current era of Islamic activism that began with the 1920s to 1940s Muslim Brotherhood in Egypt?

Other new components of Islamization have precursors, as well. Calls for shariatization of law and social policy emerged forcefully in the face of libertine 'Abbasid caliphs in the ninth and tenth centuries,[28] as well as after the Ottoman Sultan Mehmet II's wildly successful rein, which brought the Empire, including Istanbul, into the heart of Europe. In the wake of a generation of increasing secular lawmaking, his successor, Bayezit II, insisted on injecting more Islam into Ottoman law and social practice through the device of *Kanun*.[29] In this case, Islamic entrenchment emerged partly from Bayezit's ethical proclivities, partly from the effort to undermine other princes' claims to the throne, and partly in order to rebuff political and ideological Shi'ite Safavid claims to the east.

Bayezit's rule bore all the hallmarks of modern Islamization throughout North Africa, the Arab East, and into Iran and Pakistan: ideological conviction; the use of religion by regimes to co-opt opposition; and the use of reinforced traditional authenticity in international relations to limit the influence of trans-state actors—in this case, Ismail Safavi's proselytizing insurgents. Similarities are noticeable in the approaches of the Mughal Aurangzeb (1658–1707). His anticonciliatory measures against Indian non-Muslims were responses to criticisms of the *mujaddid-e alf-e sani* (renewer of the second Islamic century), Ahmad Sirhindi, who preached against Hindu practices seeping into subcontinental Islam.[30] Islamist entrenchment for internal and external political reasons also characterized the later Ottoman pan-Islamism of Sultan Abdulhamit from the 1880s to 1908.[31]

Another characteristic of modern Islamism is the emergence of lay people outside the orthodox clerical realm who nurture a form of Islamic expression containing energized social meaning in a new spatial and social locus beyond that of the state and traditional *'ulama*—the parallel sector. The same phenomenon was foreshadowed in Islamic mysticism, or Sufism.[32] Its doctrines and purveyors also were outside and parallel to those of *'ulama* Islam, preaching first a more ascetic, then a more ecstatic, but always a more spiritual approach to the godhead. More fundamentally, its mechanisms of association—such as lodges, circles, retreats, and economic enterprises—were revolutionary compared to the Islam of the *madrasas*.[33] Such associational mechanisms were exogenous to Islam, reminiscent of Christian practices. So what do we make of legal and engineering syndicates, medical clinics, and cooperatives today?

If Sufism is a form of a parallel sector, ponder its significance for the newness of today's Islamist dynamics. It proved to be the major engine for expanding the *umma* into Central and South Asia and Africa.[34] It was the chief outlet for popular (and in some cases elite) religion throughout the Ottoman centuries, and in the case of the Republic of Turkey, right through from the 1930s to the 1990s.[35]

Finally, a new aspect of today's Islamism is its emergence in an environment populated by a high incidence of secular organisms. The presence of secular compartments in Islamic societies is not new in essence, but in intensity, prominence, and self-consciousness. Classical Baghdad's *bayt al-hikma* is one example of a secular space,[36] as are Ottoman-era coffeehouses and bathhouses.[37] In *umma*-wide, long-range terms, what we have witnessed in the past generation—and are certain to see in the future—is not a return of Islam, but its sustained vitality reexpressed in familiar terms.

New Elements of Islamic Modernism

These examples are not meant to convey a sense of "same thing, different generation." There are, of course, new elements, and surveying them briefly is instructive for academicians and policymakers.

Rebuff of Modern Parameters

Western historiography—often taken over and then accepted by emerging, indigenous historiographic trends in colonized areas[38]—refers only to the nineteenth century and after as the era of Islamic reform and modernization; it belies tremendous ethno-centric conceit. Only from 1798 did Europe have a quite prominent presence in the region. Put differently, the current iteration of Islamization and renewal emerged in the shadow of European political–economic intrusion and cultural influence. In the nineteenth century, *tajdid* and *islah* were conditioned by Western parameters even while working to fend off such intrusion. In the twentieth century, Islamic activism has sought to roll back institutions and leaders seen as compromised by religious and culturally inauthentic Westernization.

Selective Rejection of Western
Cultural Influences

This is not the same as seeking to roll back modernity as a concept. That would be an antitraditional conception of *tajdid* and *islah*.[39] With the exception of examples such as the Taliban and al Qaeda—so extreme that they obscure the main thrust of re-Islamization—today there is merely selective repudiation of those aspects of Western culture that are inauthentic and disruptive to indigenous mores. Rejecting family planning, same-sex marriage, the legitimacy of homosexuality, and equalization of gender roles are not considered categorically antimodern. Some Western clergy, organizations, and democratically elected leaders reject the same things.[40]

Ideologization of Islamism

Islamism in the late twentieth and early twenty-first centuries is completely inscribed with modernity. Islamists have frequently used video and audiocassettes and today, no discussion of Islamism is complete without examining the espousal of the technologies and the culture of new media expressed by the entire gamut of Islamic activists—from apolitical Islamists to the global jihadis. Although quite important, the material accoutrements of modernity and the often-unconscious mental adaptations that come with them do not typify this aspect of today's re-Islamization.[41]

Perhaps the most characteristic and unique element in post-1960s Islamism—even in comparison with the Egyptian Muslim Brotherhood of the 1930s and 1940s—is its conscious ideological intentionality. Islamization as perceived by its elite proponents, rank-and-file adherents, and observers is an "ism" to be expressed and analyzed just as other "isms" of the Right and Left.[42] Just as observers noted that Khomeini's "guardianship of the righteous jurist-consult" (*velayet al-faqih*) was an antitraditional innovation passed off as a core principle of Shi'i Islam,[43] the ideologization of Islamist politics, economics, and violence is a singularly new, strikingly Western modern component of contemporary re-Islamization. This ideological intentionality needs to be comprehended and, when needed, countered by Western and regional leaders.

Liberation of Sacred Texts

With the exception of Iran's Islamic revolutionaries and a minority in Egypt, Islamists are products of a liberation of the religion's sacred texts from the hands of intermediaries. Although educational quality and expansion have far to go in the Islamic world, literacy has been rising in absolute terms and as a proportion of population since the 1920s in places such as Egypt, Turkey, Syria, Saudi Arabia, Iraq, and elsewhere—even as populations have continued to explode. More people are learning to read and are becoming intellectual agents and purveyors relatively autonomous from the traditional religious establishment of ulama. The latter has been functionalized and neutralized by the state, and thus implicated in authoritarian regimes in the last 60 years.

In spite of their widely differing approaches to the role of Islam and politics, lay experts—littérateurs such as Ahmad Amin, Tawfiq al-Hakim, Sayyid Qutb, and Ai Yasar Saribay, physicians such as Ayman al-Zawahiri, engineering professors such as Necmettin Erbakan, and lawyers such as Kamal Abul

Magd—have been able to read, interpret, and propagate views of the canon of Islam and its implications for modern life. Totally independent from the religion's traditional authorities, they speak in an idiom comprehensible to modern Muslims when addressing issues of concern to them. Of course, Pakistan's mullahs of the *madrasas* possess neither the modern intellectual acumen of lay Islamists, nor the systemic traditional understanding of their faith—in either its ulama form or the long-dominant sufi form of Central and South Asia.

Readiness to Pronounce Rulers as Illegitimate

The readiness to confront and pronounce as illegitimate the Muslim ruler of a Muslim state and his chosen political order is relatively new.[44] Afghans did overthrow the Safavids, the Wahhabi–Saudi alliance temporarily wrested the Hijaz from the Ottomans in the early nineteenth century, and Mehmet Ali of Egypt did attempt to assault Istanbul. But none of these was about the Islamic legitimacy of regimes. Rather, ruler/ruled relations were by and large characterized by flocks—the Ottoman *reaya*—granting dynasties fundamental, baseline legitimacy as defenders of the faith in terms of territory and orthodoxy.[45] In most cases, even 'Abbasid dissidents granted the conceptual legitimacy of the 'Abbasid caliphate, although they rebelled against its governors or edicts. Likewise, breakaway Abbasid governors in Tunisia, Egypt, or Khurasan continued to grant the conceptual legitimacy of weakened nominal suzerains in Baghdad.

Today's pronouncement that some Muslim rulers and regimes are barbaric and reminiscent of the pre-Islamic *jahiliya*, is a doctrinal innovation. Not only has *jahiliya* been dissociated from the historical referent of the time before Muhammad, but also, for violent Islamists, ridding their countries of *jahiliya* is more important than avoiding *fitna*, or discord within the house of Islam.[46] This rethinking might be considered as turning sacred texts to one's own political end, but it is also a particularly constructivist interpretation of texts.

Our discussion thus far has arrived at two important findings: first, Islamic activism is as much traditional and woven into the fabric of Islamic history as it is a new phenomenon that warrants concern. Second, several new aspects of the current iteration of re-Islamization reflect an interaction with exogenous political norms and inspiration by them. But, readiness to pronounce Muslim rulers illegitimate, the one that invites *fitna* for the sake of removing *jahiliya*, is of greatest concern to American policymakers and allies. It is important not to understate the significance of its origins, which are exogenous to Islam. Although visible events might focus on what is new and threatening in contemporary Islam, Islamization is in fact re-Islamization and has had its greatest, most historically enduring impact in the nonviolent realm.

NONVIOLENCE AND ITS IMPORTANCE IN ISLAMISM

Notwithstanding its violent and threatening aspects, one might argue that similarly, the greatest legacy of the latest iteration of re-Islamization will be in the nonviolent realm. Throughout the umma, both in the traditional Dar al-Islam (Abode of Islam) and in new Islamic vistas such as Europe and the

United States, Islamic observance and collective identification in Muslim terms are reemergent. Whether or not it reflects the failure of armed political Islam,[47] societal Islamization shows no sign of abating. This is particularly significant in the Middle East and South Asia. Continuing demographic growth is occurring in countries whose neopatriarchal, authoritarian, socio-economically, and politically top heavy states are stewarded over by regimes caught between a distrust of mass political participation and a suspicion of Western calls for reform, privatization, and democratization.

In this region, societal re-Islamization possesses political content and aspirations, mostly for inclusion into the political process. As regimes age or liberalize, nonviolent Islamists will emerge into the political arena. And, as rural-to-urban migration proceeds apace, people less touched by secularism will come into the visible political spectrum. In this respect, the victory of the Justice and Development Party in Turkey is doubly instructive. It does not merely demonstrate the political success in a secular state of a nonviolent, thoroughly modern Islamic political formation. Just as important, the Turkish government's conduct in relation to the U.S. war in Iraq shows that any given Islamist party's ethical understandings will have a large impact on its view of U.S. regional policies, as will its domestic political need to be responsive to electoral and parliamentary constituencies.[48]

Though a very different environment from Turkey, the new Iraq presents similar dynamics. Here, Islam has been built into the new state order, as the processes of elections and government formation in the midst of an insurgency have granted legitimate political power to representatives of Islamist parties. The sociopolitical capital of key nodes of loyalty is based on religious prestige. In the new Iraq, Islam—though variously interpreted—will be the idiom and substance of Iraqi nationalism. However, there will also be segments of the electorate in which one's political legitimacy will be measured against identification with Islam. Therefore, any new, fragile Iraqi government's social and foreign policies will not be able to stray too far from its constituents' assumptions about Islamic authenticity.[49]

Internal Consensus

In more general terms, the re-Islamization process, *tajdid-islah*, has several implications for regimes in Muslim majority states. Political–military elites must come to a basic internal consensus on the importance and definition of secularism as policy and environment. Though in different ways the consequences of a lack of internal consensus are most obvious in Egypt, Algeria, Turkey, Pakistan, and 1973–79 Afghanistan. Ironically, in these environments, insistence on the ruling elite's interpretation of secularism actually worked to undermine its supposed conceptual partner, namely democracy.

Open Organizational Space

Given the fundamental authenticity and legitimacy of Islam as a social idiom, religious practice, and means of association, it is likely that that the long-term, safest route requires political regimes to allow more space in society for citizen-generated and citizen-managed formations with Islamic content. This sounds like civil society, but it is much more than lingo that both opposition Islamists and regime spokesmen have come to deploy for Western audiences.[50]

A more open organizational space will require governments at the national and local levels to encourage associations outside the state and work with them as partners in the effort to provide social services and inculcate sociopolitical norms more efficaciously. Such nonviolent expressions of socially engaged Islam are no more than a recognition of reality in many regions. Yet, they create an even wider gap between nonviolent Islamists and the violent elements that need to be physically eliminated. As the costs of Islamist affiliation decrease, the benefits of abjuring anti-state activity while serving citizens will increase. Furthermore, espousing societal Islamization co-opts nonviolent Islamists by increasing needs-fulfillment for citizens, while communicating more civil norms.

Opening up more space to formations autonomous from the state must benefit non-Islamic related groups equally. Providing equal opportunities for organizations focused on gender issues, intellectual freedom, and the environment, as well as for domestic and foreign nongovernmental organizations, will work to level the playing field so that varying Islamic modes of association will have to compete with and be diluted by others.

Muslim state regimes must avoid using Islam, disguised as partnering and co-optation, in an effort to appear holier than their Islamist competition. They could attempt this by piecemeal integration of aspects of the sharia into the legal system; state press coverage of the president's attendance of Friday Prayers; peppering official pronouncements with strategically calculated support for Islam in state and society; financing violent Islamists in rival countries under the table; appointment of safe Islamists onto government boards of censor; backpedaling on gender equity and the defense of homophobia. All of these have been done throughout the broader Middle East.[51] Such confused state actions amount to a policy black hole filled by arbitrary personal power. At the same time, these moves embolden political opportunism—as opposed to maturity—among Islamists. They randomly target large swathes of the population and compromise the very principles and causes that lead toward greater liberalization of processes and norms. In short, these practices stack the deck against those very sociopolitical forces that work to prevent an Islamist monopoly on discourse and mobilization.

Political Islamism

Matters that relate to society are inextricably bound up with the polity. This is not only prima facie the case, but also doubly true in a region where states have attempted to permeate society. Islam as a religion and legitimacy resource is concerned with matters of justice, authenticity, and a community's moral, material, and political well-being. As such, societal re-Islamization will turn political. States with insufficient capacity to provide political inclusion and material welfare to societies characterized by greater urbanization, education, and exposure to transnational intellectual and ideological currents will inescapably find themselves operating in competition with Islam-motivated groups with political ends. As opposed to Syria in the 1970s–80s, or Egypt and Algeria in the 1970s–90s, a fairly large portion of the visible spectrum of political Islam is not violent in intent. Algeria is a textbook case of state repression inviting Islamist violence. Egypt is a work in progress. Depending on state responses, postviolent Islamism can turn pacifistic and still remain political.

If re-Islamization is a part of Islam and is here to stay, political Islamism is also here to stay. Regimes cannot stick their heads in the ground or deal with it coercively. Inclusion, though not the preferred route for secular leaders in Algeria, Tunisia, Egypt, Turkey, and elsewhere, is the only viable solution. And in regions approaching political transitions, such as Egypt, greater inclusion might burnish the credentials and bolster the stability of the new regime. The Hashemite Monarchy in Jordan has continued to grant legal status to the Muslim Brotherhood and other Islamist organizations, allowing them into parliament and government. The result is a neutral-to-positive impact on the legitimacy of a monarchy that not only has signed a peace agreement with Israel, but also cultivated close relations with the United States. This approach may have resulted in a dampened enthusiasm for Islamist political activists, who are at times considered too solicitous of the regime.[52]

Many opposed to political Islam's inclusion claim that Islamists will use democracy for nondemocratic aims—that political Islamists will allow "one person, one vote" one time only. Though unlikely and untested, it might be true. However, for most of the Middle East, the argument is irrelevant because there is no democracy in regimes or state structures. The outside observer needs to avoid confusing democracy with nonviolence. The latter is much more important to the survival of the region's peoples. If that sounds like a patronizing approach to foreign peoples who are not ready for what the West is, it is simply an assertion that violence is bad for people. It is conducive to instability, brutality, and irreconcilable ideological extremes that can be manipulated by rival states or non-state actors. Further, it has yet to be disproved that inclusion of a greater diversity of political aspirants in the process can reduce violence and instability, preparing the way for greater democratization of inherently nondemocratic regimes. What would have been better for the people of 1990s Algeria—keeping Islamists out of the legitimate political process or averting the terrible loss of life and damage to the political fabric and political norms?

Ultimately, the determining issue is not inclusion or exclusion of Islamists from the political process, but the values of leaders of any stripe, the autonomous strength and vitality of government and administration, and— most important—the values system animating those institutions. Government and society need to be characterized by institutions that matter, with procedures that are adhered to and that articulate civility, inclusion, respect for law, and nonviolent, nonarbitrary solution of conflict. Though imperfect, Turkey is the best example of how a focus on an ethos, as articulated by institutions and procedures, has defused the threat of violent Islamism. Intermittent inclusion of Islam-motivated politicians in the political and governmental process has driven them to adopt modes of conduct and ideas about how politics works that are consistent with their secularist rivals. Thus, rather than viewing politically inclined Islamists as a central challenge, regimes in Muslim states need to consider the reform of institutions and their values as the route to avoiding violent Islamism. It may be the case that problems of democracy, violence, and civility in the Islamic world have much, much less to do with Islamists—violent or pacifistic—than with the nature and values of regimes.

THE U.S. ROLE IN ISLAMIZATION

The United States must begin with the knowledge that Islamization is not its issue to influence directly, either rhetorically or kinetically. In short, Islamization is not about the West. If re-Islamization is a continual, metahistoric process, the United States must understand that it cannot stop it or channel it, and that its influence in the process is insignificant. U.S. policymakers should abandon hopes of crafting a sort of Islam that they want.[53] If indigenous Muslim regimes have failed at efforts to shape Islam by selectively funding mosques, seminaries, and friendly Islamization initiatives, the United States will only fare worse. To put this in perspective, a U.S. citizen would dismiss as miniscule the likelihood that any Muslim state or collection of states could influence the form of Christianity practiced in the West or the sociopolitical proclivities of practicing Christians in the United States.

Better understood as the unending process of *tajdid-islah*, early-twenty-first-century Islamic activism means that people whose foreign policies and domestic politics are influenced programmatically by Islam will become political players, candidates, parliamentarians, and rulers. Sudan and Pakistan have illustrated this development with less than ideal results. Afghanistan under the Taliban was an intolerable failure. Jordan and Turkey suggest a different possibility, and in Lebanon, parties such as Amal, and those with a terrorist wing—such as Hizbullah—are bound to continue their parliamentary presence. They speak to a material and ethical needs fulfillment among Lebanese Shi'ites much more than they are beholden to foreign sponsors such as Syria. Finally, in countries such as Egypt, where successors to geriatric rulers will have to permit some broadening of the political space, Islamist politicians will gain increased popularity, if not parliamentary representation.

Needs Determination

Although it might seem defeatism to preach the futility of staving off Islamists in politics, it is perhaps a wiser pragmatism to devise strategies that count on potential Middle Eastern partners being those very Islamists. This strategy must be supported by analytical efforts capable of truly defining concrete needs in the broader Middle East, and by measures that provide incentives to rulers to assist in their attainment. A first priority for U.S. policy is to determine what the United States truly wants and needs in the region, shorn of all of the high-flown principles and ideological blinders that have characterized pronouncements of the past several years. Three that come to mind are the global war on terror, democratization, and "not rewarding bad behavior."

In the past four years, the United States has presented the global war on terror and democratization as its two interlinked goals in the Middle East. The war on terror makes sense at home, but as a strategy it is too diffuse. Who is the enemy? All political Islam? All violent movements that target U.S. assets or fiends? All manifestations of Islamic nationalism that oppose current U.S. policies in the region? All American rivals in the region? In fact, the most concrete manifestation of the enemy is bin Ladenism. It has been defined as including not only al Qaeda, but also as "an international movement that aims to establish a puritanical Islamic order throughout the Arab and Muslim worlds, sees the United States as its principal enemy, and is empowered by transnational capabilities and a willingness to use any means available."[54]

As such, and particularly after the waning of high-intensity combat operations in Afghanistan, the enemy—now an amorphous, segregated series of groups and origins of inspiration—will never go away. Military force and diplomacy cannot succeed in eliminating it. The war on terror will lose conceptual and targeting focus. Muslim peoples have viewed it as either another American mechanism to intrude in the region and establish neoimperialist influence, or as a way to continue supporting repressive regional leaders. What the war on terror does not do is provide a concrete, realistic way forward with measurable results.

As for democratization, it too is problematic as a goal sponsored by a power exogenous to the region, especially when that power considers internal political dynamics in the region as integral to its own security.[55] Pushing democratization alienates regional leaders whose help is needed in confronting terrorism. Rather than rewarding them for assistance, it appears as— and often is—penalizing them for taking unsavory measures needed to tamp down domestic opposition to cooperation with the United States. Likewise, though Egyptians or Palestinians, for example, may dislike the methods of rule and politics used by their leaders, U.S. pressures on these leaders to democratize are interpreted as arbitrary, arrogant interventions by a foreign, Christian power. Mildly unpopular domestic leaders assume greater popularity when pressured by much more unpopular outsiders. To the extent that the United States relents on pressures for democratization, however, it appears to be hypocritical about its importance. Turks in the summer of 2003 remarked that the United States was serious about democratization in Iraq, but not serious about it in Turkey, where democratic political processes resulted in foreign policy results contrary to American desires.

Democracy as a national security strategy is much too abstract an idea, one that is not in our short- or medium-term interest. Regionally, democracy is often associated with sovereignty[56] and the assumption of power by people less ready to act as a bridgehead for Western political, military, and economic influence. Furthermore, the segments of the population in the Muslim and Arab world most receptive to genuine democratization have not supported U.S. goals in Afghanistan, Iraq, or in the war on terror. In short, pro-democratization constituencies are not pro-U.S. policy constituencies. In this respect, it is instructive to consider what democracy would mean for U.S. basing privileges, the Arab–Israeli conflict, or access to oil.

The phrase "not rewarding good behavior" is often used to explain current policies to North Korea and Iran.[57] In Iran, as well as elsewhere in the Middle East, such a stance rewards U.S. competitors and enemies. For competitors, such as France and Russia, this policy has permitted them the kind of economic and diplomatic access that the United States would need in order to wield real influence. Regarding enemies, what appears as not rewarding them actually further compromises domestic elements that, over time, would prove more tractable—in short, the United States rewards its enemies for recalcitrance.[58]

An Alternative

Rather than focusing on the global war on terror, democratization, not rewarding bad behavior, economic reform, and other agendas—which, when pushed by external powers, appear to be neoimperial intrusion—the Turkish evolution previously referred to suggests a different, less intrusive path to create conditions more conducive to pro-U.S. results in the Muslim world. The current Islam-affiliated government in Ankara arrived at the helm after a decades-long process of institutional evolution. For all its deficiencies, the Republic of Turkey, more than any other majority Muslim state, possesses institutions—such as parliament, the judiciary, the presidency, private enterprise, competitive entrepreneurism, and a system of intra- and interparty dynamics— that, at their best, manifest certain values of civility and reciprocal legitimacy in their actions.

INSTITUTIONAL REFORM

To be sure, at various times, some or all of these institutions have broken down or worked to undermine the values that ought to animate them. Yet, it may be a tribute—albeit ironic—to the reforms of Mustafa Kemal that latter-day Islamist politicians have played by the rules of the democratic game and have sought to undermine those rules no more than the secular parties.

Another priority, after needs determination, is a U.S. policy of engagement with Muslim states to focus squarely on institutional reform. Rather than manhandling existing institutions, the United States needs to communicate the values it needs in those institutions. This can be done through example and through a genuine dialogue of cultures. Homeland security must be maintained, but not by raising a wall against visitors from countries of concern whose attitudes the United States wishes to alter. U.S. policy should invite students, legislators, administrators, military officers, and even Islamists from these countries to visit U.S. political bodies, to enroll in U.S. schools of public policy, and to observe and witness the associational life that creates notions of reciprocal legitimacy, thereby invigorating democratic practices throughout society. The positive impact of existing programs that do this is so pronounced as to merit their expansion and migration into fields beyond politics and the military.

The potential yields of institutional reform with a value-oriented focus include greater efficiency of administration, greater transparency of political and fiscal processes, and increased civility and alliance formation in politics and international relations. All are essential for increasing the efficacy with which Muslim states move domestically and regionally and for increasing the credibility of existing regimes. It is a prerequisite before ideas of democratization can get any traction. In this respect, post-2001 Afghanistan and post-2003 Iraq teach that there cannot be democratization, or democrats, without democratic institutions. As Islamists enter politics, it will be necessary for them to have these norms as well.[59]

In addition to understanding what the United States wants and needs from different countries and how it will go about getting it from different kinds of interlocutors—including Islamists—the United States will require policy contingencies. They must take into account nonviolent political Islamists' domestic and foreign policy proclivities and plan realistically for working with the popularly legitimate, Islam-motivated politicians. This means that U.S. policy makers need concrete, pared-down priorities, not necessarily aligned with those of Islamists, but aligned with the art of the possible given the evolving cast of players.

Another thrust concerns the Israeli–Palestinian conflict. The absence of democratization is not the barrier to Arab–Israeli and Palestinian Israel reconciliation. Rather, the enduring Israeli–Arab conflict has acted as a brake on democratization by excusing authoritarian or totalitarian domestic policies and irresponsible foreign policies. As raw as the events of 9/11 remain for Americans, the Arab–Israeli dilemma—and particularly the Israeli–Palestinian component, focusing on holy cities such as Jerusalem, Hebron, Bethlehem, and elsewhere—is no less scarring, and not just for Arab Muslims. The United States will not have sufficient credibility in the region to drive a democratization agenda without exerting serious, painful, and politically costly efforts to equitably solve the Palestinian–Israeli conflict. The whole notion of democratization will justifiably remain suspect to Arabs and Muslims. Islamists will be entering politics in the next several years; a full-court press on the Arab–Israeli conflict cannot wait until that time. Sustainable peace might be attainable with elected, Islamist leaders in parliament and government whose concerns will be influenced by religion as well as constituents.

CONCLUSION

Islamization is re-Islamization. It is equal parts historically authentic and innovative, the latter with a Western impetus and conceptual referent. There is no Islamic wave in the sense of something that can ebb and flow. On the contrary, re-Islamization is the persistent current in the Islamic ocean. Violent Islamism may well turn out to be a historical epiphenomenon as compared to the true phenomenon of nonviolent societal Islamism, with manifold political ramifications. The most immediate of these, and worthy of practical consideration for American policymakers, is that because Islamists are a persistent social phenomenon in the Middle East, the current American initiative to democratize the region will result in them entering the political process from Tunisia to Iraq. Islamists in the political process, in either its authoritarian or participatory version, will require the United States to deal with them as points of contact and to court them as international relations constituencies with particular philosophical, ideological, and local political concerns. U.S. leaders will have to alter policies and priorities or demonstrate to Islam-influenced political leaders that American policies in the Middle East serve their interests.

NOTES

1. Fred Halliday, *Islam and the Myth of Confrontation* (London: I.B. Tauris, 1996); see also John L. Esposito, *The Islamic Threat: Myth or Reality*, 3rd ed. (Oxford: Oxford University Press, 1999); Shibley Telhami, *The Stakes: America in the Middle East* (Boulder, CO: Westview Press, 2003), 1–66; M. Hakan Yavuz, "Is There a Turkish Islam: The Emergence of Convergence and Consensus," *Journal of Muslim Minority Affairs*, vol. 24, no. 2 (2004); Jilian Schwedler "Islamic Identity: Myth, Menace, or Mobilizer?" *SAIS Review, A Journal of International Affairs*, vol. 21, no. 2 (2001), 1–17; Michael Ignatieff, "Human Rights as Policy and Idolatry," Carnegie Council on Ethics and International Affairs Merrill House Conversation, edited transcript of remarks, November 2, 2001, at www.carnegiecouncil.org/printerfriendlymedia.php/prmID/82, accessed May 2, 2005; Shibley Telhami and James Steinberg, "Fighting Binladenism," in Flynt Leverett, ed., *The Road Ahead: Middle East Policy in the Bush Administration's Second Term* (Washington: The Saban Center at the Brookings Institution, 2005), 13–20.
2. Enduring illustrations of the variegated nature of Islam and Islamic activism include Michael Gilsenan, *Recognizing Islam: Religion and Society in the Modern Middle East*, rev. ed. (London: I.B. Tauris, 2000); Clifford Geertz, *Islam Observed: Religious Development in Morocco and Indonesia* (Chicago: University of Chicago Press, 1971); and Martin Marty and R. Scott Appleby, eds., *Fundamentalisms Observed* (Chicago: University of Chicago Press, 1994).
3. The literature on this debate is extensive. For a few examples, see Carrie Rosefsky Wickham, "The Path to Moderation: Strategy and Learning in the Formation of Egypt's Wasat Party," *Comparative Politics*, vol. 36, no. 2 (2004); Wickham, "Islamist Auto-Reform: Lessons from Egypt, Jordan and Kuwait," UCLA International Institute Lecture, April 21, 2005; and Raymond W. Baker, *Islam without Fear: Egypt and the New Islamists* (Cambridge, MA: Harvard University Press, 2003).
4. Argued most forcefully by Elie Kedourie, *Politics in the Middle East* (New York: Oxford University Press, 1992), 268–280.

5. For discussions of these Arab Muslim thinkers and selections from their writings, see Albert Hourani, *Arabic Thought in the Liberal Age* (London: Cambridge University Press, 1983), 67–161; Sylvia G. Haim, *Arab Nationalism: An Anthology* (Berkeley: University of California Press, 1976), 3–34, 78–80; Charles Kurtzman, ed., *Modernist Islam: 1840–1940* (London: Oxford University Press, 2002), 31–39, 50–60, 152–157.

6. Haim, *Arab Nationalism*, 49–60; William Cleveland, *The Making of an Arab Nationalist: Ottomanism and Arabism in the Life and Thought of Sati Al-Husri* (Princeton, NJ: Princeton University Press, 1972); Bassam Tibi, *Arab Nationalism: Between Islam and the Nation-State* (London: Palgrave Macmillan, 1997); Youssef M. Choueiri, *Arab Nationalism: Nation and State in the Arab World* (London: Blackwell, 2001); and Adeed Dawisha, *Arab Nationalism in the Twentieth Century: From Triumph to Despair* (Princeton, NJ: Princeton University Press, 2003).

7. Haim, *Arab Nationalism*, 62–64.

8. Alexander Scholch, *Egypt for the Egyptians* (London: Ithaca Press, 1981); Juan Cole, *Colonialism and Revolution in the Middle East: The Social and Cultural Origins of Egypt's 'Urabi Movement* (Princeton, NJ: Princeton University Press, 1993); and Arthur Goldschmidt, *Modern Egypt: The Formation of a Nation State*, 2nd ed. (Boulder, CO: Westview Press, 2004).

9. Kemal H. Karpat, *The Politicization of Islam: Reconstructing Identity, State, Faith, and Community in the Late Ottoman State* (London: Oxford University Press, 2001), 308–373; Niyazi Berkes, *The Development of Secularism in Turkey* (New York: Routledge, 1998), 431–457; Erik J. Zurcher, *Turkey: A Modern History* (London: I.B. Tauris, 2004), 148.

10. Yitzhak Nakash, *The Shi'is of Iraq* (Princeton, NJ: Princeton University Press, 1993), 55–74.

11. James P. Piscatori, *Islam in a World of Nation-States* (Cambridge: Cambridge University Press, 1986), 35; Jean-Claude Vatin, "Popular Puritanism versus State Reformism: Islam in Algeria," in James P. Piscatori, ed., *Islam in the Political Process* (Cambridge: Cambridge University Press, 1983), 111.

12. Christophe Jaffrelot, ed., *Pakistan: Nationalism without a Nation?* (London: Zed Books, 2002); Ayesha Jalal, *Self and Sovereignty: Individual and Community in South Asian Islam since 1850* (London: Routledge, 2000), 386–421, 563–569.

13. Hillel Frisch, "The Evaluation of Palestinian Nationalist Islamic Doctrine: Territorializing a Universal Religion," *Canadian Review in Nationalism*, vol. 21 (1994), 45–55; N. Johnston, *Islam and the Politics of Meaning in Palestinian Nationalism* (London: Kegan and Paul, 1982); Yehoshua Porath, *The Emergence of the Palestinian Arab National Movement 1918–1929* (London: Frank Cass, 1974); and Yehoshua Porath, *The Palestinian Arab National Movement 1929–1939* (London: Frank Cass, 1977).

14. This is the concern of Sami Zubaida, *Islam: The People and the State: Political Ideas and Movements in the Middle East* (London: I.B. Tauris, 1993), ix–xvii.

15. Hence the pitfalls of otherwise useful works such as Aziz al-Azmeh, *Islams and Modernities* (London: Verso, 1996); and Edward Said, *Orientalism* (New York: Vintage, 1979)—not that the critiques therein are unhelpful. A.L. Macfie, *Orientalism Reader* (New York: New York University Press, 2001).

16. Douglas Little, *American Orientalism: The United States and the Middle East since 1945* (Chapel Hill, NC: University of North Carolina Press, 2004).

17. Unsurpassed in their coverage of these dynamics are Marshall G.S. Hodgson's magisterial three-volume *The Venture of Islam* (Chicago: University of Chicago Press, 1975–77); and Ira Lapidus's peerless one-volume *A History of Islamic Societies*, 2nd ed. (Cambridge: Cambridge University Press, 2002).

18. For the urban–rural disconnect, see Binnaz Toprak, *Islam and Political Development in Turkey* (Leiden: Brill Academic Publishers, 1981); for works examining similar dynamics elsewhere, see Stephanie Cronin, ed., *The Making of Modern Iran: State and Society under Riza Shah, 1921–1941* (London: RoutledgeCurzon, 2003); and Arthur Goldschmidt, Amy Johnson, and Barak Salmoni, eds., *Re-Envisioning Egypt, 1919–1952* (Cairo: American University in Cairo Press, 2005).

19. Motherland, holy, self-sacrificer, martyr, enlightened person, guide—all these are terms that have had traditionally religious meanings, but have now been desacralized in the service of sanctifying nationalism.

20. A *hadith*, or saying attributed to Muhammad, quoted in John O. Voll, "Renewal and Reform in Islamic History: Tajdid and Islah," in John L. Esposito, ed., *Voices of Resurgent Islam* (New York: Oxford University Press, 1983), 33. This remains the most concise, insightful, and readable account.

21. These issues are covered admirably well in Jonathan P. Berkey, *The Formation of Islam: Religion and Society in the Near East, 600–800* (Cambridge: Cambridge University Press, 2003), 126–129, 141–151.

22. Andrew Rippin, *Muslims: Their Religious Beliefs and Practices* (London: Routledge, 2001), 135. For an early, still valuable study of al-Ghazali, see W. Montgomery Watt, *Muslim Intellectual: A Study of al-Gazali* (Edinburgh: Edinburgh University Press, 1963).

23. Haim Gerber, *State, Society, and Law in Islam: Ottoman Law in Comparative Perspective* (New York: SUNY Press, 1994); R.C. Repp, *The Mufti of Istanbul: A Study in the Development of the Ottoman Learned Hierarchy* (London: Ithaca Press, 1986); Colin Imber, *The Ottoman Empire* (London: Palgrave Macmillan, 2002), 216–251; and Colin Imber, *Ebu's-Su'ud: The Islamic Legal Tradition* (Edinburgh: Edinburgh University Press, 1997).

24. For a recent study suggesting that the movement's founder, Muhammad ibn 'Abd al-Wahhab was much more open-minded than his latter day admirers would suppose, see Natana J. Delong-Bas, *Wahhabi Islam: From Revival and Reform to Global Jihad* (London: I.B. Tauris, 2004).

25. Moshe Gammer, *Muslim Resistance to the Tsar: Shamil and the Conquest of Chechnia and Daghestan* (London: Frank Cass, 1994); For a quite engaging journalistic account illuminating the religious Islamic aspects as well as contemporary meaning of Imam Shamil in Chechnya, see Nicholas Griffin, *Caucasus in the Wake of Warriors* (New York: St. Martin's Press, 2003).

26. Nehemia Levtzion, *Muslims and Chiefs in West Africa: A Study of Islam in the Middle Volta Basin in the Pre-Colonial Period* (Oxford: Clarendon Press, 1968); Nehemia Levtzion, *Islam in West Africa: Religion, Society and Politics to 1800* (Aldershot, UK: Variorum, 1994); David Robinson, *The Holy War of Umar Tal: The Western Sudan in the Mid-Nineteenth Century* (Oxford: Clarendon Press, 1985); and Moustapha Kane, David Robinson, David Dwyer, and Sonja Fagerberg, eds., *The Islamic Regime of Fuuta Tooro: An Anthology of Oral Tradition Transcribed in Pulaar and Translated into English* (East Lansing: Michigan State University, 1984).

27. Hourani, *Arabic Thought in the Liberal Age*; Kurzman, *Modernist Islam*; for Central Asia see Adeeb Khalid, *The Politics of Muslim Cultural Reform: Jadidism*

in Central Asia (Berkeley: University of California Press, 1998); for the Far East, see Ibrahim bin Abu Bakar, *Islamic Modernism in Malaya* (Kuala Lumpur: University of Malaya Press, 1994).

28. For a documentary example of this, see ibn al-Athir, "Puritanism in Baghdad," in Bernard Lewis, ed., *Islam: From the Prophet Muhammad to the Capture of Constantinople*, vol. 2 (Oxford: Oxford University Press, 1987), 19–20.

29. Imber, *The Ottoman Empire*, 37–44; Stanford J. Shaw, *History of the Ottoman Empire and Modern Turkey*, vol. 1 (Cambridge: Cambridge University Press, 1976), 70–79; and Repp, *The Mufti of Istanbul*.

30. Lapidus, *A History of Islamic Societies*, 377–381; Marshall Hodgson, *The Venture of Islam*, vol. 3, 83–85, 92–98.

31. Karpat, *The Politicization of Islam*, 172–188, 223–240; see also Selim Deringil, *The Well-Protected Domains: Ideology and the Legitimation of Power in the Ottoman Empire, 1876–1909* (London: I.B. Tauris, 1998).

32. The parallel sector as an analytical tool is developed by Carrie Rosefsky Wickham, *Mobilizing Islam: Religion, Activism, and Political Islam in Egypt* (New York: Columbia University Press, 2002), 93–118.

33. Annemarie Schimmel, *Mystical Dimensions of Islam* (Chapel Hill: University of North Carolina Press, 1975); J.S. Trimingham, *The Sufi Orders in Islam* (Oxford: The Clarendon Press, 1971).

34. Svat Soucek, *A History of Inner Asia* (Cambridge: Cambridge University Press, 2000), 34–39.

35. M. Hakan Yavuz, *Islamic Political Identity in Turkey* (Oxford: Oxford University Press, 2003), 133–178.

36. John R. Hayes, ed., *The Genius of Arab Civilization*, 3rd ed. (New York: New York University Press, 1992), chapters by Hamarneh and Sabra in particular; and Bernard Lewis, ed., *The World of Islam* (London: Thames and Hudson, 1976), especially the chapter by Sabra.

37. Ralph H. Hattox, *Coffee and Coffeehouses: The Origins of a Social Beverage in the Medieval Near East* (Seattle: University of Washington Press, 1985); for more on the idea of a secular space in traditional Islam, see Ira M. Lapidus, "The Separation of Church and State in the Development of Early Islamic Society," *International Journal of Middle East Studies*, vol. 6 (1975), 363–385.

38. For Middle Eastern historians adopting the Western, Orientalist perspective, see Gabriel Piterberg, "The Tropes of Stagnation and Awakening in Nationalist Historical Consciousness: The Egyptian Case," in Israel Gershoni and James Jankowski, eds., *Rethinking Nationalism in the Arab Middle East* (New York: Columbia University Press, 1997).

39. Exaggerated emphasis on Islamist atavism and antimodernity mars the otherwise superb work by Emmanuel Sivan, *Radical Islam: Medieval Theology and Modern Politics* (New Haven: Yale University Press, 1990).

40. Laurie Goodstein and Greg Myre, "Clerics Fighting a Gay Festival for Jerusalem," *The New York Times*, March 31, 2005, A1: "They are creating a deep and terrible sorrow that is unbearable," Shlomo Amar, Israel's Sephardic chief rabbi, said yesterday at a news conference in Jerusalem attended by Israel's two chief rabbis, the patriarchs of the Roman Catholic, Greek Orthodox, and Armenian churches, and three senior Muslim prayer leaders. "It hurts all of the religions. We are all against it."

41. Jon B. Alterman, *New Media, New Politics? From Satellite Television to the Internet in the Arab World* (Washington: Washington Institute for Near East Policy, 1998); John W. Anderson, "New Media, New Publics: Reconfiguring the Public Sphere of Islam," *Social Research*, vol. 70, no. 3 (2003).

42. The best example of this can still be found in Hamid Dabashi, *Theology of Discontent: The Ideological Foundation of the Islamic Revolution in Iran* (New York: New York University Press, 1993), 1–146.

43. Ervand Abrahamian, *Khomeinism: Essays on the Islamic Republic* (Berkeley: University of California Press, 1993), 24–30, 40–41; and Said Amir Arjomand, *The Turban for the Crown: The Islamic Revolution in Iran* (Oxford: Oxford University Press, 1988), 177–183.

44. Sivan's *Radical Islam* still covers this most clearly and eloquently.

45. Eloquently described in Norman Itzkowitz, *Ottoman Empire and Islamic Tradition* (Chicago: University of Chicago Press, 1972), 37–62.

46. William E. Shepard, "Sayyid Qutb's Doctrine of Jahaliyya," *International Journal of Middle East Studies*, vol. 35, no. 4 (2003), 521–545.

47. Olivier Roy, *The Failure of Political Islam* (Cambridge: Harvard University Press, 1994); and Gilles Kepel, *Jihad: The Trail of Political Islam* (Cambridge: The Belknap Press of Harvard University Press, 2002).

48. Jenny White, *Islamist Mobilization in Turkey: A Study in Vernacular Politics* (Seattle: University of Washington Press, 2002); Ali Carkoglu, "Turkey's November 2002 Elections: A New Beginning?" *Middle East Review of International Affairs*, vol. 6, no. 4 (2002); Soner Cagaptay, "The November 2002 Elections and Turkey's New Political Era," *Middle East Review of International Affairs*, vol. 6, no. 4 (2002); and Barak Salmoni, "Strategic Partners or Estranged Allies: Turkey, the United States, and Operation Iraqi Freedom," *Strategic Insights* (July 2003).

49. Yitzhak Nakash, "The Shiites and the Future of Iraq," *Foreign Affairs* (July/August 2003).

50. For work that might take too seriously the claims of Egypt's Muslim Brotherhood to already embody civil society, see Denis J. Sullivan and Sana Abed-Kotob, *Islam in Contemporary Egypt: Civil Society vs. the State* (Boulder, CO: Lynne Rienner Publishers, 1999).

51. For this phenomenon in Egypt, see Mary Anne Weaver, *A Portrait of Egypt: A Journey through the World of Militant Islam* (New York: Farrar, Straus and Giroux, 2000), 230–251.

52. Jilian Schwedler, "Political Contestation under Limited Democracy: The Islamic Action Front," in Hani Hourani, ed., *The Social History of Jordan* (Amman, Jordan: Markaz al-Urdun al-Jadid, 2002); Quintan Wiktorowicz, *The Management of Islamic Activism: Salafis, the Muslim Brotherhood, and State Power in Jordan* (Albany and Binghamton, NY: SUNY Press, 2001).

53. David A. Kaplan, "America is Spending Millions to Change the Very Face of Islam," *US News and World Report*, April 25, 2005.

54. Shibley Telhami and James Steinberg, "Fighting Binladenism," in Flynt Leverett, ed., *The Road Ahead: Middle East Policy in the Bush Administration's Second Term*, 13; available at http://www.brookings.edu/fp/saban/analysis/20050325roadahead.pdf.

55. There is far too much literature on democracy and reform in the Middle East to cite here. Two works worthy of consideration are Thomas Carothers and Marina Ottaway, eds., *Uncharted Journey: Promoting Democracy in the Middle East* (Washington: Carnegie Endowment for International Peace, 2005); and Shireen T. Hunter and Huma Malik, eds., *Modernization, Democracy, and Islam* (New York: Praeger, 2005).

56. Barak Salmoni, "Ordered Liberty and Disciplined Freedom: Conceptualizing and Teaching Democracy in Mono-Party Turkish Education, 1923–1950," *Middle Eastern Studies*, vol. 40, no. 2 (2004).

57. As just one example of this oft-repeated sentiment, see James Phillips, "Press Iran's Khatami to Follow Words with Deeds," *The Heritage Foundation Backgrounder*, no. 152 (July 23, 1998), 2.

58. See the still-valid points made in connection with Iran by James H. Noyes, "Falacies, Smoke, and Pipe Dreams: Forcing Change in Iran and Iraq," *Middle East Policy*, vol. 7, no. 3 (2000), 32–50.

59. An alternative, much more developed vision of reform is Tamara Cofman Wittes, "Promoting Reform in the Arab World," in Leverett, *The Road Ahead*, 21–36.

6

Democratic Nation Building in the Arc of Crisis: The Case of the Presidential Election in Afghanistan

Thomas H. Johnson

The United States will use this moment of opportunity to extend the benefits of freedom across the globe. We will actively work to bring the hope of democracy, development, free markets, and free trade to every corner of the world.[1]
—President George W. Bush

Democracy [is] not viable in an environment of intense ethnic preferences . . . Countries with extreme ethnic complexity experience high levels of deadly political violence, which severely strains the fabric of their democratic orders.[2]
—Larry Diamond and Marc F. Plattner

The Bush administration is significantly lowering expectations of what can be achieved in Iraq, recognizing that the United States will have to settle for far less progress than originally envisioned during the transition due to end in four months, according to U.S. officials in Washington and Baghdad. The United States no longer expects to see a model new democracy, a self-supporting oil industry or a society where the majority of people are free from serious security or economic challenges, U.S. officials say. "What we expected to achieve was never realistic given the timetable or what unfolded on the ground," said a senior official involved in policy since the 2003 invasion. "We are in a process of absorbing the factors of the situation we're in and shedding the unreality that dominated at the beginning."[3]
—*The Washington Post*

Introduction

On October 9, 2004, Afghanistan held a historic presidential election. Three and a half months later, on January 30, 2005, the people of Iraq participated in their first open election in 50 years. Both of these elections were of intense interest to the United States and the Bush administration because they represented the initial recognition of a central aspect of the radical post-9/11 shift in U.S. foreign policy strategy and tactics—the aggressive pursuit of global democracy.

A year after the tragic events of 9/11, the Bush administration published the new U.S. national security strategy.[4] This strategy was founded on three critical elements. First, in order to prevent terrorist and other possible threats to the U.S. homeland, the United States "will not hesitate to act alone, if necessary, to exercise our right of self-defense by acting preemptively." Second, the United States will maintain instruments of power, including "unparalleled military strength and great economic and political influence" to make it impermeable to challenge by any foe. "[O]ur forces will be strong enough to dissuade potential adversaries from pursuing a military build-up in hopes of surpassing, or equaling, the power of the United States." Lastly, the United States will promote democracy worldwide. "[W]e will make freedom and the development of democratic institutions key themes in our bilateral relations, seeking solidarity and cooperation from other democracies while we press governments that deny human rights to move toward a better future."[5]

The U.S. policy of reserving the right to wage preemptive war as well as other aspects of the new strategy met with resistance from many international quarters. When compared to previous U.S. foreign policy experience, the new strategy represents "an entire new set of ideas and principles" that challenges notions of multilateralism, self-determination, and sovereignty, as well as one of the founding principles of the UN: no preemptive war.[6] Additionally, the United States and its policy appear unable to translate its position of global dominance into instruments that can effectively manage various troubling parts of the international system.[7]

The purpose of this chapter is to focus on one aspect of the new national security policy—the promotion of democracy—relative to that policy's initial test case in Afghanistan. Specifically, it examines a central component of the U.S. promotion of democracy in Afghanistan—the presidential electoral process as well as the meaning of its results to future democratic development. The analysis of this case raises important questions as to the problems facing the United States as it pursues the promotion of global democracy.

Politics in Afghanistan have traditionally been driven by local concerns. Ethnic and sectarian identities define boundaries for Afghan personal and group interactions and drive local concerns. Ethnicity and the issues that arise from ethnic fragmentation are key challenges facing any nation-state that is attempting to construct modern state institutions and norms. Those nation-states with more than one ethnic group that still rely on tribal structures find it more difficult to accomplish this task. This has been the case not only in Afghanistan but also in Africa, Asia, and parts of Eastern Europe. As long as groups within the state place more importance on their ethnic identities than on their national ones, there will continue to be conflicting loyalties that will greatly complicate national democratic development. As I argue later, Afghanistan is a prime example of the way in which ethnicity can directly impact state formation and determine the success or failure of government. How the United States addresses such concerns within its framework of democratic promotion is critical. Critical theoretical issues concerning ethnicity and democratic development underlie the analysis.

ETHNICITY, SECTARIANISM, AND DEMOCRATIC STATE FORMATION: SOME THEORETICAL CONSIDERATIONS

> [Afghanistan] consists of a mere collection of tribes, of unequal power and divergent habits, which are held together more or less closely, according to the personal character of the chief who rules them. The feeling of patriotism, as it is known in Europe, cannot exist among Afghans, for there is no common country.
>
> —Sir Henry Rawlinson, nineteenth-century British diplomat/colonialist[8]

According to Adrian Hastings, "nation, ethnicity, nationalism, and religion are four distinct and determinative elements within world history."[9] They are core concepts for every human and help guide individual and group motivations while determining how these entities will react to certain situations. All four are closely linked to each other, and as Hastings argues, it is difficult to separate one from the others.[10] History would clearly suggest that a society's culture and ethnicity could become dominant factors in the approach to state formation and ideas of governing. In tribal societies, ethnicity plays an even greater role in the everyday life of individuals and their interactions with others.[11] Afghanistan is a seemingly prime example of a society with ethnic cleavages that represent significant obstacles to the creation of a democratically cohesive and legitimate government.[12] According to Diamond and Plattner, "ethnicity is the most difficult type of socio-political cleavage for democracy to manage."[13] The underlying failure of many states plagued by ethnic fragmentation has been the uneven inclusion of minority groups in the rule of government and the government's willingness to favor one ethnic group over another.[14] These ethnically charged relationships can lead to conflict within societies and form an insurmountable barrier to democratic state formation.

Similarly, religion and sectarianism are important factors that help define an individual's identity and, in many cases, reflect directly on the individual's ethnicity. Throughout history, religion has affected the creation of nation-states and, in some cases, has even been the basis for forming a common bond between different ethnic groups and forging unity when no other force was capable of the task. Moreover, religion has produced the predominant character of many states,[15] such as Afghanistan. Today, the Middle East and Central Asia illustrate this phenomenon. Islam has become directly tied to both ethnicity and nationalism and has helped form the state structures in the region.

Ethnicity and religion are important elements in the formation of a litmus test to determine the probability of success for the creation of a stable and successful government. A national identity is often difficult to construct among ethnically diverse nation-states. The national identity must supersede ethnic loyalties in order to avoid infighting between competing groups vying for political power. Today's successful nation-states have populations that have placed national identity before ethnic identity, whereas most failed (or failing) states have remained ethnically defined, hindering the forging of unity and cohesiveness among the populace.

There is little doubt that a major challenge for democracy, as well as the Bush administration's global pursuit of it, is ethnic conflict.[16] Such ethnic conflict may exist for a variety of reasons. Diamond and Plattner posit that ethnic conflict erupts

> because ethnicity taps cultural and symbolic issues—basic notions of identity and the self, of individual and group worth and entitlement—the conflicts it generates are intrinsically less amenable to compromise than those revolving around material issues . . . they revolve around exclusive symbols and conceptions of legitimacy, they are characterized by competing demands that cannot easily be broken down into bargainable increments.[17]

Hence, ethnicity is viewed as the individual's and group's identity and defines their view of entitlement. This has clearly been a significant historical dynamic in Afghanistan where the Pashtuns of the south have considered themselves as the only legitimate rulers of Afghanistan and have been the sole producers of kings and emirs that have ruled for the last 300 years.[18]

The underlying factor for the creation of ethnic conflict in the majority of multiethnic societies has been the degree to which all parties are included in the ruling structure of the state. In severely divided societies, ethnic identity provides a clear line of demarcation as to who will and who will not be included; these lines seem to be unalterable.[19] If Horowitz's theory is correct, then exclusion produced by ethnic differences is the single most difficult barrier for multiethnic nation-states to overcome. "In deeply ethnically divided societies, in contrast to other lines of cleavages, such as class or occupation, the lines appear to be permanent and all-encompassing, predetermining who will be granted and denied access to power and resources."[20] Further complicating this situation are the historical memories of these groups, predominantly those of the excluded or minority groups, and the resulting deeply rooted animosity toward the ruling or historically dominant group within the nation-state.[21]

Ethnicity and its possible conflicts become increasingly negative factors in the implementation and development of democratic structures and ideals within nation-states. As long as individuals value ethnicity more than nationalism and a struggle for power exists between separate groups, the chances for the creation of a democratic government and civil society are less likely. This is true not only in Africa, but also in the republics that were created after the fall of the Soviet Union and in the Balkans. Given the chance, it appears that most groups will choose to side with their own ethnic heritages and fight for control of the political system. If so, then multiethnic societies that lack feel-ings of nationalism are not conducive to forming democratic governments.

Tilly argues, "the absence of extensive kinship or tribal organization favored the development of the nation-state in Western Europe."[22] Brinbaum and Badie suggest, "Third World states generally face societies that maintain the persistence of tribal or tribal structures, the crucial importance of kinship, and the limited individualization of property rights in land."[23] Intense ethnic identity is *not* conducive to the growth and development of democratic insti-tutions that stress the importance of the whole populace over that of the indi-vidual or the group. "[T]he tribe or ethnic group gives primary importance to ties of kinship and patrilineal descent, whereas the state insists on the loy-alty of all persons to central authority."[24]

According to Rubin in his analysis of Afghan fragmentation, "democracy, in the liberal tradition, consists of procedures for making the government accountable to society so that society can govern itself by means of the state."[25] He continues to say, "the inclusion of citizens in the polity's institu-tions and opportunities to contest power define a democratic regime."[26] If the state shows preference to one group or another or includes only a certain group, that group gains a larger share of the distribution of important mate-rial and nonmaterial goods, including prestige. This increases the chance that "ethnic politics" will slow the development of democratic structures.[27]

Another obstacle in developing and maintaining a multiethnic democratic state is the sheer difficulty for any regime in promoting an all-inclusive gov-ernment and superimposing it on an ethically divided society.[28] Democracy, as a concept, stresses majority rule, which in multiethnic societies means there will always be groups that feel left out of the political arena. Successful democracies build into their systems procedures and mechanisms that allow minority groups to have a voice within government and thereby feel included in the overall governing process. The primary shortfall of many states facing ethnic conflict has been the ruling group's failure to allow the sharing of power with others within the nation-state.

AFGHANISTAN: THE EPITOME OF AN ETHNICALLY FRAGMENTED SOCIETY

Afghanistan is a country with a diverse ethnic composition that complicates democratic as well as state formation. The present boundaries of Afghanistan were created to serve as a buffer between the British and Russian Empires as Afghanistan confronted modernity through its forced integration into an Euro-centric state.[29] These "virtual" borders were not drawn along ethnic, linguistic, or religious lines, resulting in an externally imposed "state" com-posed of a complicated mix of people who were mostly living in small, kin-based communities outside of the limited urban areas. "The state was only able to impose its will upon the tribes and occupy its own territory thanks to the financial subsidies and weapons which were freely provided by the English between 1880 and 1919."[30] Consequently, the Afghan people were embittered about modernity and all that it entailed. Complicating the situation was the adoption of this modernity process by many Afghan leaders in recent history. In the end, according to Olivier Roy, it was not modernization that failed the Afghans but the rulers' notions of modernity. Simply put, he argues, "it is not modernization which brings problems, but modernity, the hypothesis which holds that modernity must necessarily involve a 'cultural revolution,' a transformation of the way of thinking and adoption of new social paradigms."[31]

Along with modernity came new concepts to Afghanistan and its people, both on social levels as well as on governmental ones. Ideas such as women's rights, separation of church and state, property rights, implementation of secular laws, and basic regulations, which historically were dealt with on the tribal level, were now being forced from the center outward. In the end, modernization was rejected by the traditionalist Afghans, mistaking it for modernity, a social concept. This wholesale rejection led to the weakening of many Afghan regimes, which were unable to propel the state from a draconian mindset to a more ideologically advanced social structure and organization.

Power sharing also undermined many regimes throughout the last hundred years of Afghan history. Rulers turned to various sociopolitically influential groups (such as the *ulema*, the chiefs of the Pashtun confederation, or other prominent personalities) that were in favor of attaining more direct control and authority.[32] This weakening of central power and its inability to co-opt the powerful and influential segments of society further decreased the chances of creating a lasting and fully independently operating state system. Afghans saw that they were better off supporting their local leaders and tribal elites, who provided them with security and economic relief, rather than supporting a central government that was dependent on the same leaders and elites to survive. In the end, this cycle undermined both the state and local leadership by creating a nonfunctioning government and establishing in the psyche of the Afghan the notion that no modern state system can successfully govern by bringing together both local and national level governing structures.

Currently, traditional legitimacy exists at tribal levels throughout Afghanistan. It is based on the sanctity of traditions and the legitimate rule of the tribal elders acting under those traditions.[33] Traditional legitimacy is effective at the tribal level, but will not be effective for the government of a modern state. Much of Afghan society today, especially the rural areas of the country, continues to live within the governing structures of tribes and clans. Roy states, "the tribes see the state as existing on the periphery, responsible for administering land whose boundaries are constantly fluctuating on account of conquests carried out by the tribal confederations, in respect of which the state is no more than the means of continuity."[34] Rubin further develops this notion by suggesting, "the tribal model depicts tribes as largely self-governing groups of people united by a 'group feeling' based on a belief in common kinships[.] [W]hile the state claims authority over society within a territory, a tribes claims jurisdiction over a set of persons bound by kinship relations."[35] The tribes of Afghanistan see the central government as nothing more than a foreign and unfamiliar power trying to force control in areas of society that traditionally are governed by tribal codes of conduct. Most tribes and villages have remained self-sufficient and autonomous, accepting central control only when in their material interest or when faced with overwhelming force.[36]

Tribal Makeup of Afghanistan

Today, Afghanistan is made up primarily of Pashtuns who would like to see a strong and Pashtun-run central state, Tajiks who focus on power sharing in the central state, and Uzbeks and Hazaras who desire recognition of their identities and mechanisms of local government.[37] Although some of these groups are ethnically and linguistically distinct, they are not necessarily different in terms of culture.

Historically, the Pashtun tribes of the south, forming the largest demographic bloc within Afghanistan, have ruled and governed the country.[38] Unlike other ethnic groups, the Pashtuns stress pronounced tribal structures and codes at state expense. The Pashtun dominance of government has created an atmosphere of tension between them and the remaining ethnic groups in Afghanistan—mainly Tajiks, Uzbeks, and Hazaras. These tensions have led to conflict, as well as repressive measures to quell the power struggle of these ethnic minority groups.

Minority ethnic groups have played specific roles within the society as a whole and within the government. But not until the Soviet Union's invasion of Afghanistan did they truly gain power within the overall societal structure and establish themselves as a political and military force that the Pashtuns could no longer ignore. In the past, fighting for control of the state had occurred primarily between Pashtuns (i.e., Durranis versus Ghilzais). But as other ethnic groups rose in importance and made stabs at governing, a great struggle arose within Afghanistan that eventually led to outright civil war and the collapse of the Afghan government and state structure.

Since the beginning of modern Afghanistan, Afghan rulers have manipulated ethnic groups in their attempts to control the state. For example, "to weaken the Barakzais, Ahmed Shah, the 'father' of modern Afghanistan appointed a separate khan for the Achakzais, making the clan into a separate tribe, a status that they retain today."[39] Successful Afghan ruling authorities have been artful in underscoring and exploiting the differences of these groups, including encouraging conflict between them in order to maintain control. This manipulation is similar to that during the British history in Iraq. In order to control remote areas, the British identified points of contact among the tribesmen and farmers in rural areas and effectively created tribal leaders. The government co-opted the leaders for social status and other benefits of upper-class inclusion. This "divide and conquer" technique further fragmented the society and lessened the likelihood of collective action among the tribes in Afghanistan.

Past attempts at Afghan modern state formation that have directly challenged the local tribal and religious structures of society have resulted in ethnic backlash and state failure. The underlying problem for Afghanistan's governments has been their inability to create a sense of genuine national unity in times other than crisis.[40] This lack of nationalism, compared to the deeply rooted ethnic identity the majority of Afghans feel, reflects the reality of how difficult it is for ethnically fragmented societies to coalesce into one unified front.

Further complicating the dynamics of Afghan society are the relationships between the tribes themselves and between the varying ethnic groups that compose the nation-state. Simply put, the relationship among tribes are generally marked by "competition and outright animosity," according to Christie.[41]

The Bonn Agreement and Process

In December 2001 the precursor to Afghanistan's first nationwide election was held in Bonn, Germany, under the auspices of the UN Special Representative for Afghanistan. The Bonn conference was organized soon after it became clear that the United States and the Northern Alliance were going to defeat the Taliban regime. The goal of this conference was to systematically map Afghanistan's future.

After nine grueling days of meetings and deal-making between various Afghan factions,[42] a UN-brokered agreement was signed establishing provisional arrangements for Afghanistan pending the reestablishment of permanent government institutions. It established an interim government for Afghanistan until a nationwide election could be held. Pashtun tribal leader Hamid Karzai was chosen to serve as head of an interim power-sharing council, which took office in Kabul on December 22. Karzai was clearly the U.S. favorite for this position. Especially after the Taliban's assassination of Abdul Haq in the fall of 2001, Karzai was the one Pashtun leader with whom the United States felt comfortable. Washington lobbied vigorously in Bonn to secure Karzai's position as the leader of the interim government.[43]

Although the Bonn Agreement—viewed by many as a "peace agreement"— laid the groundwork for Afghanistan's future political processes and institutions of governance, it did not bring together the warring parties of al Qaeda, the Taliban, and the Northern Alliance. Rather, Bonn coalesced Afghan groups opposed to the Taliban and al Qaeda. Ironically, these factions were also historically opposed to each other. Hence, although Bonn did represent a new level of commitment and political will by both Afghans and major powers and did establish the agenda and process for the establishment of permanent governance institutions, it did not attempt to resolve many root problems, most notably Afghan ethnic fragmentation and distrust.

Moreover, as noted by some critics, Bonn codified de facto power relations, disregarding their legitimacy or illegitimacy.[44] This was particularly pronounced in the allocation of key ministries to the Tajiks and Northern Alliance who, at the time of the Bonn conference, controlled Kabul in the immediate aftermath of the Taliban's demise.[45] The Northern Alliance received the three most powerful ministries within the interim government.

Younis Qanooni, leader of the Northern Alliance's delegation, was made interior minister. The Alliance's commander-in-chief, General Mohammad Fahim, became head of the Defense Ministry, and Dr. Abdullah Abdullah retained his position as foreign secretary. The 30-member cabinet included 11 Pashtuns, 8 Tajiks, 5 from the Shi'a Hazara population, and 3 Uzbeks. The remaining three were drawn from other minorities. Northern Alliance cabinet members appointed at Bonn were primarily ethnic Tajiks and former militia leaders from the Panjshir Valley, base of the famed Afghan resistant leader Ahmed Shah Massoud, who was assassinated on September 9, 2001. Since the defeat of the Taliban, these Panjshiris have dominated the Afghan security forces.

One could rightfully argue that neither the Bonn meeting nor the interim government it chose was very representative of the demographics and traditional power centers in Afghanistan. In particular, relatively few Pashtuns were given seats of power.[46] Pashtuns assumed that this imbalance would be corrected. They expected Karzai to shift the balance of power back their way and give their former king a prominent national role. This did not happen.

Emergency *Loya Jirga* and the Resulting Transitional Government

A central component of the Bonn Agreement charted the course for the future democratic elections to be held in Afghanistan. Section I (4) stipulated that, in the meantime,

> [a]n Emergency *Loya Jirga* [national political assembly] shall be convened within six months of the establishment of the Interim Authority . . . . The Emergency *Loya Jirga* shall decide on a Transitional Authority, including a broad-based transitional administration, to lead Afghanistan until such time as a fully representative government can be elected through free and fair elections to be held no later than two years from the date of the convening of the Emergency *Loya Jirga*.[47]

The Emergency *Loya Jirga* was also to elect a head of state for the transitional administration.

On June 24, 2004, the Afghan transitional government and administration of Hamid Karzai were installed during formal ceremonies in Kabul. Karzai had easily won the June 13 election at a national political assembly, or emergency *Loya Jirga* called for by the Bonn Agreement. The *Loya Jirga*, consisting of 1,500 representatives elected or appointed from 32 provinces, debated the political future of Afghanistan over a seven-day period.

Two main issues concerning government composition faced the Emergency *Loya Jirga*: the role of former King Zahir Shah and his representatives, and the role of the Panjshiris who have controlled most of the Afghan security services in and near Kabul since the defeat of the Taliban. Both of these issues were resolved in rather interesting ways.

The former king's support for the election of fellow Pashtun Karzai as the Afghan transitional head of state somewhat diffused ethnic issues. Subjects such as religion, the role of parliament, stability, and economic development dominated the *jirga* debates. But, this dissipation of ethnic suspicions and rivalry was short-lived, as Karzai would try to appease the various factions in the cabinet appointments he made.

The most problematic and sensitive appointments were in the area of security. Karzai renamed Mohammed Fahim, a leader of the Northern Alliance forces based in the Panjshir Valley, as defense minister.[48] Karzai further strengthened Fahim's position by appointing him as one of three vice presidents. This move was a clear indication of the Tajiks' power—as well as the Northern Alliance—and signaled Karzai's acceptance of the Panjshiris as necessary partners in his militarily weak government. Karzai recognized that he could not maintain stability during the fragile transition period without the help of powerful factional leaders such as Fahim. However, the relationship between Karzai and Fahim quickly became contentious and had the potential to bring down the Transitional Government.

For all practical purposes there was only one key change to the interim cabinet as a result of the *loya jirga*—the departure of Interior Minister Yunus Qanooni, a Tajik.

Qanooni played a key role during the Bonn meeting in securing initial support for Karzai's candidacy among leaders of a powerful, Tajik-led political and military coalition. The dismissal of Qanooni from the powerful interior ministry met with considerable controversy. When Karzai announced Qanooni's replacement was Taj Mohammed Wardak, an elderly governor and ethnic Pushtun, Panjshiri soldiers and policemen in the ministry initially resisted with roadblocks and work stoppages. Karzai recognized the implications of alienating the Tajiks, as well as the considerable military strength of the Northern Alliance and especially the Panjshiris. He resolved the crisis by appointing Qanooni as adviser for internal security, a newly created post, and as minister of education.[49]

Fahim, Qanooni, and Ahmad Wali Massoud were all vying for the leadership of the Panjshiris (Shura-i Nazar), and relations among them reportedly were not good. The demands by Pashtuns for Karzai to reduce these men's power exacerbated relations, in particular between Fahim and Qanooni. Yet, the basic reality was that, were it not for the U.S. and coalition presence, the Panjshiris could replace Karzai anytime they wanted—and a lot of them were chafing under the constraints of the coalition.

Karzai's choice of cabinet members also clearly represented a compromise between stability and change. Many Pashtuns expected that he would make major changes to the interim cabinet chosen during the Bonn meeting by removing factional leaders and appointing a balanced and professional cabinet more in line with the desires of the Pashtun community. Ultimately, this proved to be an impossible task. The leaders of the Northern Alliance were less than accommodating to change that would diffuse the considerable power they had received in Bonn. The cabinet reflected Karzai's recognition of the importance of striking a balance between the Pashtuns and Tajiks. Karzai was intimately aware of this after leading Afghanistan's interim government for six months in an uneasy partnership with leaders from the Tajik-led Northern Alliance. He was faced with the extremely difficult task of assembling an administration that would satisfy all major ethnic groups while meeting the country's desperate need for professional governance after years of ruinous conflict.

The cabinet's composition also highlighted the Pashtuns' continuing disorganization and lacked a level of leadership acceptable to broader groups. Considering that Kabul had traditionally been ruled by Pashtuns, the composition of the cabinet represented a significant shift in traditional power relationships. But then, alliances and ideologies are fluid, one reason why Afghanistan has had nothing resembling a stable central government for much of its existence. Nevertheless, the Tajik-dominated Northern Alliance recognized their ability to achieve practical superiority over the Pashtuns who, superior in numbers, had held them at bay for years. In the end it appeared that the *Loya Jirga*'s main achievement was to lend legitimacy to Hamid Karzai's transitional government—an end-state seemingly consistent with the desires of the United States and other international actors.

Alienated Pashtuns?

The new power of the Tajiks did not sit well with the Pashtuns and alienated many in Karzai's critical Pashtun power base. Whereas former king Zahir Shah was named by Karzai as "Father of the Nation," many Pashtuns were dismayed and angered that none of his aides had been given senior posts.[50] Other than Karzai, very few Pashtuns held positions of power in the Afghan cabinet. In July 2002, a *Washington Post* article titled "Pashtuns Losing Faith in Karzai, U.S."[51] suggested that the Pashtuns were "becoming rapidly disillusioned by a series of developments that have reinforced the power of rival ethnic Tajiks and militia leaders, left the former king politically sidelined and a Pashtun vice president assassinated, and subjected Pashtun villages to lethal U.S. air attacks."[52]

Pashtuns reportedly did not feel welcomed in Kabul where the officials they saw did not speak Pashtu. Padsha Khan Zadran, a powerful Pashtun leader/warlord in the important Khost Province,[53] summed up the sentiments of many Pashtuns when he asked, "Why are they humiliating Pashtuns? We're the majority. They placed Hamid Karzai at the top as a representative of Pashtuns. But in reality he's no longer a Pashtun. He's sold himself out. He's a traitor. Pashtuns cannot sit around waiting. They will react and will claim their rights."[54]

AFGHANISTAN'S HISTORIC OCTOBER 2004 ELECTION: PRECURSOR OF DEMOCRATIC DEVELOPMENT?

According to the Bonn Agreement, Afghan national elections were to be held on June 24, 2004 ("no later than two years from the date of the convening of the Emergency *Loya Jirga*").[55] These elections were to determine Afghanistan's president, and National Assembly and Provincial Councils, all to be held concurrently.[56] The presidential election was separated from the other two most certainly because multiple provincial contests would probably, "see an increase in factional violence as local power structures are challenged and, in some cases, long-term rivals put in direct competition."[57]

Electoral infrastructure delays, continuing instability, the claimed reemergence of the Taliban, and Kabul's lack of control over the rural areas eventually led to the postponement of the simultaneous elections. However, the primary reason for the delay in elections was concern over overall security. In particular, antigovernment activity and cross-border attacks from Pakistan meant the situation was judged not sufficiently stable in June 2004 to allow for free and fair elections. Eventually, the presidential election was postponed until September 2004, and then once again rescheduled for October 2004. The National Assembly and Provincial Council elections—viewed as a much more complex undertaking than the presidential election—were also postponed.

In the spring and summer months preceding the presidential election, new violence was witnessed, especially toward election workers. A poll conducted for the Asia Foundation in July 2004 by Charney Research—a New York polling firm, which also conducted a voter education planning survey in Afghanistan—suggested that 81 percent of Afghans intended to vote. Afghans' apparent

> eagerness to participate was confirmed by the rapid progress of voter registration since May, when it began in the rural areas (home to four-fifths of the population). In three months, registration soared from 1.5 million to 8 million of the estimated 9.5 million eligible voters. It continues at a pace of up to 125,000 per day, despite Taliban remnants opposed to the vote who threaten and even kill registrants.[58]

Whereas Taliban threats drew the media's attention, warlords and their armed militias posed greater threats to the elections and people.

> According to a survey of Afghan voters conducted by the relief organization CARE, 87% said that the government should do more to reduce the powers of Afghan commanders, and 64 percent said the most important way to improve security was to disarm the militias. Only 17 percent said that Afghans would face pressure on how to vote, but of those, more than 85 percent said the pressure would come from commanders. Interestingly, only 0.84 percent said that Islamic clerics would influence their vote.[59]

Threats to voters by regional power brokers were commonplace. For example, in September 2004 in southeastern Khost province, elders of the Terezai tribe announced on Khost radio that all tribe members must vote for Hamid Karzai. Tribal families who voted against Mr. Karzai would have their houses burned down.[60] As suggested earlier, tribal elders, as well as the collective identity of the Afghan tribes, often determine the positions of individuals.

> Deference to tribe is a common attitude all across southern Afghanistan, where the largest ethnic group, the Pashtuns, live. Individuals such as Sayid Amir, an astrologer waiting for loaves of bread at a bakery in Qalat, know that the new Afghan Constitution allows them full personal rights. But he still says he must defer to his tribal elders with his vote. "It depends on our tribal leaders," he says. "Yes, I know it is my right to choose whom I want. But in my region, the tribal leaders will all get together and choose whom they will vote for, and then everyone will vote for that person."[61]

Such a context with its accompanying behavior and attitudes is inconsistent with Western concepts of democracy.

Eventually 9 million of the eligible 9.8 million eligible voters registered. In fact, "in the provinces of Khost, Nooristan, Paktia, and Paktika, voter-registration rates exceeded eligible voters by 140 percent. In 13 of the 34 Afghan provinces voter registration exceeded the number of eligible voters."[62] Voter registration fraud and voting irregularities were cited by many observers. It is also worth noting that the Organization for Security and Cooperation in Europe (OSCE) refused to send election monitors to Afghanistan because they believed that "the present conditions in Afghanistan [were] significantly below the minimum regarded by OSCE . . . as necessary for credible election observation."[63]

Although the training and recruitment of election staff was slower than originally anticipated, eventually, there were 4,807 polling centers manned by a staff of approximately 120,000. Finally, on October 9, 2004, the presidential election took place in an atmosphere of great anticipation. Eighteen eligible candidates were listed on the Afghan presidential ballot. Around eight million voters, some waiting in lines for hours, voted. Harmid Karzai garnered 55.4 percent of the vote and his main opponents Yunus Qanooni, Haji Mohammed, and Abdul Rashid Dostum received 16.3, 11.7, and 10 percent, respectively. There were, however, complaints about voter intimidation—especially in the Pashtun south and east—voting procedures, multiple voting, and other counting irregularities in some areas. Also, 15 of the candidates initially called for the election to be suspended because of alleged fraud and "intimidation by Mr. Karzai's supporters, and [a] charge that the faulty ink pens have made it possible for Afghans to vote multiple times."[64] Most of these candidates eventually backed away from their complaints after a series of meetings with U.S. Ambassador Zalmay Khalilzad.[65] Eventually, an Impartial Panel of Election Experts concluded that the outcome had not been affected by these problems.[66]

Even with these controversies, the Afghan election was viewed by most as a historic watershed event and a resounding success. High voter turnout, low levels of violence, and the participation of women even in conservative Pashtun southern areas pointed to many positives. The simple fact that the election was held was important considering that Afghanistan ranks at the bottom of nearly all development indices, has no extended tradition of universal franchise, and has experienced almost a quarter century of continual conflict in its immediate past.

But, there is an important question concerning the election. What do the election results mean for the development of democracy in Afghanistan? Evidently, the answer to this question is not clear.

Figure 6.1 presents two maps that seem germane to the answer. The upper map in figure 6.1 represents a geographical breakdown of ethno-linguistic groups in Afghanistan. As suggested by this map, the Pashtuns primarily occupy the mountain belt that extends along much of the border with Pakistan and the Registan Desert southwest of Kandahar. The Tajiks primarily live in the eastern range of the Hindu Kush Mountains in the extreme northeast of the country. The Shi'a Hazaras occupy the central Hindu Kush range in the center of Afghanistan. Finally, the Uzbeks occupy the area east of Badghis—both the desert of Faryab and its plain that extends northward into central Asia (in the north and center of the country). When one compares this upper map in figure 6.1 with the lower map representing the provinces carried by each of the presidential candidates, an extremely interesting pattern emerges. Considering that each of the four leading Afghan presidential candidates belonged to a different ethno-linguistic group— Karzai (Pashtun), Qanooni (Tajik), Mohaqiq (Hazara), and Dostum (Uzbek)— the maps track ethnic representation quite nicely. Unlike a two-colored American electorate map, Afghanistan's has four hues. Intuitively, it appears that the results of the Afghan presidential election merely reify traditional ethnic splits in the country.

In order to more explicitly explore the notion that the results of the presidential election primarily reflect long-standing ethnic divisions, provincial election data for each of the four leading candidates was gathered. Data was also collected for each of the 34 Afghan provinces relative to their ethnic breakdown or composition.[67] Correlation analysis was then performed on these data representing provincial voting results and provincial ethnic composition. The correlation results of this analysis are presented in table 6.1.

The results are telling. The analysis clearly supports the notion that the results of the Afghan presidential election represent and reflect historical ethnic patterns that have long driven conflict dynamics in the county. No candidate received significant support outside of his particular ethno-linguistic group.

As can be seen in table 6.1, each ethnic group voted for the explicit candidate from their own group, with correlations (r) of ethnic parochial voting ranging from between .84 and .91. These results are statistically significant with a $p < .0001$ meaning that these results could not have occurred randomly. Whereas such an analysis does not imply causation, it does suggest clearly that traditional ethnicity remains at the forefront of Afghan politics, at least as represented by recent presidential voting patterns.

An examination of table 6.1 also indicates other notions of the vital importance of ethnicity in Afghan politics and governance. It is interesting to note

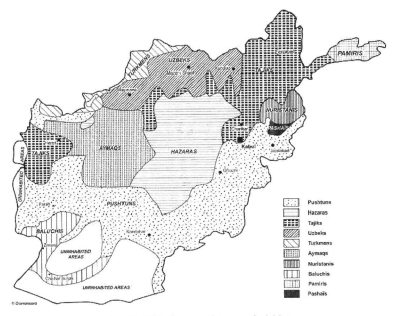

Simplified distribution of macro-ethnicities.

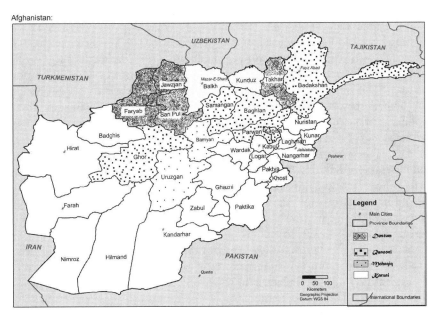

Figure 6.1 Afghan ethno-linguistic groups and Afghan October 2005 Presidential Election results.

Source: Afghan Elections Project—The Joint Electoral Management Body, www.elections-afghanistan.org.afl.

Table 6.1 Correlation coefficients (Pearson r) for Afghan presidential candidates at the provincial level

	Ethno-linguistic provincial votes received (%)			
	Pashtun	Tajik	Hazara	Uzbek
Hamid Karzai	.88 ($p<.0001$)	−.44 ($p<.01$)	−.45 ($p<.01$)	−.54 ($p<.001$)
Yunus Qanooni	−.54 ($p<.001$)	.84 ($p<.0001$)	−.14 ($p<.42$)	.01 ($p<.96$)
Haji Mohaqiq	−.34 ($p<.05$)	−.20 ($p<.26$)	.91 ($p<.0001$)	−.06 ($p<.72$)
Rashid Dostum	−.45 ($p<.01$)	−.10 ($p<.58$)	.14 ($p<.41$)	.88 ($p<.0001$)

Note: SAS 9.1 procedure "proc corr" was used to produce the Pearson Correlation Coefficients ($n − 34$). Thanks to Adrianne Casebeer for assistance with the correlational analysis.

not only the high positive correlations between the different ethno-linguistic groups with their respective ethnic candidate (represented by the correlation results in the table's diagonal), but also the negative correlations that show the candidates for whom the various ethnic groups were not likely to vote. The Pashtuns have significant negative correlations ($r = −.44$–$−.54$) relative to their probability of supporting a candidate from a different ethnic group. The chance of a Pashtun voting for any of the other candidates was indeed very slight and reflected their solidarity in voting patterns. Likewise, the Tajiks had a very slim chance of voting for a Pashtun ($r −.54$ with a p $<.001$). These results suggest that the two most influential Afghan ethno-linguistic groups—traditional rivals—will not only vote for their own candidate, but also against the other. This is not an encouraging finding for the success of a strong presidential system based on the primacy of one ethnic group in deference to others. In fact, it has been argued that a strong presidential system can actually be a recipe for disaster in countries such as Afghanistan where political elites are deeply divided, for it effectively permits only one winner, while potentially generating many disgruntled losers.[68]

The Afghan governmental system mapped by the Bonn Agreement could fail miserably if Karzai were to take advantage of the opportunity of his powerful office to advance the causes of his own ethnic group, the Pashtuns. This would be disastrous for Afghanistan. Not only would it likely reinforce factionalism and deepen the rifts between ethnic groups, but also eventually result in civil war or secession.

This analysis suggests that Afghanistan faces an extremely difficult challenge: how to unify its fragmented society and foster the development of a national identity while each ethnic group continues to attempt to gain a foothold in government, sometimes at the expense of other groups. This ethnic approach, rather than a regional or national one, will continue to fragment society until one dominant ethnic group controls all of the governmental power or ethnic politics will make way for increased internal conflict.

As the analysis above bears out, the presidential election appears to have been more procedural than substantive. With Afghan ethnic groups voting mostly along ethnic lines rather than crossing over to candidates from other ethnicities, the election made little headway toward uniting the divided country behind a single candidate. Although Karzai was elected with a majority of the overall vote, he was not elected with a majority of the vote within any ethnic group outside his own, the dominant Pashtun. Hamid Karzai's claim that he is a truly national candidate that has support across ethnic lines is not borne out. Less populous, but no less important, ethnic groups such as the Uzbeks, Tajiks, Hazaras, and Turkmen did not "forget" their own interests and vote for Karzai in an attempt to unite the country.

Although the American administration assumes the election of an Afghan president is the first step on a path toward democracy, ethnic divisions, unless properly addressed, threaten to derail any long-term hope of a democratic Afghanistan. Unwilling to vote outside ethnic boundaries and come together in compromise, Afghan citizens have begun a voting trend that does not portend well for any future parliamentary government.

The burden falls on the political elites to reach compromise independently or face continued intractability on all ethnically divisive issues, which in Afghanistan translates as almost all daily business. Rather than letting the situation deteriorate, the elected leaders must reach compromises that are mutually and constitutionally guaranteed, so those minority groups feel vested in the various government institutions.[69] On issues that include rather than exclude them, Afghan minorities will demand compromise. Additionally, changes should come from the bottom up. Inherent here is the belief that government is most effective when it is open to its citizenry. If the citizenry views the government as ineffective, they will have no incentive to participate and will come to view the government negatively.[70]

All is not bleak, however. Afghanistan does have two major factors in its favor for democratic development. First, it is a multiethnic society composed of a handful of groups rather than two opposing forces. With four major ethnic groups, the Afghan polity has many sources from which to form coalitions to bridge the ethnic divide.[71] Second, the timing of the government-building process allows each group to enshrine collective rights that will protect political interests and share economic ones.[72]

CONCLUSION

While the United States pushes Afghanistan toward a democratic government, not just in name, but also in practice, the Bush administration would be well advised to look closely at the complexity involved in building a lasting democracy in ethnically divided Afghanistan. In a society fragmented by ethnic groupings where concerns over rights of the group dominate the rights of the individual, a Western-style liberal democracy, designed to promote and protect individual rights, is viewed as doing little to address to the needs of the groups.[73] Indeed, as Horowitz points out, young democracies often fall victim to the problems of their past as they appropriate colonial institutions or Western constitutional provisions, neither of which takes into account the reality facing the new nation.[74] In Afghanistan's case, addressing the ethnic divisions that permeate the country is paramount if democracy is to take hold.

Rather than endorse a procedural democracy that only highlights the completion of events, such as elections, the Bush administration must force the Afghan government to address the issues that divide the citizenry with earnest concern and grave attention.

Over the past 100 years, national politics have not been of much concern to the ordinary Afghan who made decreasing the state's influence at local levels his number one priority.[75] This constant deflection of central authority in the everyday lives of Afghans allowed traditional governing structures to remain largely intact and slowed their evolution to more modern structures. As the central government fought to gain access to these local structures, it was met with increased resistance and eventual revolt. The cycle repeated itself through many different Afghan regimes using varying models of government.

The challenge facing the current Afghan government is the task of uniting the Afghan people while not repeating the mistakes of the past. The concept of national identity needs to be bolstered, but not at the expense of marginalizing ethnic traditions and norms that are deeply valued by the Afghan people. As long as people are divided by ethnicity or religion, there will be injustice, corruption, and discontent. The goal in every budding democracy should be to create a strong sense of national identity above all else. Governments must foster the common identity and remove all ethnic and religious aspects of government. In Afghanistan, Shi'a, Sunni, Pashtun, Tajik, Uzbek, and Hazara leaders must fully cooperate in a quest for unity. It is only then that all citizens will achieve a common sense of national belonging and democracy will be able to thrive. In the end, this tightrope act will determine whether or not Afghanistan succeeds in forming a modern nation-state with democratic institutions and a large civil society.

NOTES

1. *National Security Strategy of the United States* (Washington, DC: The White House, September 2002).
2. Larry Diamond and Marc F. Plattner, eds., *Nationalism, Ethnic Conflict, and Democracy* (Baltimore: Johns Hopkins University Press, 1994), xix.
3. Robin Wright and Ellen Knickmeyer, "U.S. Lowers Sight on What Can Be Achieved in Iraq," *The Washington Post*, August 14, 2005, A01.
4. *National Security Strategy of the United States.*
5. For an excellent analysis of this strategy, the Bush administration's foreign policy and "neo-conservatism," see James Mann, *Rise of the Vulcans: The History of Bush's War Cabinet* (New York: Viking, 2004).
6. Ibid., 330.
7. See Thomas H. Johnson and James Russell, "A Hard Day's Night?: The United States and the Global War on Terror," *Comparative Strategy*, vol. 24, no. 2 (2005), 127–151.
8. Preston Mendenhall, "After the Taliban, What Next?" MSNBC; available at http://msnbc.com/news/64306.asp.

9. Adrian Hastings, *The Construction of Nationhood* (Cambridge: Cambridge University Press, 1997), 1.

10. Ibid.

11. Smith defines ethnicity as a "community with a collective proper name, a myth of common culture, shared historical memories, one or more differentiating elements of common culture and an association with a specific (although not necessarily residence in) homeland." See Anthony Smith, *The Ethnic Origins of Nations* (Oxford and Melden: Blackwell Publishers Inc, 1986), 94.

12. "Legitimacy" can be defined as the belief of the citizens that the authority of the government is just and credible. Legitimacy rests on a belief in the legality of rules and the authority of those who hold offices created under those rules. Citizens are obedient to the authority of legally established rules and offices, not to particular individuals.

13. Diamond and Plattner, *Nationalism, Ethnic Conflict, and Democracy*, xvii.

14. Donald L. Horowitz., "Democracy in Divided Societies," in Diamond and Plattner, *Nationalism, Ethnic Conflict, and Democracy*, 48.

15. Hastings, *Construction of Nationhood*, 4.

16. Horowitz, "Democracy in Divided Societies," 35.

17. Diamond and Plattner, *Nationalism, Ethnic Conflict, and Democracy*, xviii.

18. Since the modern formation of the country of Afghanistan, only two non-Pashtuns have ever reigned in Kabul. Habibullah Ghazi, a Tajik, briefly held power in 1929 until he was overthrown and Pashtuns returned to power. Burhanuddin Rabbani Tajik, leader of the *Jamiat-i-Islami*, was an ineffectual *Mujahideen* president of Afghanistan from June 1992 until the Taliban took Kabul in September of 1996. Rabbani then led the Northern Alliance.

19. Horowitz, "Democracy in Divided Societies," 35.

20. Diamond and Plattner, *Nationalism, Ethnic Conflict, and Democracy*, xix.

21. Ibid., xviii.

22. Barnett R. Rubin, *The Fragmentation of Afghanistan* (New Haven and London: Yale University Press, 2002), 9.

23. Ibid., 9.

24. Ibid., 10.

25. Ibid., 4.

26. Ibid.

27. Horowitz, "Democracy in Divided Societies," 35.

28. Ibid., 42.

29. Rubin, *Fragmentation of Afghanistan*, 5.

30. Olivier Roy, *Islam and Resistance in Afghanistan*, 2nd ed. (Cambridge: Cambridge University Press, 1990), 17.

31. Roy, *Islam and Resistance in Afghanistan*, 16.

32. Willem Van Schendel and Erik J. Zurcher, eds., "Identity Politics in Central Asia and the Muslim World," in Gabriele Rasuly-Paleczek, ed., *The Struggle for the Afghan State: Centralization, Nationalism, and Their Discontents* (New York: I.B. Tauris & Co Ltd, 2001), 149.

33. Max Weber, *The Types of Legitimate Domination*, vol. 1 (Berkeley: California University Press, 1978), 215.

34. Roy, *Islam and Resistance in Afghanistan*, 14.

35. Rubin, *Fragmentation of Afghanistan*, 10.

36. Jeffrey J. Roberts, *The Origins of Conflict in Afghanistan* (Westport and London: Praeger Publishers, 2003), xii.

37. Rubin, *Fragmentation of Afghanistan*, 11.
38. The Pushtuns, representing 42% of the population, make up the largest ethnic group in Afghanistan. Ethnic Tajiks represent 27% of the population. The Hazaras represent another 9%. Other groups—such as the Aimaks, Turkmen, Baluch, Uzbek, and others—comprise the rest. The country is almost totally Muslim, with the Sunni Muslims representing 80% of the population and Shi'i Muslims representing 19%. See "Afghanistan," *The World Factbook 2004* (Washington: Central Intelligence Agency, 2004).
39. Rubin, *Fragmentation of Afghanistan*, 46.
40. John C. Griffiths, *Afghanistan: Key to a Continent* (Boulder: Westview Press, 1981), 78.
41. Kenneth Christie, *Ethnic Conflict, Tribal Politics: A Global Perspective* (Surrey: Curzon Press, 1998), 5.
42. Key factions at Bonn were the Northern Alliance (primarily Tajik), the Rome Group (representing the former king, Mohammed Zahir Shah), the Cyprus Group (allegedly Iranian-backed), and the Peshawar Group (primarily Pashtun).
43. Interview of senior U.S. government official.
44. Barnett Rubin, "Afghanistan and Threats to Human Security," an essay adapted from a speech delivered in Tokyo on December 15, 2001, at the International Symposium on Human Security: "Human Security and Terrorism—Diversifying Threats under Globalization"—from Afghanistan to the Future of the World, www.cfr.org./public/reource.cgi?pers!1841, accessed February 2, 2005. Although not explicitly stating so in the Bonn Agreement, Lakhdar Brahimi, the special representative of the UN secretary general suggested that the role of the Emergency *Loya Jirga* after six months was to remedy some of the defects in the interim government originally chosen at Bonn. One such defect was that the original interim government did not closely reflect the demographics of the country.
45. See Thomas H. Johnson, "The Loya Jirga, Ethnic Rivalries and Future Afghan Stability," *Strategic Insights*, vol. 1, no. 6 (Monterey, CA: Center for Contemporary Conflict, Naval Postgraduate School, August 2002). Much of the following discussion is pulled from this article.
46. It is interesting to note that even the Rome group of Zahir Shah, the former king, had very heavy non-Pashtun representation, including the group's leader in Bonn.
47. *Agreement On Provisional Arrangements in Afghanistan Pending the Re-Establishment of Permanent Government Institutions*, accessed August 4, 2005.
48. Fahim, a Tajik from the Panjshir Valley, replaced Massoud as the military leader of the Northern Alliance after the legendary Afghan leader was assassinated. He played a key role in the ground war against the Taliban. The United States, however, had reportedly reevaluated its relationship with the Northern Alliance and its view of Fahim. One Western official with extensive experience in Afghanistan stated, "The U.S. government is making a terrible mistake in supporting Fahim . . . The U.S. has the resources to understand this is not a reliable partner and that he could easily be replaced . . . Fahim's tendencies are those of a street thug." Susan B. Glasser and Pamela Constable, "Tension Rises between Two Key Afghans: Defense Chief Is Seen as Threat to Karzai and Nation's Stability," *The Washington Post*, August 5, 2002, A12. Fahim has an interesting past. Fahim reportedly replaced Najibullah as the head of KhAD (the Soviet's puppet PDPA's brutal secret police and intelligence agency during the Soviet occupation). He is close to the Russians (he was the clear Russian favorite to lead the Northern Alliance after the death of Massoud) and is extremely disliked by many Pashtuns, Hazaras, and Uzbeks.

49. *The Washington Post*, Foreign Service, "Karzai Swears in New Afghan Cabinet," Monday, June 24, 2002.

50. Ibid.

51. "Pashtuns Losing Faith in Karzai, U.S.," *The Washington Post*, June 13, 2002, A-1.

52. Ibid.

53. At the time, Zadran was reported to control the three southeastern provinces of Khost, Paktia, and Paktika—traditional Pashtun strongholds. Zadran had been part of a continuing conflict, in part, concerning the governorships of these three provinces. See "Warlord Pushes for Control of a Corner of Afghanistan," *New York Times*, August 6, 2002.

54. BBC Correspondent Kate Clark in Khost, Afghanistan, "Pashtuns Demand Greater Role in Afghanistan," *BBC News*, July 25, 2002.

55. See Section (1) 4 of *Agreement on Provisional Arrangements in Afghanistan Pending the Re-Establishment of Permanent Government Institutions.*

56. The concurrency of these elections was a last minute concession and controversial. See Barnett Rubin, "A Brief Look at the Final Negotiations on the Constitution of Afghanistan," January 4, 2004, at www.kabulreconstructions.net/ index.php?id = 293.

57. International Crisis Group, "Afghanistan Elections: Endgame or New Beginning?" *Crisis Group Asia Report*, no. 101 (July 2005), ii.

58. Craig Charney, "Afghan Success Story," *The Washington Post*, July 30, 2004, A19. On June 25, 2004, suspected Taliban fighters killed 17 people in Uruzgan province because they registered to vote.

59. Scott Baldauf, "Afghan Voters Face Threats," *Christian Science Monitor*, October 4, 2004.

60. Ibid.

61. Ibid.

62. Ibid.

63. Ibid.

64. Scott Baldauf, "Boycott Threatens Afghanistan's Foray into Democracy," *Christian Science Monitor*, October 12, 2004.

65. Ibid.

66. See International Crisis Group, *Final Report of the Impartial Panel Concerning Afghanistan Presidential Elections 2004*," November 1, 2004, at www.elections-afghanistan.org.af/.

67. Official Afghan election data was drawn from Joint Electoral Management Body, "Afghanistan Presidential Election Results-2004," at www.elections-afghanistan.org.af/Election%20Results%20Website/english/english.htm; for information on the provincial ethno-linguistic data, see the following: www.aims.org.af/; Ludwig W. Adamec, ed., *Historical and Political Gazatteer of Afghanistan*, vols. 3–5 (London: HMSO, 1914, revised and reprinted Graz, Austria: Akademische Druck-u. Verlagsanstalt); Thomas H. Johnson et al., *Afghanistan: The Northern Provinces* (Silver Spring, MD: The Orkand Corporation, 1988), chapter 3; Thomas H. Johnson et al., *Afghanistan: The Southern Provinces* (Silver Spring: The Orkand Corporation, 1989), chapter 4 and; Thomas H. Johnson, dir., *Afghanistan: The Western Hinterland Provinces* (Silver Spring: The Orkand Corporation, 1989), chapter 4. Provincial ethno-linguistic data also came from expert judgments in some provinces.

68. William Maley, "Executive, Legislative, and Electoral Options for Afghanistan," at www.cic.nyu.edu/pdf/E9ExecLegisElectoralOptionsMaley.pdf, accessed June 10, 2005.

69. Anne Marie Goetz, Mary Kaldor, and Robin Luckham, "Democratic Institutions and Democratic Politics," in Sunil Bastian and Robin Luckham, eds., *Can Democracy Be Designed?* (London: Zed Books, 2003), 42.

70. Robert A. Dahl, *Polyarchy: Participation and Opposition* (New Haven: Yale University Press, 1972), 120.

71. Ibid., 115–116.

72. Ilan Peleg, "Transforming Ethnic Orders to Pluralist Regimes: Theoretical, Comparative and Historical Analysis," in Adrian Guelke, ed., *Democracy and Ethnic Conflict: Advancing Peace in Deeply Divided Societies* (New York: Palgrave Macmillan, 2004), 21.

73. Ibid., 10.

74. Donald L. Horowitz, "Democracy in Divided Societies," *Journal of Democracy*, vol. 4, no. 4 (1993), 35.

75. Ibid., 168.

REGIONAL SECURITY AND STABILITY

7

The Arab–Israeli Conflict and Regional Stability

Ellen Laipson and Emile Hokayem

The long saga of Israel, the Palestine, and their immediate Arab neighbors has shaped the politics and the psychology of security for the wider region from North Africa to South Asia. Despite Herculean efforts by the United States and other Western powers, the failure to resolve the territorial and existential conflict between Israel and Palestine in particular must be seen as one of the key factors in shaping the security environment of the wider region. Several generations of Arabs and Israelis have been profoundly affected by the conflict and by the occasional breakthroughs in resolution efforts. The enduring conflict, which has religious, historic, demographic, and social dimensions, is also all about security: the perceptions of personal and national security of each of the players, the tragic history of five Middle Eastern wars, the dominance of military officers in national decision making, the emergence of Palestinian terrorism in the 1970s, and the more recent explosions of violence stemming from Palestinian frustration and Israeli efforts to impose a unilateral security regime on the territory it controls.

It is debatable how much the new violence perpetrated by al Qaeda and apocalyptic Islamic radicals also draws sustenance from the legacy of failed peace efforts and the epic myth of Palestine.[1] This debate has become part of the political discourse between neoconservatives in the United States. Is the Arab–Israeli conflict the inspiration for the violence and political despair that permeates the region's recent history? Or is it possible to disaggregate the causes of the region's instability? Some argue that terrorism and political violence derive principally from failed governance on the Arab side, and such violence has been used relentlessly and counterproductively by Arab regimes and societies as a political weapon for decades.[2] From this perspective, only when a more stable political culture is established can the Arab–Israeli conflict be solved. Others believe that the humiliation and defeat of Arab armies by Israel's military superiority has generated politics of despair and created a fertile ground for terrorism and destructive ideologies. Thus, two competing perceptions prevail about the causality of the region's predicament: is it Palestine as a festering wound that has spread relentlessly throughout the region, or is Palestine its own microclimate, less relevant to the passions and politics of the broader region, neither affected by nor able to affect other storms and weather systems in the region?

This chapter is premised on the assumption that one must avoid a one-dimensional view and resist the temptation to say either that the Arab–Israeli conflict explains everything bad that happens in the region or that it is irrelevant. For the four million Palestinians living in the West Bank and Gaza and the four million Palestinian refugees living mostly in neighboring countries, isolated in recent years and now managing a critically important leadership transition, there is no other topic. But for 22 Arab countries and 280 million Arabs, it is important to assess honestly the difference between a rhetorical and emotional construct, and an evolving reality, in which maturing nation states are increasingly differentiating their national interests and agendas from the pan-Arab myth of shared history and purpose.

This chapter argues that one can increasingly disaggregate security issues that derive directly from the Arab–Israeli conflict and the failure of the "peace process" on the one hand, and those that affect current realities and practical security considerations in changing Arab societies removed from the immediate Arab–Israeli zone, on the other. It aims to explore how the Arab–Israeli conflict shapes the current and prospective security agenda in the region, and how it does not. To identify areas for constructive improvement even if the Arab–Israeli conflict remains unresolved, it is critically important to separate the historic legacy and accumulated grievances shared across the Arab world from the real world in which many increasingly differentiated Arab governments and societies now operate. Each achievement of the peace process (such as the 1978 Camp David Accords, 1979 Israel–Egypt Peace Treaty, 1993 Oslo Accords between Israelis and Palestinians, and 1994 Jordan–Israel peace treaty) led many Arab states to establish new policies and practices that have had significant security consequences. Several key Arab states no longer plan for future Arab–Israeli combat, and in pan-Arab gatherings, the peace process and the question of Palestine appear to be less dominant on the agenda than was previously the case.

FRAMING THE ISSUES: ASSUMPTIONS AND DEFINITIONS

To begin the exploration of how the Arab–Israeli issue affects the region's security, it is important to lay out some assumptions and definitions.

The Palestine Question

For current and future policymakers, the Arab–Israeli conflict of nearly a century's duration now centers on the single issue of Palestinian statehood. The broader issues of Israel's recognition as a state and its ability to conduct normal state-to-state relations with neighbors that are not parties to the territorial dispute are largely resolved, even though the process has been halting and a far cry from the "New Middle East" vision of social and economic interaction much heralded in the mid-1990s in a period of active and effective peacemaking. For the twenty-first century, the focus is on the last, and hardest, problem: how will Israel and a new Palestinian state coexist in a small territory with limited resources? At its most mechanical, the question of the legal status of the West Bank and Gaza Strip is forefront. Beyond territory are more intangible issues: the right of return of the Palestinian diaspora, the rights and obligations of the two societies with respect to movement of people, the right to own property, the settlement of outstanding claims, the stewardship of holy sites in both territories.

The unilateral Israeli withdrawal from Gaza in 2005 will create new uncertainties about the sovereignty of Gaza and will probably reduce the prospects for a further Israeli withdrawal from most of the West Bank, thus complicating plans for a viable Palestinian state with an easily defined territory.

Furthermore, with the death of Yasser Arafat in 2004, Palestinian politics entered a new era. The January 2005 elections were well regarded as an open exercise of democratic choice. Mahmoud Abbas, a loyal Arafat lieutenant, was elected president and enjoyed local and international support in his first year in office. But his lack of charisma and his apparent inability to act as the agent of real change in internal Palestinian politics could lead, by the next elections, to a change from the "old guard" that he represents to new leaders with a different experience of the Arab–Israeli struggle. The new generation of Palestinian leaders waiting in the wings is mainly a product of the first Intifada (1988–90) and of the first stages of Palestinian autonomy (1990s). They have a more direct experience of the Israeli occupation, and their ties to Israeli society are also stronger. Contrary to Arafat, a larger-than-life figure who viewed himself as an important actor in international and regional politics, the younger generation entertains more local ambitions. The new leadership will have to demonstrate its ability to govern the Palestinian autonomous areas more efficiently and more transparently than before. As much as Israeli intentions, good governance and progress on security issues will determine the future of the Palestinians.

One State or Two?

Peace process activists have worked with the parties to define a large agenda of issues.[3] But hovering above that daunting set of issues is an emerging discourse among Palestinians questioning the very structure of the formal negotiations. Some argue for turning the clock back to the period before the establishment of the Israeli state, when intellectuals debated the merits of a single, binational state, a democracy with Jews, Christians, and Muslims as equal citizens.[4] The death of Yasser Arafat may lead to a confusing period when his successors struggle to define his legacy and demonstrate their loyalty to his mission. Will they interpret his refusal to agree to the offer in 2000 as a mandate to reopen the basic terms of the bargain? Or will they work within the paradigm of a two-state solution?

Defining the Region

There are three distinct subregions in the Arab world, which generally coincide with the distinct geographic zones of North Africa, the Mediterranean littoral of West Asia, and the Arabian Peninsula. Egypt is the pivotal state that links the three subregions. For purposes of this analysis, the focus is on Egypt as a leadership state, the Levant (Israel, Lebanon, Syria, and Jordan), and the Gulf (the Arabian Peninsula, Iraq and Iran). Less attention is given to the francophone Arab states of the Maghreb and Libya. Iran and Israel are considered as the major non-Arab powers. Turkey as a member of NATO, will most likely continue to orient its own security policies in that transatlantic context, but would likely be an important actor in new Middle Eastern security arrangements.

Different Kinds of Security

One of the most profound lessons of the long Arab–Israeli history is that military superiority does not necessarily bring security. Since the 1967 war, Israel has enjoyed a security relationship with the United States that has enabled Israel, through access to NATO-equivalent systems and its own technological prowess, to maintain its status as a world-class military power. Israel also possesses nuclear capabilities and possibly other nonconventional programs, which combined make it the most modern and capable force in the region. Nonetheless, for over a decade and a half, Israel's security in most of its aspects—the safety and well-being of its citizens, the stability of its economy, and the quality of its relations with its neighbors—has been severely compromised by low-technology war from terrorism and the long-running insurgency called the *intifada* (Arabic for uprising).

In the Middle East region, one can find every kind of security threat and the full spectrum of security responses by the states. The region has experienced conventional wars between states at least once a decade for over 50 years; the last one involving Israel was 1982. In the last quarter century, there have been Arab–Arab wars (Iraq's 1990 invasion of Kuwait), an Arab–Iranian war (1980–88), and two wars between Iraq and a coalition of regional and non-regional states (1991 and 2003). The region has unresolved border disputes, particularly in the Arabian peninsula, suffers from environmental scarcities that could well lead to wars over water or arable land, and has experienced internal political violence in many states due to poor governance that has led to interference by neighbors and conditions of mistrust among states.

At least three other factors beyond the Arab–Israeli conflict contribute to a regional environment characterized by profound security challenges. Regional organizations, from the Arab League, the Gulf Cooperation Council, and other subregional fora, have proven to be very weak in addressing security issues. Second, at least four of the region's states (Israel, Iran, Syria, and Egypt) are known to be in possession or pursuit of weapons of mass destruction, creating uncertainties about their intentions and capabilities to act aggressively toward neighbors and extraregional powers. A third factor is the nearly complete absence of intraregional trade, which in other parts of the world serves to mitigate conflict.

In assessing prospects for a new security architecture for the region, one must therefore employ a wider lens than simply imagining how the question of Palestine shapes security; the region faces a series of security problems that can be separated from the indisputably powerful emotional and political pull of the Palestine problem. Security is primarily a national government function and responsibility, although this chapter also considers supranational security arrangements that may include some transfer of sovereignty for security outside the nation state. It also considers human security as an increasingly important dimension of how nation states and societies create conditions that foster peace and security.

Regional Security Concepts

For the decades since the departure of the British as the recognized security guarantor of the Gulf, Western experts have examined and articulated many different concepts for regional security. At the abstract level, these concepts range from hegemony by an outside power, hegemony by a regional power, balance of power among the regional states, and variations on regional security regimes, which could include developing the Gulf Cooperation Council into a regional equivalent of NATO.[5] In actuality, the United States has served as the main outside power for over 30 years, and has experimented with additional approaches that do not neatly fit into these academic concepts. In the 1970s, there was the two-pillar policy, developing deep security ties to Saudi Arabia and Iran as the regional powers. This approach collapsed with the fall of the shah. Later there was dual containment, positing that Iran and Iraq, after their bloody war, were both sources of regional instability and were best dealt with by sanctions and containment.[6] At present, the United States works closely with several small Gulf States willing to cooperate militarily, perhaps against a shared threat (e.g., Iraq under Saddam Hussein prior to 2003) or perhaps against an unspoken threat from instability in Saudi Arabia or an aggressive Iran. In any case, this cooperation coexists with often acute anti-Americanism, as in Qatar, home to both a large U.S. Air Force presence and the pan-Arab television station Al-Jazeera. U.S. long-term plans for an important security presence in Iraq are not yet articulated, and will be a function of the ability to quell the anti-coalition insurgency that arose there following the 2003 war.

At important historic junctures, new thinking has emerged about smarter and more effective ways to manage the security challenges of the region. After the Gulf War and the regional Madrid conference, for example, there was much optimism about establishing a new security architecture that would allow the states in the region greater transparency regarding each other's defense structures and policies, thus permitting higher confidence in each state's ability to understand the threat environment and plan appropriately. It would encourage more cooperation against shared threats, and less contingency planning for bilateral disputes that could turn into conventional wars. At that juncture, in the early 1990s, there was also talk of beginning a dialogue about the region's nonconventional capabilities that could create dynamics for arms reductions and the eventual elimination of weapons of mass destruction.

The post-Saddam moment may provide another such opportunity for new thinking about regional security. Scholars and practitioners in the West have dusted off their theory books and returned to some big-picture thinking.[7] What is notable, however, is the small role that the regional states play in this discourse. Regional views are eagerly sought, but throughout the region, with a few exceptions (Israel, Egypt, Turkey, Iran), there is an absence of a robust security community that would permit policy options to be debated outside of government. Citizens are generally quite passive about security matters, assuming that their strong states will continue to monopolize this topic. Even within presidential palaces and royal diwans, there is a presumption that the great powers (the United States and to a lesser extent Europe), will take the lead on grand strategy, and that national security depends on adapting to the preferences of powerful outside actors. It seems that one of the necessary missing ingredients of regional security is a security community that is capable and confident enough to express national and regional preferences, and to advise policymakers on ways to transfer the real responsibility for regional security to the local sovereign actors.[8]

THE EVOLVING PLACE OF THE ARAB–ISRAELI CONFLICT IN ARAB POLITICS

The assumption that the foreign and domestic policies of Arab states have been heavily determined by the Arab–Israeli conflict originates from the belief that the Arab world shares a set of political norms that constrain and guide the behavior and choices of Arab states.[9] Throughout the 1950s, 1960s, and 1970s, Arab leaders were constrained by norms that restrained their ability to devise independent policies, whether domestic or foreign. These norms were thought to be not only constraints but also the expression of a shared Arab identity that shaped the behavior of all actors, molded their expectations, and drastically limited the autonomy of states and their leaders.

The Arab–Israeli conflict was central to this intellectual framework. When Egyptian President Gamal Abdel-Nasser laid down "the three no's"—no peace with Israel, no negotiations, no recognition—at the 1968 Arab summit in Khartoum, he had simply spelled out the underlying principles that characterized the Arab world's position vis-à-vis Israel. After the failure of Arab states to defeat the Jewish national movement in 1948, pan-Arab norms required apparent solidarity with the Palestinian people as well as constant awareness of "the Zionist threat." In the eyes of many, the plight of the Palestinians came to personify the humiliation of the Arab world at the hands of Western imperialists and to echo the Arab world's enduring backwardness. In the hands of Arab regimes, it also became a convenient tool to discredit domestic criticism and external rivalry.

From 1948 until 1967, Arab states dominated and often manipulated the Palestinian issue. The Palestinian national movement was highly dependent on the agendas of the states that harbored Palestinian refugees and guerillas, especially Egypt, then the cradle of Arab nationalism. The stunning defeat of Arab armies during the 1967 Six-Day War provoked the rise of a Palestinian liberation movement led by Yasser Arafat. Arafat's independent agenda led to a series of confrontations with Arab states worried about the military power of the Palestinian Liberation Organization and Arafat's brinkmanship.[10] Whereas Arafat relentlessly advocated "revolution until victory," Arab regimes, preoccupied first and foremost by their survival, refused to adopt his strategy. These divergences escalated into armed confrontation among the PLO and Jordan, the Lebanese government, and Syria. Finally, the ineffective Arab response to the Israeli invasion of Lebanon in 1982 and the Syrian–Palestinian armed confrontation of 1983 validated the view, in Palestinian eyes, that Arab states would not stand by them at critical moments.

By occupying non-Palestinian Arab lands (in Lebanon, Syria, Jordan, and Egypt), Israel gained considerable leverage on Arab states and locked them in bilateral dynamics that further undermined the shaky foundations of Arab solidarity. States with territories occupied by Israel had logically to adapt their agendas and their strategies to the new situation. The Palestinian issue was in effect demoted, although it figured prominently in the general theme of the confrontation with Israel. In 1979, Egypt signed a peace agreement with Israel in exchange for the return of the Sinai Peninsula. By violating Arab norms and betraying the Arab cause, Egypt isolated itself from the rest of the Arab world. This also undermined the credibility of the Arab League, and resulted in increased tensions between Arab states, now suspicious of the others' intentions. It also vindicated the Palestinians' apprehension that Arab states would seek arrangements with Israel at their expense.

At the same time, more immediate security developments in the Persian Gulf captured the attention of Arab Gulf States. The 1971 British withdrawal from the region, the 1978 Soviet invasion of Afghanistan, the 1979 Islamic revolution in Iran, and the beginning of the Iran–Iraq War in 1980 required the Gulf States to conceptualize their security separately from the Arab–Israeli conflict. It also allowed them to preserve their autonomy vis-à-vis secular, pro-Soviet Arab nationalist states that continued to dominate Middle East politics.

By occupying Kuwait in 1990, Iraq ended the illusion of an Arab system based on brotherhood. Saddam Hussein sent shockwaves throughout the region by threatening other Arab states and denouncing any allied with the United States. Furthermore, the PLO's backing of Saddam Hussein alienated Gulf States that funded Palestinian political and social organizations and hosted Palestinian workers. The Palestinian street, and its leadership, almost unanimously sided with Saddam Hussein during the war. By doing so, they also vented their frustration with and contempt for Arab leaders incapable of achieving substantive results on the Arab–Israeli front. Consequently, anti-Palestinian sentiments grew in Gulf countries and funding and political support for the PLO considerably diminished in the post–Gulf War period.[11] After the expulsion of Iraqi troops from Kuwait, the Palestinian cause lost its main backers. Its leadership—particularly the PLO—was ostracized.

The U.S. victory during Gulf War I considerably altered Arab regional politics: the George H.W. Bush administration built strong alliances with Arab Gulf States and launched Arab–Israeli peace talks at the Madrid conference. It also resulted in the reintegration of Egypt on the Arab scene and a Syrian repositioning. The prospects for a durable and comprehensive Arab–Israeli détente or even peace changed the security priorities of many Arab states. The 1990s were marked by the 1993 Oslo agreements, the signature of the Israeli–Jordanian peace treaty, and significant progress on the Syrian question.[12]

The PLO's strategic decision to pursue bilateral talks with Israel rather than seek a comprehensive regional agreement signaled Yasser Arafat's desire to disassociate the Palestinian issue from the larger Arab–Israeli conflict. The assumption that the Palestinians would hold more influence and leverage if they moved quickly and independently from other Arab states seemed to be validated, as observers expected the establishment of a Palestinian state in short order.

THE CURRENT SECURITY ENVIRONMENT: SECOND INTIFADA, 9/11, THE IRAQ WAR, AND GLOBALIZATION EFFECTS

The Second Intifada

The second Intifada began in September 2000. It opened a new era of instability in the Middle East that wiped out the declared optimism of the previous decade. As violence erupted in the West Bank and Gaza, accompanied by acts of terror directed at Israeli civilians, renewed Israeli–Palestinian hostilities threatened to poison relations between Israel and Arab states, including those at peace with the Jewish state. The risk that these renewed tensions between Israel and its neighbors would escalate into armed confrontation was minimal, but the uprising was seen as a setback that could reverse political and economic advancements and endanger the relative stability of the region.

This cycle of violence started after the breakdown of the final status talks between Palestinian and Israeli negotiators at Camp David in the final days of the Clinton presidency. Distrust and frustration between the parties had been building for years, with confidence-building measures constantly undermined by the use of terrorism by Palestinian groups and the expansion of Jewish settlements in disputed areas. The 2000 Intifada was largely confined within Israel and the Palestinian territories, and was led by the Palestinian

Authority (PA), which had gained legitimacy as a state-like entity in the middle to late 1990s.

From September 2000 until the death of Arafat in November 2004, there was little substantive action from Arab governments and few mass demonstrations in Arab capitals, as if the decade of negotiations and conciliation between Palestinians and Israelis had freed Arab states from perceived or expected responsibilities toward the Palestinian people, allowing them to focus on their own agendas. Therefore, the collapse of the peace process did not provoke extreme reactions on the part of Arab regimes. Moderate Arab states, including Egypt and Jordan, continued their official relationships with Israel. Radical states, such as Syria, blamed the Palestinian failure to establish an independent, sovereign state on the PA decision to pursue bilateral negotiations with Israel rather than to seek a comprehensive peace agreement including Syria and Lebanon. The official Arab response to the second Intifada reflected these profound divisions as well as continued Arab distrust of Arafat and the PA. As an observer rightly noted, "This [Arab] level of political support did not go as far as Jordan or Egypt suspending ties with Israel over the reoccupation of the Palestinian territories in 2002, nor did it go as far as Gulf states shutting off oil supplies as they did in 1973 to protest US support for Israel."[13]

Arab peace efforts amounted to three relatively modest initiatives: the short-lived Abdallah proposal that pledged normalization of ties with Israel in return for a complete withdrawal from all occupied Arab lands;[14] vain Jordanian and Egyptian crisis management plans intended to support the efforts of the Quartet—an informal group composed of the United States, the United Nations (UN), Russia, and the European Union that put forward a peace plan known as the "road map"—by brokering ceasefires with Palestinian radical groups[15] and the timid Arab backing of the ephemeral Palestinian cabinet headed by Mahmoud Abbas.[16]

Political Islam and the Repercussions of 9/11

The rise of political Islam and the threat of al Qaeda–related terrorism are also mitigating the perception of the Arab–Israeli conflict as the main source of instability in the Middle East. For countries with no territorial disputes with Israel, the imminent threat to their security is materializing as internal contestation linked to a transnational Islamist organization with unprecedented appeal. The nature and immediacy of the Islamist threat differs substantially with the perceived Israeli threat. It requires Arab states to adapt their security postures and define a new, more complex enemy to their populations. As the enemy within becomes more menacing than the enemy without, Arab states must rethink their domestic policies and find ways to discredit Islamists with real and immediate grievances and demands.

The 1980s and 1990s were marked by the rise of militant Islamist movements in the Middle East. As a result of the Islamic Revolution in Iran and the war in Afghanistan, Arab regimes confronted a new form of violent political contestation, led by dedicated Islamist fighters, fueled by a sense of Islamic revival and the failure of existing Arab regimes, and sustained by established Islamist political parties. Islamic militants posed existential threats to regimes in Syria in the early 1980s and Algeria in the 1990s, and caused significant damages to the economy and stability of Egypt and Morocco during both decades. By the end of the 1990s, however, they had achieved none of their declared goals, leading some to conclude the Islamist star was already in decline.[17]

In the 1990s, Islamist terrorism emerged as a global threat. The terror campaign specifically targeted U.S. interests at home (the 1993 World Trade Center bombings) and abroad (the bombings of the U.S. embassies in Africa in 1998 and the USS *Cole* in 2000). It culminated with the al Qaeda–engineered attacks of September 11, 2001. Driven by hatred for the United States, intense dislike of Middle Eastern regimes, and strict adherence to the most rigid interpretation of Islamic scriptures, al Qaeda and groups directly or loosely associated with it command little genuine and operational support in the Middle East, but their anti-American ideology coupled with a enduring sentiment of oppression rally some rhetorical support in Islamist and non-Islamist circles.

In itself, the Arab–Israeli conflict plays a relatively secondary role in shaping the beliefs driving these militants. Osama bin Laden has used much broader historic reference points to justify his action, ranging from the loss of Muslim Spain (Al-Andalous) to the sanctions imposed on Iraq in the aftermath of the 1991 Gulf War. The sources of Islamist grievances against the United States are multiple: presence of U.S. troops on Saudi soil; humiliation and oppression of Arabs in general; Western support of corrupt Arab regimes; moral depravity of the West; and suffering of the Iraqis and the Palestinians. According to al Qaeda, confronting the main oppressor—the United States—will bring down its proxies in the Middle East, including Israel. In bin Laden's view, the United States and its relationship with Saudi Arabia was the source of evil:

> For more than seven years the United States is occupying the lands of Islam in the holiest of its territories, Arabia, plundering its riches, overwhelming its rulers, humiliating its people, threatening its neighbors, and using its bases in the peninsula as a spearhead to fight against the neighboring Islamic peoples.[18]

In a 1996 *fatwa*, he targeted specifically, "Americans occupying the land of the two holy places." In 1998, he called for the killing of "Americans and their allies, civilians and military . . . in any country in which it is possible to do it." In his October 2004 statement, he traced back his hatred of the United States to 1982, charging that it supported Israel during the invasion of Lebanon, but he did not refer to earlier Arab–Israeli wars.

In his videotaped statements prior to the 9/11 attacks, Osama bin Laden made the Arab–Israeli conflict important, but not central to his belief system. His subsequent emphasis on the Arab–Israeli conflict was viewed as essentially opportunistic and as an attempt to garner popular support by tapping into distrust of the United States and associating it with the plight of the Palestinians. For their part, worried about being identified with bin Laden's apocalyptic terrorism, Palestinian groups have struggled to dissociate their fight from al Qaeda's. Even Islamist Palestinian organizations have stopped short of endorsing his actions for fear that the global campaign against terror would equate them with al Qaeda.[19]

Religion has never dominated the ideology of the Palestinian national movement. The main Palestinian groups leading the fight against Israel were mostly secular, adopting ideologies ranging from Marxism to pan-Arab nationalism. Their influence remained unquestioned until the mid-1990s, when the failure of the PA to capably govern Palestinian autonomous areas swelled the ranks of its Islamic contenders: Hamas and the Palestinian Islamic Jihad. Even Arab states that confronted Israel did not portray their struggle with the Jewish state as mainly a civilizational one. The anti-Semitism they too often displayed was a provision of political mobilization, but they seldom viewed the conflict as pitting religions and civilizations against each other. Rather, during the Cold War, it was Arab nationalism and socialism that dominated the political discourse.

The main Islamic group opposing Israel during the past two decades was the Shi'a Lebanese Hezbollah. Although Hezbollah conducted acts of global terror, the movement's stated objectives remained limited to regional and territorial considerations. Its dependency on Syria and Iran limited its freedom of action. During the 1990s, Hezbollah was widely considered as Syria's best negotiating card in its attempt to recover the Israeli-annexed Golan Heights, not as its primary tool to export Islamic fundamentalism.

The repercussions of the 9/11 attacks on Middle East affairs were immense. Most importantly, the war on terrorism exposed the profound problems that affect Arab societies—which are separable from the Arab–Israeli conflict. It focused global attention on the Arab world's political and economic backwardness. Most Arab states are dictatorships that restrict freedom of expression and deny their citizens the right to participate in the political process.[20] The military and security services play a crucial role in defining and running the domestic, security, and foreign policies of most Arab countries. Elected parliaments are rare, and play an insignificant role in public affairs. Rights of ethnic and religious minorities, as well as women, are barely respected. The higher education sector is underdeveloped, which clouds the prospects for economic growth. Indeed, the economic performance of the Arab world is dismal: according to the World Bank, since 1980 the GDP per capita growth in the Middle East and North Africa region averages 0.9 percent, less than that of sub-Saharan Africa.[21]

GLOBALIZATION EFFECTS

Two additional factors shape the ways in which the Arab–Israeli issue is changing in local perceptions and priorities. Whereas media coverage is raising awareness of the Arab–Israeli conflict in the Middle East, generational change is bringing to power people with immediate economic and political needs detached from the conflict. Although these trends can be construed as conflicting, they can also be drawn together, depending on progress on the peace and reform front.

Media Effects. With the introduction of satellite television in the Middle East in the mid-1990s, the media has emerged as a central actor in regional and local Arab politics.[22] Previously, states monopolized information as they sought to manipulate news to advance their interests and to limit and filter access to information that could threaten their authority. The Arab media, especially satellite television, has brought images and stories to private homes and public cafes. This revolution in mass culture is promoting new political discourses. In a region where print media is still subject to heavy state censorship and local television controlled by central governments, satellite television has become an outlet of choice for expressing dissenting views and debating issues long controlled by states.

Predictably, the Arab media has embraced and promoted the Palestinian and Arab causes, providing ample coverage of the Arab–Israeli conflict and the developments in the Palestinian occupied territories.[23] The beginning of the second Intifada in September 2000 marked the real debut of Arab satellite television in regional politics. With images of street battles in the West Bank and Gaza, interviews with Palestinian inhabitants and officials, and live (and sometimes emotional) comments by television correspondents, the Israeli–Palestinian conflict has taken on a new reality for Arab viewers and has increased awareness of the plight of the Palestinian people. The coverage of the conflict remains overwhelmingly pro-Palestinian, and anti-Israeli rhetoric fills TV shows. But for the first time, the Arab audience is also exposed to Israeli narratives and arguments. Television shows often invite comments from Israeli experts and politicians, as well as Arab critics of the PA and Arab governments.

The rise of pan-Arab satellite television has had two contradictory effects. By broadcasting throughout the Arab world, networks have created a sense of immediacy and proximity to the Arab–Israeli conflict and revived pan-Arab sentiments among viewers. Previously, the Arab–Israeli conflict was an abstraction for Arabs as much as a pretext for political manipulation by Middle Eastern states. Satellite television has also allowed for—and encouraged—Iraq and Palestine to become twin issues, juxtaposed in media reporting and in the minds of many in the region.

On the other hand, Arab attention has become divided: coverage of important political and local issues, terrorism, and the Iraq crisis are capturing headlines and competing for air time with the Palestinian issue. Demand for news and talk shows that address governance and socioeconomic topics is on the rise.

Demographic and Leadership Effects. A generation of Arab heads of state that was closely identified with the Arab–Israeli conflict is rapidly ceding power to younger, less ideological rulers with fewer political and emotional ties to this conflict.[24] The consequences of this change could be substantial for the Arab–Israeli conflict. Hafez al-Assad of Syria, King Hussein of Jordan, and Hosni Mubarak of Egypt were major actors in the Arab–Israeli conflict for decades. They have been involved in wars and peace negotiations, and while in power they have determined their security and foreign policies according to their perception of the regional balance of power and domestic political aims.

Their successors' histories differ significantly, but the survival of the regimes of Abdallah of Jordan and Bashar al-Assad of Syria is highly dependent on the conflict. The stability of their regimes depends greatly on their perceived legitimacy and stance vis-à-vis the Arab–Israeli conflict. King Abdallah of Jordan came to power in 1999 after Jordan signed peace with Israel. Abdallah, a relative newcomer with little experience in public affairs, derives part of his legitimacy and popular support from the fact that his wife, Queen Rania, is of Palestinian origin. Syrian President Bashar al-Assad succeeded his father thanks to a tailored constitutional change destined to preserve the security and economic interests of the regime. Bashar lacks serious military credentials and suffers from an untested anti-Israeli record. To consolidate his power, he is compelled to adopt hard-line positions on the Arab–Israeli conflict, vehemently criticizing Israel and offering support to radical Lebanese and Palestinian groups.[25] This results in a paradox: Bashar, who has little personal history with the Arab–Israeli conflict, needs to appear more intransigent than his father to deflect accusations of weakness.

Elsewhere in the Arab world, new leaderships demonstrate little interest in the Palestinian issue. In Iraq, the implications of regime change for the Arab–Israeli conflict are substantive: as the country struggles to rebuild itself and faces daunting security challenges, the new Iraqi leadership shows little interest in, or even sympathy for, the Palestinian cause. Whereas Saddam Hussein was directly engaged in armed confrontation with Israel in 1981 and 1991 and integrated the conflict into his political discourse, Prime Minister Iyad Allawi's statement that Iraqi normalization with Israel had to wait until a comprehensive peace agreement was more a gesture to gain legitimacy in the Arab world than a threat to Israel. By doing so, Iraqi leaders signal their desire to distance themselves from the Arab–Israeli conflict, focusing instead on rebuilding their country and security issues in their immediate neighborhood.

Generational change is not limited to the leadership. The population surge in the Arab world is creating a new class of people with no connection to Arab nationalism and the Arab–Israeli conflict, but with economic and social needs that states are unlikely to meet given the current political and economic backwardness of the region. Some 55 percent of Egypt's population is under age 25, as is 62 percent of Syria's, and 58 percent of Saudi Arabia's.[26] These youth have no direct memories of Arab nationalism or the Arab–Israeli wars that marked the histories of their nations (and their current leaders).

PARADIGM SHIFT IN U.S. POLICY AND
ITS IMPLICATIONS FOR SECURITY

The Bush approach to the Middle East after the 9/11 attacks differed considerably from those of his predecessors. The 2003 Iraq War was fought on the premise that factors other than the Arab–Israeli conflict affect regional stability and international security. An Israeli analyst observed:

> At the grand strategic level, the American offensives in Afghanistan and Iraq and against al Qaeda are predicated on a notion [. . .] that the real Middle East dynamic around which US policy should be organized is not the Israel–Arab or Israeli–Palestinian dispute, but rather the need to counter Islamic terror, WMD, and radical rogue states, all of which directly threaten American security.[27]

The Clinton administration had operated under the assumption that the resolution of the Arab–Israeli conflict would create the conditions for a more stable and prosperous Middle East. Therefore, priority was given to the peace process, and Iran and Iraq were subjected to a containment policy destined to weaken the regimes and curtail their capacity to undermine regional stability. Instead of resolving the Palestinian issue first thus creating conditions conducive to progress in the Arab world, the Bush administration set out to transform the regional environment first. The Bush administration identified the nexus among terrorism, weapons of mass destruction, and rogue states as the ultimate threat to international order and U.S. interests.[28]

The Bush administration also postulated that domestic factors in Arab countries, particularly Middle Eastern authoritarianism, produced the Islamic ideology responsible for the 9/11 attacks. It identified lack of freedom as the main obstacle to greater stability and defined an aggressive strategy to democratize the Middle East:

> Sixty years of Western nations excusing and accommodating the lack of freedom in the Middle East did nothing to make us safe—because in the long run, stability cannot be purchased at the expense of liberty. As long as the Middle East remains a place where freedom does not flourish, it will remain a place of stagnation, resentment, and violence ready for export. And with the spread of weapons that can bring catastrophic harm to our country and to our friends, it would be reckless to accept the status quo. Therefore, the United States has adopted a new policy, a forward strategy of freedom in the Middle East.[29]

On the Palestinian issue, President Bush rejected the Clinton strategy of aggressively engaging the parties, endorsed the idea of a change in Palestinian leadership, and sanctioned the Sharon government's decision to build a security fence and isolate Yasser Arafat. In a June 2002 speech, President Bush conditioned his administration's involvement to a change in Palestinian leadership. This explains the limited efforts of the Bush administration to restart a peace process, aside from the "road map," an initiative that never enjoyed the full backing of the White House, or genuine attempts to build momentum.

With the attention of the United States focused on proliferation, terrorism, Afghanistan, and Iraq, the Arab–Israeli dispute was demoted on the U.S. agenda during the first Bush term. Events in the region, including Arafat's passing, provided the context for President Bush to embrace a more activist stance, at least rhetorically, by 2005. He welcomed President Abbas to the White House in May 2005, praising the quality of the Palestinian people's commitment to democracy, and pledging renewed U.S. support for the road map. The president named special envoys to help the Palestinians with security and with economic development and investment.

DIVERGENT REGIONAL VIEWS ON SECURITY AND THE SALIENCE OF THE ARAB–ISRAELI CONFLICT

The importance of the Arab–Israeli conflict is reflected in the threat perceptions and security agendas of the Arab states, which vary in the three major subregional zones associated with the issue: Egypt, the Levant, and the Arab Gulf States.

Egypt

The largest and most influential Arab country, Egypt, remains a central actor in the Arab–Israeli issue. Because it commands considerable influence with the Palestinian national movement and esteem from Israel as the first Arab state to sign peace with it, Egypt is solicited by both parties to reduce violence or create conditions conducive to peace talks. Its involvement in the peace effort is substantial: Egypt hosts major summits on behalf of the parties to the conflict, it conveys messages and facilitates negotiations, and its diplomats and security officials play key roles in mediating intra-Palestinian disputes.

Yet, Egypt's own security agenda is less and less identified with this conflict. After the 1978 Camp David Accords, Egypt recovered its occupied lands and built a strategic partnership with United States that translated into substantial economic and military benefits. Despite concerns about the enduring imbalance of power in favor of Israel, Egypt derives strategic benefits from its alliance with the West that alleviate its former existential fears.

As a middle power with significant influence in its neighborhood, Egypt aspires to play a role beyond the Arab–Israeli issue and become a privileged partner of the West. Based in Cairo and headed by Egyptian secretaries general, the Arab League is under heavy Egyptian influence. For some, it represents the pan-Arab element of Egypt's foreign policy that allows Cairo to pander to Arab public opinions while pursuing pro-Western policies. Egypt is very involved in African affairs, and its relationship with Sudan is critical to the resolution of the 30-year-long civil war that plagues that country. Egypt is also attempting to deepen its relations with the Maghreb. Moreover Egypt is a Mediterranean power that seeks to affirm its position as a pivotal participant in regional politics by hosting summits and actively engaging in the Euro-Mediterranean dialogue. Indeed, Egypt carefully nurtures its relations with key European countries, particularly France and the United Kingdom. But Egypt's ambitions extend to the global scene, as it actively lobbies for a permanent seat at the UN Security Council, an achievement that would consecrate its foreign policy efforts.

Nevertheless, Egypt is not immune to geopolitical changes. Regional developments could heighten tensions between Egypt and Israel. Should Iran and other Arab states acquire nuclear capabilities, Egypt might feel compelled to follow the trend to preserve its image and enhance its strategic posture.[30]

Instability in Egypt could spring from domestic sources. In recent years, internal threats to the Egyptian regime have considerably diminished. The Islamist menace to the Mubarak regime has receded with the failure of Egypt's Islamic Jihad to score decisive victories or to enroll popular support. By co-opting nonviolent Islamist movements, the Mubarak regime has preserved its authority but has made concessions to conservative groups at the expense of more liberal and secular political parties. But in the absence of political reforms, the issue of succession could reinitiate a cycle of domestic unrest. Succession in Egypt is emerging as a real challenge, but with little connection to the Arab–Israeli conflict. Hosni Mubarak's failing health might precipitate change in the mid-term. The fall 2005 presidential elections became the focal point for increased international attention to the democracy deficit in Egypt, and as of mid-year, it was unclear if President Mubarak would run again and whether the new electoral law would be implemented in a way to permit true competition and multiple presidential candidates.

The Levant

The Levant (Syria, Lebanon, Jordan, Israel, and the Palestinian territories) is the core zone of the Arab–Israeli conflict, and the security of each state is still profoundly affected by the outcome of the Arab–Israeli issue.

Lebanon and Syria continue to deny the existence of the Jewish state. For Israelis, the blatant official and popular anti-Semitism is an expression of absolute rejection of their existence as an established nation and evidence of an enduring Arab desire to annihilate their state.

The continuing occupation of Arab territories by Israel is the most concrete illustration of the conflict. Aside from the disputed Palestinian territories, since 1967 Israel has occupied the Syrian Golan Heights. Despite UN certification, Lebanon claims that Israel's withdrawal from Southern Lebanon was incomplete and demands the return of an area known as the Shebaa Farms. Because of Syrian caution and fear of military escalation, the Golan remains the quietest front line in the conflict, but Southern Lebanon has emerged as a flashpoint for clashes between Israel and Syrian-backed Hezbollah.

At the military level, the Levant is characterized by the great imbalance of power between Israel and the Arab states.[31] Israel's military exceeds the military capabilities of its Arab neighbors by far.[32] Arab militaries have been repeatedly defeated by the strategic and operational mastery of the Israel Defense Forces. Syria's efforts to achieve strategic parity ended with the collapse of its Soviet patron.[33] But this gap in conventional capabilities has informed the Syrian decision to acquire weapons of mass destruction.[34] Despite its policy of "strategic ambiguity," Israel is believed to possess an arsenal of 400 nuclear warheads, a key asset to deter any state-based existential threat. Furthermore, Israel's advantages are supplemented by its very strong alliance with the United States. This imbalance extends to the economic domain. Israel's economy generates an annual GDP of approximately US$110 billion compared to Syria's 20 billion and Jordan's 10 billion. As a provider of high-end products and services, Israel is fully integrated into the global economy.

Levant states have attempted to rectify this imbalance of power by resorting to asymmetric warfare. Palestinian groups have used terrorism and guerilla tactics in the occupied territories, and in the 1970s, terrorist groups were able to act independently from states. Since the 1980s, state-sponsored terrorism and guerrilla actions emerged as preferred methods to break Israeli resolve and expel the Israeli Defense Forces from Lebanon.[35] Despite Israel's withdrawal in May 2000, tension on the Israeli–Lebanese frontier periodically escalates into limited but worrisome violence. Syria and Hezbollah also financially and politically support Palestinian organizations located in the West Bank and Gaza.

Another potentially explosive issue relates to the presence of Palestinian refugees in the three countries. In the past, Palestinian refugees have caused instability in Lebanon and Jordan, and they could potentially disrupt any peace arrangement with Israel. Discriminated against and living in dismal conditions, they have espoused the most radical forms of political contestation and have little hope of returning to their lands after decades of exile. If denied the right to return to their villages, these refugees will need permanent settlement in the countries that host them or other countries willing to accept them. Outbursts of violence are likely to occur during this process.

Domestic political stability in Jordan, Syria, and Lebanon is still precarious. Regime security continues to be their overriding concern. In Jordan, King Abdallah appears to be in control, but unrest within the Palestinian community is possible. He also faces serious challenges from the Islamists and disenfranchised people, as was the case in 2002 during the riots in Maan.[36] In Syria, Bashar's top priority remains the survival of the Assad regime.[37] As a minority regime, the Assad power must cope with myriad threats, including that of political Islam. The March 2004 Kurdish uprising illustrated the resilience of domestic contestation despite 35 years of absolutist power.[38] Bashar must improve Syria's dire economic situation that is heightening domestic discontent and manage the effects of Syria's forced withdrawal from Lebanon in April 2005. Finally, post-Syria Lebanon, still struggling to devise a fundamental political formula that guarantees the rights of all sects, must address issues as complex as the post-Syria security situation, the Hezbollah challenge, the rise of Muslim extremism, and the integration of Palestinian refugees.

In this context, Syria remains a pivotal state whose fortunes are linked to both the Arab–Israeli conflict and, more recently, the situation in Iraq. It views these challenges as connected, and grounds its national security outlook in the old paradigm of the Arab–Israeli issue. For Syria, the U.S. presence in Iraq and Israeli belligerence combine to pose an existential threat to the regime. As a result of strategic miscalculations and U.S. actions, Syria is now militarily and politically encircled. Under pressure from the international community after the February 2005 assassination of former prime minister Hariri, Syria was forced to withdraw its troops from Lebanon in April 2005. Its fierce and vocal opposition to the U.S. occupation of Iraq has heightened tensions with the United States. Infiltration of foreign fighters into Iraq from Syria and Syrian harboring of anti-American and anti-Israeli groups has become a key item in the discussions between the two countries, and Syria could be, according to its critics, actually facilitating a connection between those with long experience in fighting Israel, and the insurgency in Iraq. The 2003 bombing of a Palestinian camp outside Damascus by the Israeli Air Force and the 2004 assassination of a senior Hamas leader in the Syrian capital illustrate that Syria remains a hot zone in the enduring Israel–Arab struggle. Border clashes continued in the summer of 2005 and resulted in casualties on both sides. Israel launched air strikes in the last week of June on militant positions in response to attacks by Hezbollah fighters on Israeli posts in Shebaa Farms.

The Arab Gulf States

In the past two decades, the Arab Gulf States' threat perceptions have evolved. Confronted with state-born threats, anxious to defend their own model against the Arab "core states," and worried about Islamist-generated turmoil, the Arab Gulf States (Saudi Arabia, Kuwait, Qatar, the United Arab Emirates (UAE), Bahrain, and Oman) have over time developed security agendas distinct from the Arab–Israeli dispute.[39]

Despite apparent uniformity, Arab Gulf States are hardly similar. Over the past two decades, their economic and political fortunes have significantly differed. Saudi Arabia, previously the unquestioned hegemon among Gulf Cooperation Council (GCC) states, is now facing serious challenges to its stability and to its regional leadership. The smaller Gulf States benefit from more flexible domestic environments and maintain closer ties to the United States. Incapable of providing for their own security and too small to operate without an external patron, they maintain close links to the United States. Qatar now hosts the U.S. Central Command's forward headquarters; Bahrain, the U.S. Fifth Fleet; the UAE, the U.S. Air Force; and Kuwait, US Army and Marine units.

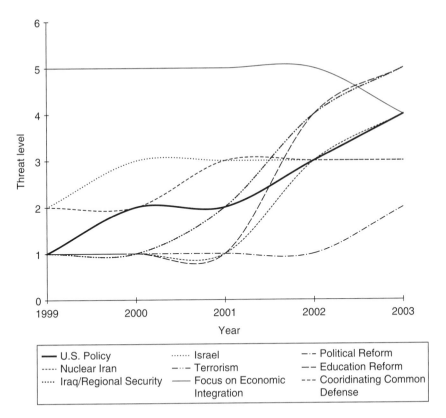

Table 7.1   GCC Threat Perceptions, 1999–2003

Note: Threat levels have been adapted from John Duke Anthony's Reports on the Annual GCC Summits, 1999–2003.

Source: Gulfwire Perspectives found on-line at www. arabialink.com.

Nevertheless, the Gulf States can be conceptualized as a distinct analytical unit because of common security perceptions, shared regional preferences, and organizational and normative commonalities. Despite the lack of transparency in Gulf policymaking, it is possible to identify the evolving threat perceptions of GCC states by examining deliberations during the annual GCC summit meetings. Table 7.1 illustrates one interpretation of the evolving threat perceptions of the GCC countries, as adapted from annual reports on GCC summits.

Arab Gulf States have never participated in military actions against Israel or suffered from Israeli attacks. But they offered substantial political and financial support to Palestinian organizations, and, most importantly, they imposed an embargo on shipments of crude oil to Western countries after the 1973 Yom Kippur war to protest Western backing of Israel.

The Arab Gulf States' shift away from the Arab–Israeli conflict originates from a series of regional strategic developments in the 1980s, including the

Iranian Islamic Revolution and the Iran–Iraq War. Iran's desire to export its revolution and the two countries' struggle for regional hegemony threatened to destabilize Arab Gulf regimes. Although Saudi Arabia, the largest Arab Gulf country, is generally considered a status quo power in the Persian Gulf, Iran and Iraq have always had hegemonic ambitions and huge militaries. Preventing the rise of a hegemon therefore compelled the Arab Gulf States to enter into delicate political balancing acts. Moreover, inspired by Iran, Shi'a movements, long suppressed by Sunni governments, became more assertive, even resorting to terrorism. Indeed, the threat was a real and present danger. With their oppressed Shi'a populations (9 percent of the total population in Saudi Arabia, 25–30 percent in Kuwait, 65–70 percent in Bahrain), the authoritarian Gulf regimes could not underestimate the influence of the Iranian Revolution.

For a while, it seemed that the Arab Gulf countries envisaged security as emanating from collaborative efforts. The creation of the Gulf Cooperation Council in 1981, a direct response to the Iranian threat, suggested that Arab Gulf States would cooperate on defense and internal security issues. Security cooperation in the context of the GCC had one overriding priority: regime survival against domestic and foreign threats. As Emile Nakhleh put it, "Gulf security in the context of the GCC is directly equated with the continued stable existence of the present regimes and forms of governments in the Gulf States."[40] The primacy of that goal influenced the security policies of the different member-states, as well as those of the organization. Security cooperation was threefold: internal security, interstate relations, and military collaboration. Interestingly, the GCC, an often-decried organization, proved effective at fighting Shi'a unrest in the 1980s. Nakhleh even traces the establishment of the GCC to domestic concerns: "The real impetus for security cooperation, in fact, came not from the Iran–Iraq War per se but from internal instability, namely militant Shi'a activity."[41] Because they favored bilateral cooperation over integrated approaches, the counterterrorist record of the 1980s was mixed, but the GCC did provide a forum for interior ministers to coordinate their work.

Gulf War I demonstrated the limited effectiveness of a common security policy to deal with external threats. Despite a decade of cooperation, Arab Gulf States proved incapable of deterring Iraq and protecting one of their own. Rather, they had to rely on a Western power, the United States, to liberate Kuwait and provide a shield against Saddam Hussein's ambitions.

Since 9/11 and the Iraq War, the Gulf security agenda is dominated by the situation in Iraq, the Iranian nuclear challenge, and the Islamist terrorist threat. Security decision-making in the Gulf is monopolized by the top leadership, with little outside consultation. No national security community, composed of independent analysts and professionals, exists to inform policies. Even at the regional level, given the opaque decision-making process, it is difficult to evaluate the extent of security cooperation, whether on internal issues (terrorism, border control, crime) or on defense issues. Key strategic and operational decisions are usually not publicized.

Yet, the multiplication of terrorist attacks in Saudi Arabia as well as the proximity of Iraq require enhanced cooperation on internal security issues. Al Qaeda–related terrorism and Shi'a activism can inflict serious damage to the Gulf States' stability and economy. Because of the transnational nature of these threats and the fear of contagion from Iraq, intelligence and police co-operation will be essential to any collective security initiative. Gulf States already cooperate on border controls and maritime security, but better intelligence sharing will prove critical to their success in disrupting internal threats to their regimes.

New state-born threats from Iran and Iraq to Gulf security also top the region's agenda in the twenty-first century.[42] The fall of Saddam Hussein's regime in Iraq has removed a main source of regional instability, and the presumed threat from Iraq's Weapons of mass destruction (WMD). But the fear that instability and chaos in Iraq can spread throughout the region provokes new anxiety. This concern explains the Gulf States' desire to see the emergence of a central authority capable of keeping the country unified and stable.

After the détente in GCC–Iranian relations in the late 1990s, Iran's nuclear ambitions might disturb the delicate balance-of-power that Arab Gulf States seemed to favor over other models of regional security. Iran's nuclear program is widely believed to have a military intent. Like Iraq, it entertains hegemonic aspirations in the Gulf and has territorial disputes with the UAE. Iran's rationale for developing a nuclear option seem related more to its search for a deterrent from external powers than from any perceived threats from Arab Gulf States, but will undoubtedly affect the regional balance of power.[43]

The Arab–Israeli conflict occasionally resurfaces in national rhetoric when acute security crises occur. After a terrorist attack in Saudi Arabia in 2004, for example, Saudi Crown Prince Abdallah assigned the level of blame on "the Zionists" at 95 percent.[44] The struggle against al Qaeda in Saudi Arabia is fought on the grounds of Islamic legitimacy by the Saudi regime. By accusing Zionists of acts of terror, Abdallah might have attempted to make an improbable link between movements that deny any Islamic legitimacy to the regime and Israel, widely accused of threatening Islam and occupying Muslim Holy sites. The Arab–Israeli conflict also affects the Arab response to the Iranian nuclear challenge, which testifies to the resilience of anti-Israel norms. Gulf Arab states, predictably anxious about the prospects of a nuclear Iran, have remained largely quiet. With Israel still perceived by many in the Arab public opinion as an existential threat, the foreign policies of the Arab Gulf States are constrained despite the urgency of the crisis.[45]

The question of whether GCC states have developed a common and genuine desire to collectively combat perceived threats is key. At present, the GCC is getting better at tactical-level cooperation. From border controls to maritime security, GCC states are increasingly integrating their systems and sharing information. More importantly, Arab Gulf States are efficiently working together to combat terrorism. In this respect, interior ministries have enhanced intelligence sharing and police coordination. The Gulf States ratified in May 2004 a counterterrorism agreement to enhance security coordination in the Gulf. This success is due to perceived domestic benefits: terrorism is indeed the most acute threat to the stability of their regimes and economy, but as authoritarian states, the Gulf countries can use a vast array of tools to dismantle terrorist cells with little public protest.

However, at a strategic level, the diverging internal and foreign agendas of the GCC states and the role of the United States as security guarantor reduce the prospects of a larger and more dependable strategic community. The inability of the GCC to train and deploy a credible military unit to provide for collective security despite huge defense expenditures during the 1990s illustrates the reluctance of the Gulf States in this matter. At present, there are no signs of NATO-like security cooperation, with a high degree of institutionalization and considerable authority and resources.

Policy coordination on state-based threats, such as the Iranian nuclear challenge, is more difficult to achieve because of divergent preferences, apathy, or continuing reliance on an external actor to guarantee stability. Moreover, profound disagreements between Saudi Arabia and some of the small Gulf States might inhibit progress on security matters. Anxious to protect its power over the GCC, Saudi Arabia is attempting to empower this organization to prevent the development of bilateral relations, whether formal or informal, between the United States and the small states.

TWO ALTERNATIVE FUTURES REGARDING THE POSSIBLE IMPACT OF THE ARAB–ISRAELI CONFLICT ON REGIONAL SECURITY

Let us consider two different interactions between the Palestine problem and current dynamics in regional security, one where regional security arrangements will gradually evolve, independently of the outcome of the stalled peace process, and a second where the linkage is stronger and more destructive.

Regional Security Cooperation Advances Despite Stalemate in Palestine

Below the threshold of grand strategy or a radical transformation of the region's political culture, there is much incremental and constructive work in the security arena that could be achieved, even if no progress occurs in resolving the Palestine conflict. Much work has been done to identify practical areas for security cooperation among regional states at the subregional level (such as Gulf States, or North African states) and at the region-wide level (with all Arab states, Iran, and sometimes Turkey and Israel included).[46] Since the optimism of the early 1990s, when the Madrid conference led to the establishment of regional working groups, including the Arms Control and Regional Security (ACRS) group, a modest literature has developed drawing on hundreds of hours of interaction among regional security experts. Topics explored have included environmental threats to security, lessons from the U.S.–Soviet experience on arms control, counterterrorism, maritime security, and civil defense. These conversations, which continue under nongovernment auspices, rarely address conventional military balances, or concrete ways to reduce threats from weapons of mass destruction; rather, they operate in a safety zone where national policies are not scrutinized or criticized. Although the ACRS process and its Track II successor cannot claim to have produced dramatic breakthroughs, it has quietly contributed to creating a virtual community of regional experts who have established personal and professional relationships and could become important non-governmental security voices when political openness permits more public discussion of security issues.

This process could be reinvigorated with the willingness of the regional parties and some outside support and encouragement. In early 2005, three factors provided encouragement that such a renewed initiative could be productive: first, the tensions in the region of 2003–04 are beginning to wane, despite Iraq's daunting domestic problems; second, the international community has found a formal process, through the European Union (EU) and the International Atomic Energy Agency (IAEA), to set some terms for negotiating with Iran over its nuclear activities; and third, the death of PLO Chairman Yasser Arafat creates some new possibilities for more fruitful engagement with the Palestinians.

Such a new effort, building on the work of the past decade, would most likely focus on counterterrorism cooperation and other immediate and acute threats to the security interests of states. It would focus on gradual enhancements to national and regional capacities through bilateral or regional exchanges of information, technical assistance, and technology. In June 2004, the NATO summit in Istanbul extended an offer of technical assistance and cooperation to the Gulf States, expanding and building on the Mediterranean dialogue on security that has existed since 1994.

Such a capacity-building approach would be less susceptible to being undermined due to the Arab–Israeli issue than other, more ambitious security initiatives. It could operate "under the radar screen" of the high politics of the region.

Efforts to Advance Security Arrangements Falter Due to Political Violence by Joint Palestinian–Arab–Iranian Saboteurs

A darker scenario could emerge if the insurgency in Iraq galvanizes and is galvanized by regional radicals bent on undermining any positive new activity in the Palestine–Israel arena. The territory of Syria finds itself a critical bridge between the Palestine and Iraq theaters, and the Syrian government appears unwilling or unable to prevent the movement of non-state actors and their arms. Greater Iranian involvement and Syrian–Iranian coordination, through resources, training, and possibly manpower, could connect the dots between the Palestine issue and Iraq, with deadly and dangerous consequences.

This narrative, which some believe is already playing out, and could be accelerated with Iran's election of a hard-line conservative president, would conflate opposition to Israel's occupation of the West Bank and American presence in Iraq, and would posit that a coordinated effort could reap results on both fronts. The Palestinian and Lebanese experience in insurgency and terrorism gained over many years of violence against Israel would be transferred in part to the Iraq theater, and would encourage a political linkage of the two conflicts. While Iraqi insurgents are proving highly capable of lethal activity without significant outside help, a linkage to the long-suffering Palestinians might attract more Iraqi followers to the insurgent cause, and support in the other direction would energize the non-Fatah activists in the post-Arafat era, leading them to believe that they (Hamas' Al-Aqsa Martyrs Brigade, in particular) are the natural successors to the PLO.

In this perfect storm, U.S. investments in the security of key states—Israel, Saudi Arabia, Iraq, and Jordan—are at risk. The prospects for regional security would be seriously reduced, even if the demand for security cooperation in preventing the movement of fighters across the region would become an urgent imperative. Under such conditions, there would be little appetite for planning and establishing new security architecture. Instead, there would be further polarization in the region, with pressure on key Arab states to join in coalition action to squelch the rising violence.

Such a dramatic outcome is, sad to say, not implausible, and makes more critical the efforts to work simultaneously on the peace process and on building stability in Iraq. It may require some important infusions of security support to a new Palestinian government, and possibly closer coordination with Israel's counterterrorism policies to prevent working at cross purposes, and to try to persuade Israel to avoid counterproductive policies that exacerbate tensions and provide incentives for more violence. Persuading Syria to avoid nasty entanglements with the region's bad actors would be a high priority.

CONCLUSION

The Middle East region faces daunting security challenges: acute challenges such as the insurgency in Iraq, terrorist threats in the Arabian peninsula, and continued violence between Israel and Palestinians; and strategic challenges such as Iran's nuclear program and the possibility of further WMD proliferation in the region. Security issues are therefore foremost on the agendas of regional states and external players. At the same time, the region is also in a dynamic phase due to leadership transitions, the emerging consensus over the need for political and economic reforms, and the effects of globalization in changing local social and political norms. The intersection between the daunting security challenges and these other concurrent factors makes for a volatile and dangerous mix, but may, paradoxically, create more incentives for cooperation and more willingness to consider new approaches to security.

The Arab–Israeli issue, in our view, is in strategic decline as the key determinant of regional behavior. Although it retains a powerful hold on the culture and the social psychology of the region, the Arab states provide evidence of a desire to set increasingly distinct and separate national agendas, and for the states not directly bordering Israel, the fate of Palestine is shifting downward as a priority and preoccupation. At the state level, this can be explained as result of Arafat's strategic mistakes, the passage of time, and the fatigue factor that sets in after decades of devotion to this cause. To be sure, there are some counterindications, such as the impact of pan-Arab media on the perceptions of young people, who are now exposed to detailed coverage of violence and tension between Israel and the Palestinians. It is possible, but not probable, that these young people, from North Africa to South Asia, will remain deeply committed to the Palestinian cause as a motivator of their political preferences, as opportunities to express those preferences develop.

One of the critical factors in enhancing security decision-making in the region is developing greater local capacity. For now, matters of security are the purview of a select few. Security policy is the monopoly of incumbent power, and there is virtually no engagement of civil society. To some extent, this is true even in Western democracies, where security issues that concern law enforcement, intelligence, and military professionals are not debated in full public view. But in the Middle East region, the secrecy and power of the security bureaucracies has been particularly strong, and the absence of non-government experts capable of debating security issues has impeded consideration of a wider range of policy options.

Outside powers, including the United States, could do more to encourage the emergence of a robust security community in the region. The network of regional security professionals that was nurtured a decade ago could be mobilized for greater responsibility, as track two activities or more directly as advisors to governments. More cross-fertilization of ideas and more cross-training of military and other security disciplines would help governments as they face such a daunting list of security challenges. The United States needs to find ways to encourage a more open and sophisticated security debate. At times, such a debate will appear to be sidetracked by the enduring saga of Palestine and other contentious issues where U.S. policies are seen as part of the problem. But progress in improving the security of the citizens and states of the region over the long run will require a more open and honest discussion of all the issues.

NOTES

1. In a statement released in October 2004, Osama bin Laden traced his hatred of the United States to the Arab–Israeli conflict: "Allah knows that it had never occurred to us to strike the towers. But after it became unbearable and we witnessed the oppression and tyranny of the American/Israeli coalition against our people in Palestine and Lebanon, it came to my mind. The events that affected my soul in a direct way started in 1982 when America permitted the Israelis to invade Lebanon and the American Sixth Fleet helped them in that. This bombardment began and many were killed and injured and others were terrorized and displaced. I couldn't

forget those moving scenes, blood and severed limbs, women and children sprawled everywhere. [. . .] And the whole world saw and heard but it didn't respond. In those difficult moments many hard-to-describe ideas bubbled in my soul, but in the end they produced an intense feeling of rejection of tyranny, and gave birth to a strong resolve to punish the oppressors. And as I looked at those demolished towers in Lebanon, it entered my mind that we should punish the oppressor in kind and that we should destroy towers in America in order that they taste some of what we tasted and so that they be deterred from killing our women and children." These comments were met with great skepticism, as many Arabs sought to dissociate themselves from bin Laden and stressed the low priority that bin Laden had given the issue so far. Full text available at http://english. aljazeera.net/NR/exeres/79C6AF22–98FB-4A1C-B21F-2BC36E87F61F. htm.

2. Michael Scott Doran, "Palestine, Iraq and American Strategy," *Foreign Affairs*, January/February 2003; and "Is Palestine the Pivot?" *foreignaffairs.org*, March 16, 2005.

3. For a detailed account of the peace process, see Dennis Ross, *The Missing Peace: The Inside Story of the Fight for Middle East Peace* (New York: Farrar, Straus and Giroux, 2004), 801–805. At the end of his mandate and in a last effort to reach an agreement, President Clinton put forward the Clinton parameters, a set of observations on the unsettled issues that are thought to be the basis of any future peace negotiations.

4. Michael Tarazi, "Two Peoples, One State," *New York Times*, October 5, 2004.

5. Michael Kraig, "Assessing Alternative Security Frameworks for the Persian Gulf," *Middle East Policy Journal*, vol. XI, no. 3 (Fall 2004).

6. Martin Indyk, "The Clinton Administration's Approach to the Middle East," Speech to the Washington Institute for Near East Policy, May 1993; and Anthony Lake, "Confronting Backlash States," *Foreign Affairs*, March/April 1994.

7. *Alternative Strategies for Gulf Security* (Muscatine, IA: Stanley Foundation, 2004); Kenneth Pollack "Securing the Gulf," *Foreign Affairs*, July/August 2003; Andrew Rathmell, Theodore Karasik, and David Gompert, *A New Persian Gulf Security System* (Santa Monica, CA: RAND, 2003).

8. A new initiative by the International Institute for Strategic Studies, the Gulf Dialogue, convened in Bahrain in December 2004 and worked to identify new opportunities for intraregional security cooperation. See "The Need for a New Framework for Gulf Security," by John Chipman, *Financial Times*, December 9, 2004.

9. For a discussion of norms in the Arab world, see Michael Barnett, *Dialogues in Arab Politics* (New York: Columbia University Press, 1998).

10. For a history of the Palestinian national movement, see Barry Rubin, *The Transformation of Palestinian Politics: From Revolution to State-Building* (Cambridge, MA: Harvard University Press, 1999).

11. Most Palestinian workers left or were expelled from Kuwait following the 1991 Gulf War. According to Human Rights Watch, only 100,000 out of 350,000 Palestinians before the war had remained in Kuwait in July 1991. Palestinians were deported to Iraq or sent to Jordan. *Middle East Watch*, "Nowhere to Go: The Tragedy of the Remaining Palestinian Families in Kuwait," October 23, 1991.

12. For an analysis of the peace negotiations during the 1990s between Israel and the Arab states, see Samuel Segev, *Crossing the Jordan: Israel's Hard Road to Peace*

(New York: St. Martin's Press, 1998); Helena Cobban, *The Israeli–Syrian Peace Talks: 1991–96 and Beyond* (Washington: U.S. Institute of Peace Press, 2000); and Ross, *The Missing Peace*. For a history of Arab–Israeli peace efforts since 1948, see Itamar Rabinovich, *Waging Peace: Israel and the Arabs, 1948–2003*, 2nd ed. (Princeton: Princeton University Press, 2004); and William Quandt, *Peace Process: American Diplomacy and the Arab–Israeli Conflict since 1967* (Washington, DC: Brookings, 2001).

13. Riad Kahwaji, "Only Sympathy Remains," *Bitter Lemons*, August 2004, at www.bitterlemons-international.org/inside.php?id=207.

14. During the 2002 Arab summit in Beirut, Saudi Crown Prince Abdallah put forward an ambitious peace proposal that called for complete normalization of ties between the Arab League countries and Israel, should the latter agree to a full withdrawal from all Arab territories occupied since the 1967 war. This initiative proved a non-starter: many suspected that the Saudi plan was primarily intended to improve relations with the United States after the terrorist attacks of September 11, 2001. Syria, a key actor in the Arab–Israeli conflict, made clear its displeasure with the proposal.

15. Egypt in particular hosted several meetings between PA officials, PLO militants, and Hamas and Islamic Jihad leaders to broker ceasefires and reform the Palestinian security apparatus. Despite brief periods of calm, Egyptian efforts did not decisively alter the security environment.

16. In June 2003, the United States and its key Arab allies met in Sharm el-Sheikh to demonstrate their support to the newly designated Palestinian Prime Minister Abbas. Abbas's efforts to consolidate his power and reform the security apparatus were undermined by Arafat. He also found little concrete support from Israel, the United States, or the Arab states. He resigned in September 2003 after five months in power.

17. For an analysis of the rise and decline of Islamism, see Gilles Kepel, *Jihad: The Trail of Political Islam* (Cambridge: Harvard University Press, 2002); and Olivier Roy, *L'Echec de l'Islam politique* (Paris: Le Seuil, 1992).

18. For an analysis of Osama bin Laden's motives and objectives, see Bernard Lewis "License to Kill: Usama bin Ladin's Declaration of Jihad," *Foreign Affairs*, November/December 1998.

19. International Crisis Group, "Dealing with Hamas," *Middle East Report*, no. 21 (January 2004), 24–25.

20. Freedom House, *Freedom in the World 2004*, at www.freedomhouse.org/research/survey2004.htm.

21. World Bank, *Better Governance for Development in the Middle East and North Africa*, September 2003.

22. For a discussion of the emergence and role of the media in the Arab world, see Jon Alterman, *New Media, New Politics? From Satellite Television to the Internet in the Arab World* (Washington, DC: Washington Institute for Near East Policy, 1998); Naomi Sakr, *Satellite Realms: Transnational Television, Globalization and the Middle East* (London: I.B. Tauris, 2001); and William A. Rugh, *Arab Mass Media: Newspapers, Radio, and Television in Arab Politics* (Westport, CT: Praeger, 2004).

23. Abbas El Tounsy, "Reflections on the Arab Satellites, the Palestinian Intifada, and the Israeli War," *Transnational Broadcasting Studies*, no. 8 (Spring/Summer 2002).

24. For an analysis of leadership change in the Arab world, see Daniel Byman, "The Implications of Leadership Change in the Arab World," in Nora Bensahel and

Daniel Byman, eds., *The Future Security Environment in the Middle East: Conflict, Stability, and Political Change* (Santa Monica: Rand, 2004).

25. Bashar al-Assad's anti-Semitic diatribe during Pope John Paul II's visit to Syria in May 2001 and his frequent meetings with Hezbollah leaders, something his father rarely did, suggest that he attempts to build legitimacy by tapping into the Syrian public opinion's hatred of Israel and the immense political credit garnered by Hezbollah during the Israeli occupation of Southern Lebanon.

26. US Census Bureau, International Data Base, September 2004, at www.census.gov/ipc/www/idbnew.html.

27. Yossi Alpher, "Until Now, Israel Has Benefited," *Bitterlemons*, May 3, 2004.

28. "The National Security Strategy of the United States of America," White House, September 2002, at www.whitehouse.gov/nsc/nss.html.

29. President George W. Bush, Speech to the National Endowment for Democracy, November 6, 2003, at www.whitehouse.gov/news/releases/2003/11/20031106-2.html.

30. For an examination of Egypt's nuclear policy, see Robert Einhorn, "Egypt: Frustrated but Still on a Non-Nuclear Course," in Campbell, Robert Einhorn, and Reiss, eds., *The Nuclear Tipping Point: Why States Reconsider Their Nuclear Choices* (Washington, DC: Brookings, 2004).

31. Eliot Cohen, Michael Eisenstadt, and A. J. Bacevich, *Knives, Tanks and Missiles: Israel's Security Revolution* (Washington, DC: Washington Institute for Near East Policy, 1998).

32. Kenneth M. Pollack, *Arabs at War: Military Effectiveness, 1948–1991* (Lincoln: University of Nebraska Press, 2002).

33. Michael Eisenstadt, *Arming for Peace? Syria's Elusive Quest for "Strategic Parity"* (Washington, DC: Washington Institute for Near East Policy, 1992).

34. Ellen Laipson, "Syria: Can the Myth Be Maintained without Nukes?" in Campbell, Einhorn, and Reiss, *The Nuclear Tipping Point.*

35. Judith Palmer Harik, *Hezbollah: The Changing Face of Terrorism* (London: I.B. Tauris, 2004); and Hala Jaber, *Hezbollah* (New York: Columbia University Press, 1997).

36. International Crisis Group, *Red Alert in Jordan: Recurrent Unrest in Maan*, February 2003; and "The Challenge of Political Reform: Jordanian Democratisation and Regional Instability," *Middle East Briefings*, October 2003.

37. Volker Perthes, *Syria under Bashar Al-Asad: Modernisation and the Limits of Change*, Adelphi Paper Volume 366 (London: International Institute for Strategic Studies, 2004); International Crisis Group, *Syria under Bashar (I): Foreign Policy Challenges*, Middle East Report no. 23, February 2004, and *Syria under Bashar (II): Domestic Policy Challenges*, Middle East Report no. 24, February 11, 2004.

38. Gary Gambill, "The Kurdish Reawakening in Syria," *Middle East Intelligence Bulletin*, April 2004.

39. Gary Sick and Lawrence Potter, eds., *Security in the Persian Gulf: Origins, Obstacles, and the Search for Consensus* (New York: Palgrave Macmillan, 2002).

40. Emile Nakhleh, cited in Michael Barnett, "Identity and Alliances in the Middle East," in Peter Katzenstein, ed., *The Culture of National Security: Norms and Identity in World Politics* (New York: Columbia University Press, 1996).

41. Emile Nakhleh, cited in Michael Barnett, "Identity and Alliances in the Middle East," in Peter Katzenstein, ed., *The Culture of National Security: Norms and Identity in World Politics* (New York: Columbia University Press, 1996).

42. John Chipman, "The Need for a New Framework for Gulf Security," *Financial Times*, December 9, 2004.
43. Emile El-Hokayem, "The Arab Gulf States and the Iranian Nuclear Challenge," *The Daily Star*, January 15, 2005.
44. MEMRI Dispatch, May 2, 2004, at www.memri.org/bin/articles.cgi?Page=archives&Area=sd&ID=SP72604.
45. See Saudi Foreign Minister Saud al-Faisal's speech to the Gulf Dialogue conference, "Towards a New Framework for Regional Security," December 2004.
46. For summaries of this work, see *Middle East Policy*, vol. XI, no. 3 (Fall 2004), a special issue entitled Alternative Strategies for Gulf Security.

8

IRAQ AND THE NEW REGIONAL
SECURITY DYNAMIC

Judith S. Yaphe

When the United States went to war in Iraq in March 2003, the professed goals were to end the repressive rule of Saddam Hussein's regime, uncover the long-hidden weapons of mass destruction that had eluded a decade of UN-led inspections, and prevent further cooperation between Baghdad and the Islamist extremists responsible for the 9/11 attacks. Less mentioned, but by no means absent, was the intention of introducing real democratic values and institutions to Iraq and making the fledgling successor government a beacon for the region to emulate. Some representatives of the Bush administration, dubbed neoconservatives or "neocons," claimed that the war would be quick, that the Iraqis would welcome the Americans as liberators, not conquerors, and shower them with rose petals and rice, and that the Iraqis, as the region's staunchest democrats, would quickly turn the new Iraq into a democratic showplace that was the envy of the region. In the Pentagon, Secretary of Defense Donald Rumsfeld was equally determined to make the war in Iraq a showcase of what a transformed military force could accomplish with smaller deployments and greater mission integration. The war of shock and awe was to illustrate a twenty-first-century response to a twenty-first-century threat: the asymmetric warfare of terrorism.

The images of the mission's goals and intentions in Iraq did not match the reality of Iraq. Iraq's military was quickly defeated, but there were no weapons of mass destruction found, no confirmed evidence of the new terrorist networks that had caused 9/11, and no quick and easy transition to democratic rule. Although most Iraqis were happy to see Saddam and his family dethroned, gratitude for liberation was a short-lived and transitory sentiment. The U.S.-led coalition force found itself unable or unwilling to deal with the postwar climate of violence, looting, sabotage, and terror. Understaffed on both the military and civilian sides and captive of the neoconservative strategic outlook, U.S. forces were unprepared to deal with the Iraq they entered and occupied. Instead of a warm welcome resembling the liberation of France in 1945, the American invasion force encountered determined resistance to their presence, which quickly grew in strength and

sophistication. The first American administrator for Iraq, Jay Garner, anticipated using Saddam's ministries and civil servants to administer the same
kind of health and human services programs they had managed under 12 years
of UN-imposed sanctions. He also expected to downsize and depoliticize the
400,000-man army and employ those released in public works projects, all on
salary. Instead, he found burnt buildings, missing records, and no one to
manage anything. This clash between ideology and reality would haunt U.S.
efforts to restore political governance, begin economic reconstruction, and
define an exit strategy. This chapter examines the reasons for the clash and
the implications war, regime change, and occupation in Iraq had and will
have for U.S. strategy and security in this vital region.

U.S.–IRAQ RELATIONS NEVER STABLE

American–Iraqi relations have followed an uneven course since the 1958
revolution that removed the pro-British monarchy and installed the first of
several pro-Soviet revolutionary dictatorships. For a number of reasons, Iraq
has shunned close encounters with the outside world, in part because of a
strong sense of historical pride and independence, a suspicion of Western
intentions, and a fear of neocolonialism by the more powerful great powers.
It never joined the United Arab Republic as envisioned by Egyptian
President Gamal Abd al-Nasir and Syria, and it belonged to the Central
Treaty Organization (CENTO) and the Baghdad Pact only briefly. Iraq was
instrumental in forming the rejectionist front in 1978 following Egyptian
President Sadat's signing of a peace treaty with Israel. It convened a summit
of Arab states in Baghdad, ended aid to Egypt, and helped create the rejectionist platform of the states on the frontline with Israel. A few months later,
Baghdad broke once again with Damascus when Saddam Hussein announced
he was assuming the presidency and purged the party of a number of alleged
traitors whom he accused of plotting his overthrow with Syria.

The United States, for its part, rarely viewed Iraq as a reliable partner
when it sought allies or surrogates in the Persian Gulf. Iran under the shah
and Saudi Arabia were critical components of President Nixon's "Twin
Pillars" strategy. Nixon preferred to work through local surrogates to maintain regional stability, but did not regard Iraq as a benign state. Iraq broke
relations with the United States after the 1967 Arab–Israeli war. They were
reinstated briefly in the 1980s when Iran appeared to be on the verge of
defeating Iraq in their eight-year-long war. Iraq had powerful advocates in
Saudi Arabia and the small Gulf Arab states that urged the United States to
help Iraq because it was fighting to stem efforts by the revolutionary regime
of Ayatollah Khomeini to export the Iranian Islamic revolution across the
Gulf.[1] During the Reagan administration, the United States reopened its
embassy in Baghdad and offered Iraq help in its war effort. Iraq was not able
to purchase components in the United States for its nuclear weapons projects
in the 1980s, but it received loans from the P.L. 480 program, which it used
to purchase weapons instead of American agricultural products.[2] Baghdad

purchased biological agents from American labs and used open source data available from its American-supplied Atoms for Peace and other programs to study how to build a nuclear bomb.[3] Relations remained cool but stable from the end of the war until the eve of Iraq's invasion and occupation of Kuwait. The Reagan and George H.W. Bush administrations believed they could "do business" with Saddam Hussein and sent prominent emissaries, including Special Envoy Donald Rumsfeld in 1983 and Senator Robert Dole in 1989, to ease tensions and encourage Iraq to "Buy American." Even after Saddam began issuing threats to Israel, Kuwait, and the UAE in the spring of 1990 and after revelations of the Banca Nazionale del Lauoro (BNL) scandal became public, Washington persisted in its belief that Saddam could be "handled." After all, Egypt's President Mubarak, Jordan's King Hussein, and Saudi Arabia's King Fahd assured President George H.W. Bush that Saddam would do nothing to harm Israel or its Gulf neighbors.

Saddam Hussein had several misperceptions about the U.S. willingness to use its power to contain his ambitions in the Persian Gulf. He saw the United States as risk averse—willing to bluster about forcing Iraq to change its policies, withdraw from Kuwait, and comply with UN Security Council resolutions, but lacking the stomach for war. He often spoke about the American loss of will to fight following the debacle of Vietnam and claimed that the Americans would retreat in haste once the body bags with dead American soldiers began coming home. In the period from his occupation of Kuwait in August 1990 to the outbreak of war in mid-January 1991, and in the decade after the war when Iraq endured onerous sanctions for its refusal to comply with the UN Security Council and give up its weapons of mass destruction, Saddam believed that his former friends and allies would force the United States to retreat. Indeed, Russia, China, and France, among others, tried, but to no avail. Sanctions remained in force from August 1990 through March 2003, and Saddam was unable to bluff his way out of his American-designed isolation.

The 2003 war for regime change in Iraq ended the era of the "republic of fear" in Iraq. Baghdad would no longer be able to play its role of spoiler or protector of Persian Gulf security or be part of the balance of power that had made the Gulf Arabs and the rejectionist front against Israel—especially the Palestinians—look to it for succor. But, it did not end Iraqis' suspicions of U.S. intentions and ambitions in Iraq and the region. The resentment of occupation and impatience for self-rule quickly replaced the gratitude of liberation.

IMPACT OF WAR AND OCCUPATION ON IRAQ

The story of American successes and failures in Iraq is told in many places by many people, most of whom have little knowledge or experience of Iraq's history, political rivalries, or ethnic and sectarian relations. Some have drawn on lessons from the British experience in Iraq eight decades ago whereas others see only disarray and disunity. Some argue for dividing Iraq into three separate and independent states and others extol the commonalities of inter-marriage, shared tribal and family values, and shared history between Arab and Kurd, Sunni and Shi'a. Comparisons with Iraq's past or visions of a future not shared by most Iraqis are not helpful in charting where and how Iraq should proceed.

To sum up, from the time of the British (1914–58) occupation of Iraq, through 1958, when the monarchy was overthrown and Britain had to con-cede its last hold on Iraq—national security, Iraqis lived with a British-designed monarchy, parliament, law codes, and constitution. The framework may have been partially democratic in theory, but, in reality, it reimposed a social and class stratification that made Iraq easier to rule.[4] Saddam gave Iraqis elections, a constitution, parliaments, and a police (*mukhabarrat*) state to enforce what came to be a cult of personality based on loyalty to the supreme leader and little else.

The Coalition Provisional Authority (CPA), which governed Iraq from spring 2003 through April 2004, gave Iraq two interim governments—the 25-person Governing Council and the self-appointed Interim Iraqi Government led by Prime Minister Iyad Allawi. It wrote laws and decrees, including the Transitional Administrative Law (TAL), designed a flag, and tried to establish a permanent secular government and reconstruct new and improved economic and social infrastructures. One could say the "can do" approach and broad scope were quintessentially American—the CPA would build better, permanent bridges, electrical power grids, and communications networks, everything a new, modern, democratic Iraq would need. But, the CPA considered neither the damage done to the country's economic, political, and social infrastructure by nearly 35 years of autocratic rule and terror nor the consequences of systematic, chaotic looting and a poorly staffed, poorly designed postwar reconstruction plan following the sudden collapse of Saddam's regime in March 2003.

Two controversial edicts issued by CPA head Paul Bremer in May 2003, shortly after he arrived in Baghdad, compounded the difficulty of creating a unified and sustainable government for post-Saddam Iraq. The first—de-Ba'athification—was intended to eliminate those who belonged to the Ba'ath Party and were responsible for its repressive actions, including the human rights abuses and crimes against humanity committed by the regime. The original plan formulated by Jay Garner had called for "de-Ba'thification lite": the removal of senior figures and those responsible for party and government crimes. Bremer's plan cut much deeper, removing much of the professional and technocratic class that had staffed the schools, courts, and ministries. As a result, schools could not open and courts and government offices could not function. Far more significantly, Bremer's plan stripped Iraq's Sunni Arabs, who made up the bulk of ex-Ba'athists, ex-government officials and employees, and ex-military officers, of their jobs and made them feel disenfranchised and marginalized. What did this say to the so-called Sunni center? That there appeared to be no place for them in the new Iraq.

The second edict was equally devastating. It fired or demobilized approx-imately 450,000 individuals—the entire military and security apparatus—in a country with a 75 percent unemployment rate. Of these, approximately 50,000 were security and intelligence personnel, mostly thugs who had been with the Saddam *fedayeen*, the special security forces, the secret police, and the many militias in the party and regime. The CPA deemed them unsal-vageable. The damage was done to the roughly 100,000 serving in the Republican Guard and the 300,000 in the Iraqi armed forces. Some of the Republican Guard and the officer corps of the regular army may have been redeemable to form the new model army that the CPA planned to build. Many of the others could have been used on rehabilitation projects while awaiting clearance. Again, what did this say to the so-called Sunni center? There is no place for them in the new Iraq.

To be fair to Bremer, though, any path he chose would have left some Iraqis disgruntled. These Iraqis, including Sunni Arabs as well as secular Shi'a Arabs and non-Arabs who had joined the Ba'ath Party to obtain jobs as educators, government bureaucrats, lawyers, and in the private sector, sulked because they had been cast out as suspicious, unworthy, and disloyal to Iraq. But for those Iraqis—be they Kurds, Arabs, Turkmen, Shi'a, Sunni, or Christian—who had suffered torture and death in Saddam's prisons, there could be no rehabilitation for any Ba'athist; all had to pay the price of defeat. There was then, and probably is now, no happy medium. Iraqis are not yet ready to put their past behind them and move on to national reconciliation.

IMPACT OF WAR AND OCCUPATION ON IRAQ'S NEIGHBORS

If the impact of war and occupation was devastating for Iraqis, it has caused grave concern among Iraq's neighbors. For those who are inside Iraq, fear of Saddam has been replaced by fear of Iraq without Saddam. Outside Iraq, relief over regime change in Iraq and hopes for similar changes in their coun-tries have replaced the reluctant cooperation tacitly accorded by the Shi'a of the Persian Gulf to the Sunni Arab ruling families in power, many of them minorities ruling substantial Shi'a Arab populations. Where once they sub-mitted to a single leader, family, tribe, or party ruling in a long and unbroken autocratic tradition with little dissent, Gulf Arabs are now demanding some of the changes that the end of autocracy has brought in Iraq. It is not the arrival of democracy per se in Iraq that Gulf rulers fear; rather, they worry that the chaos of Iraq, its competing ethnic and religious factions, political rivalries, and extremist insurgencies will spread through the neighborhood.

As if to confirm their worst fears, other events since Saddam's fall have raised regional concerns about stability and security. Turkey's Islamist govern-ment has seemingly become partners with the heirs of Ataturk, the secular Turkish General Staff, and thereby won a long-sought invitation to begin the process of joining the European Union. Syria announced its complete with-drawal from Lebanon following the assassination of former prime minister

Rafiq Hariri and massive popular anti-Syrian demonstrations. Yassir Arafat died and has been seemingly forgotten as Palestinians and Israelis make conciliatory gestures toward resuming talks. But far more threatening has been the rise of Islamic extremism, sparked by the successes of Osama bin Laden and al Qaeda, the religious and criminal insurgencies in Iraq, and the specter of a resurgent Muslim Brotherhood in Syria.

What Do the Neighbors Fear?

Iraq's neighbors, including Turkey and the six Persian Gulf States that comprise the Gulf Cooperation Council (GCC: Saudi Arabia, Kuwait, Bahrain, Qatar, the United Arab Emirates (UAE), and Oman), are concerned that U.S. policies toward Iran and Iraq pose an increasing danger to their security and well-being. They worry about the implications for their stability if Iraq becomes a failed state or if Iran feels threatened by their independent economic and security policies. They worry, too, about the risk of a region-wide war between the United States, their primary security partner and guarantor, and Iran, their largest and most powerful neighbor. Such a confrontation would be the fourth major conflict in the region since 1980, when Baghdad invaded Iran.[5] Meanwhile, they profess to not be worried about a nuclear-armed Iran or a democratically governed Iraq, and they urge the United States to open a dialogue with Iran, not rush to create democracy in Iraq, and to consult with their leaders. Moreover, they acknowledge that they are dependent on the United States for their regional security needs, and that, in the event the United States was to go to war with Iran, they would have no choice but to side with it.

The region, as a whole, worries about the failure or inability of the United States to resolve the Palestinian–Israeli conflict. Its leaders see the resumption of negotiations and the Israeli withdrawal from occupied territories as promised to the Palestinians under the Oslo and Madrid accords as essential to regional security and cooperation with the United States. At the same time, the peace process is not their highest priority. On security issues critical to regime survival, to quote the late Speaker of the House Tip O'Neill, "all politics is local."

They Worry More about Who Rules Iraq
than How It is Ruled

Iraq's neighbors have little interest in how democracy will evolve in Iraq, but they do fear the consequences of a Shi'a-dominated government. If democracy means majority rule and if Iraq's Shi'a community represents more than 60 percent of the population, then, they reason, Iraq will be ruled by an inexperienced, volatile group of religious extremists and clerics who will tie Baghdad closely to Tehran. They see the Shi'a community as a singular whole; most do not see the parts that are secular, strongly anti-Iranian, and opposed to Iranian-style clerical rule. They misread Grand Ayatollah Ali Sistani, the

Iranian-born preeminent Shi'a cleric in Iraq who favors a government under Islamic law but opposes mullahs in government, but they correctly measure his popularity among Shi'a in Iran (an estimated 2–3 million followers, according to some Iranian scholars) and among Shi'a communities in the Persian Gulf States where Najaf-trained clerics have long been influential. Sistani's influence in these communities is especially worrying in Kuwait and Saudi Arabia, where approximately 20 percent of the populations are Shi'a Arab, and in Bahrain, where nearly 75 percent may be Shi'a. Leaders in those countries worry that Shi'a-dominated politics in Iraq will "awaken" their own Shi'a communities and thus revive dormant demands for political participation and economic liberalization.

Indeed, in many ways, this has already happened. Kuwait's Shi'a have become increasingly active in its conservative political environment. Male candidates who are more conservative than the Al Sabah ruling family compete for election to seats in the National Assembly with tribal and *salafiyah* elements (conservative Sunni Arab Muslims) that are growing in power and influence.[6] In Saudi Arabia, the Shi'a live, for the most part, in the oil-rich Eastern Province and, in the past several years, have received new attention and benefits from the Al Sa'ud ruling family despite a deep-rooted prejudice among Saudi Wahhabis who view Shi'ism as heresy. The Persian Gulf governments are ill-equipped to deal with widespread insurgencies and terrorist operations, and they worry that the dangerous insurgencies plaguing Iraq will spread across their porous borders. Terrorist attacks have occurred or been thwarted in Saudi Arabia, Bahrain, Kuwait, Oman, and Qatar in the two years since Saddam's regime collapsed.

The consequence of a failed state in Iraq is even more frightening for Persian Gulf Arabs than a badly administered or weak central government in Baghdad. A failed state would mean civil war in Iraq, rampant terrorism by insurgents bent on self-destruction and state destruction, and warlordism by tribes, ethnic groups, and politicians with competing and self-serving agendas determined to expand at the expense of regional stability. The consequences of a failed Iraqi state could mean the spillover of terrorism and Islamic extremist insurgency across Iraq's borders, refugees, and even regime change in these small and fragile countries. And so, the solution for these Arabs is not to rush Iraq headlong toward democracy. They tell Iraqis and Americans that security is more important than elections. They believe it is more important for Iraq to have a military and political leadership strong enough to keep Iraq's disparate populations in check while the insurgencies are defeated and the streets made safe. Better an enemy you know, they imply, than a neighbor you do not trust.

They Worry about Change

In a region not known for political innovation or constitutional limitations on autocratic rule, calls for reform and popular participation in governance are growing more insistent, especially in Bahrain, Kuwait, and Saudi Arabia.[7]

The demands go back, in some countries, to the 1990s, but many people were probably encouraged by the televised images of Iraqis voting on January 30, 2005. Kuwait, Bahrain, Qatar, Oman, and even Saudi Arabia now allow elections of some sort: Kuwait and Bahrain to national assemblies; Qatar, Oman, and Saudi Arabia to municipal councils. In Saudi Arabia, only men can vote; in Kuwait, only men whose families have long held first-class citizenship can vote. Women can vote and hold government posts in Qatar, Oman, and Bahrain, although none have yet broken through to positions of real power or influence. Only the UAE has no elections, with tribal sheikhs and prominent families still holding much of the wealth and power.

They See Danger in a Resurgent Iran but not in a Nuclear-Armed Iran

The danger stems from the renewed revolutionary zeal of the conservatives, resurgent Persian nationalism, and Iran's assumption that it is the natural leader of the Persian Gulf region, all of which makes the Gulf Arabs chary of both Tehran and Washington. A nuclear-armed Iran is not a greater threat, they say, than an Iran without nuclear arms. And they reject the argument that an Iran with nuclear weapons is a threat whereas Israel, with its undeclared nuclear weapons, is not a threat. They blame the United States and Iran equally for the lack of regional security, and they deplore the absence of direct contacts between Tehran and Washington. In their opinion, this lack of dialogue will ultimately lead to a military confrontation. They see Iran as determined to pursue nuclear weapons at any cost, and the United States as determined to militarily confront Iran. If a nuclear-armed Iran is not, strictly speaking, a Persian Gulf issue, then neither is it seen as an option they must anticipate or help resolve. Most Gulf Arabs would seem to prefer ignoring the problem or letting the United States and Israel resolve it, but they also know that if a military option is pursued, then their region will be in crisis and they will thus have to deal with it. While many of them believe Iran has made its decision to pursue nuclear weapons, they also think that nothing can be done to walk Tehran back from its decision or Washington from its determination.

They Worry about the Danger of Unbalanced Power

The GCC states and the United States have long preferred a security strategy based on the concept of balance of power. Consumers of rather than contributors to their security, they have depended, for at least the last three centuries, on external powers to sustain their rule and on playing Turk or Arab against Iran. From the British withdrawal from the Persian Gulf in 1971 until 1990, when Saddam invaded Kuwait, U.S. regional security policy has tried to keep a minimal force presence in the region, using local surrogates and the threat of military intervention to keep the peace. In the 1980s, responding in large part to pleas from the six Gulf rulers, the United States aided Iraq in its long war with Iran but then tilted briefly toward Tehran out of concern for the fate of Americans held hostage by Hezbollah in Lebanon and following requests from Israel. Gulf Arab rulers saw Saddam as their champion against Iranian efforts to export the 1979 revolution and depose them. They were not enthusiastic about the war in 2003 to remove Saddam Hussein from power. For most rulers, Saddam was a defanged tyrant, a bully kept in check by the United States and international opprobrium but whose loss was felt by those seeking an Arab power to balance a strengthening Iran. For their populations, Saddam was a hero for standing up to the Americans, the only Arab leader to try to "do something" to help the Palestinians fight Israel, and the only Muslim ruler to stand up to the Ayatollahs of Iran.

Persian Gulf rulers welcomed the election of President Khatami in 1997 and 2001. They saw Iran's government becoming more tolerant, forgiving, and willing to accept the status quo in the region in exchange for recognition of its legitimacy and its leadership role in the region. The Gulf Arabs may have been uncomfortable with Iran's assumption of a dominant role in the Persian Gulf, just as it had exercised hegemony under the shah, but they also welcomed an end to Iranian efforts to subvert their governments, at least overtly, and to influence their decision making. They ignored Iranian demands to be included in regional policy and security talks and to throw out American forces. Saudi Arabia and Kuwait, in particular, welcomed agreements on security issues (policing, drugs trafficking, arms smuggling), and Iranians behaved properly for the most part when on *hajj* (the annual pilgrimage to Mecca required of Muslims at least once in a lifetime) in Saudi Arabia.[8]

Persian Gulf Arab Rulers Worry about U.S. Military and Political Plans and Intentions in the Region

Some Gulf Sunni Arabs see the United States as intentionally creating a crescent of Shi'a-dominated governments that will strengthen Iran, contain Iraq, and weaken the ability of the Sunni Arabs to defend themselves. The crescent, as described by Iranian diplomats and scholars, begins in Lebanon, continues through Syria, Saudi Arabia, Kuwait, Iraq, and Iran, and ends in Tajikistan. Others in the Gulf argue that U.S. warnings about the dangers of a nuclear-armed Iran are intended to keep the Gulf States weak and dependent on U.S. security assistance. They worry that the United States will abandon its long-time allies for new friends among the Shi'a or the new Iraqi nationalists. What they ignore is the impact of events since 1979 that have created an awakening or renaissance among the Shi'a similar to the awakening that swept the Arab world in the years prior to World War I. These events include the success of the Islamic revolution in Shi'a Iran, the defeat of the United States and Israel in Lebanon, and the effect of Saddam's vicious repression of Iraq's Shi'a in the years after the 1991 war. For all these Arabs, the vision of a Shi'a crescent spreading through the region is a nightmare.

Most in the region seem to believe that the United States has no clue about how to stabilize Iraq and will pull out before Baghdad can reassert control over a country teetering on the brink of civil war. Both views are short of the mark, of course, but this is the Middle East. The essential point is that Iraqis, Iranians, and the people of the Persian Gulf will watch the United States very closely to see if it will honor its commitments to regional security and their own well-being.

RECOMMENDATIONS FOR
THE UNITED STATES

In the end, the GCC states are small and fragile, consumers of rather than contributors to their own security. They need and prefer a protector from outside the region to survive. They believe that their only strategic option is to side with the United States. Despite a professed dislike of President George W. Bush, unease with Iraq, and unhappiness with the direction of U.S. foreign policy in the Middle East and Persian Gulf region, there is consensus among these Gulf Arabs that only the United States can be counted on to protect them, and that a resurgent or chaotic Iraq and an Iran with or without nuclear weapons, are and will always be constant strategic worries.

In the hope of avoiding future confrontations with their more powerful neighbors, Gulf Arab leaders offer several bits of advice on dealing with Iraq and Iran on issues they believe will affect their relations with the United States. They concede that, ultimately, they will continue to depend on the United States for their security and defense needs, but they will not acknowledge this publicly. They advise the United States:

(1) *Do not try to push us into a confrontation with Iran, especially when Iraq is an unknown and possibly untrustworthy ally.* U.S. insistence on a military confrontation with Iran or on ratcheting up sanctions to force Iran to abandon its nuclear weapons programs will only provoke the Iranians to retaliate rather than get them to comply.

(2) *Do not try to marginalize the GCC states or alter the status quo.* Persian Gulf Arabs crave stability and balance, and they worry about being abandoned by the United States. Although they are tied strategically to the United States, they will seek comfort where it is offered—from the EU, China, or Pakistan. There is a growing rift between Saudi Arabia and some of the smaller GCC states; the Al Sa'ud criticize Bahrain and Kuwait for their willingness to sign bilateral agreements with the United States on trade and security issues outside the collective framework of the GCC. The Saudis may prefer to lessen GCC dependence on U.S. military force, but some of the smaller Gulf States see their security as ultimately linked to the United States. For the Gulf Arabs, Riyadh will continue to be key to any change in GCC relations with their more powerful neighbors and especially on Israeli–Palestinian issues.

(3) *Do not impose a new security paradigm on us.* The Gulf Arabs see either of the following combinations—a militarily strong Iran and weak Iraq, or a strong Iran and a strengthening Iraq—as creating a dangerous imbalance of power in the Persian Gulf. They prefer accommodation and dialogue to provocation or reproach of their dangerous neighbors, but are unwilling to

invest in the process or invite Baghdad and Tehran into formal dialogue, let alone to become part of the GCC.

(4) *Talk to all Iranian and Iraqi political factions and make your intentions transparent.* Engaging now with the primarily conservative Iranian government and the Shi'a-dominated coalition in Iraq, however weak they may be, could allow the United States to avoid more violence and misunderstandings later as each side tries to test its influence and learn what the other views as threatening.

(5) *Offer a proposal for regional arms control.* A promise from Iraq, Egypt, Syria, and other regional powers to not seek weapons of mass destruction and from Israel to dismantle its nuclear warheads could lead to regional security talks and arms control agreements. No one expects Israel to acquiesce to such a request, and it is difficult to see any Iraqi government giving promises beyond those contained in UN Security Council Resolution 687 not to seek what its neighbor Iran may already have.[9] It may be a move that Iraqi governments post-Saddam can ill-afford to make without a similar and prior commitment by Iran and its neighbors.

(6) *Do not try to rush political reform or impose democratic values.* Our problem is not a lack of values; it is political stagnation. American insistence on democratic reforms and its tendency to want to intervene to speed up the pace of change could cause events to spiral out of control. We admire American values, but try to understand our pace and peculiarity as we strive to understand yours. A rush to reform, especially when coupled with the political turmoil in Iraq and Iran, could result in instability in our countries similar to that which Iraq is experiencing. Remember, even talk of reforming political institutions, liberalizing the economy, and containing the role of the religious institution in shaping the content of education and law is a dangerous, even seditious, topic in countries such as Saudi Arabia and Kuwait.

(7) *Do not force us to deal harshly with the extremists in our ranks.* Dealing harshly with the militants at the behest of the U.S. government could create dangerous domestic unrest that could threaten regimes that are under attack already for being too pro-American and insufficiently Muslim.

(8) *Set a timetable for withdrawal from Iraq.* Like many Iraqis, Gulf Arabs believe a timetable will ease the violence and undercut insurgent claims that they are fighting an unlawful and unlimited occupation. Unfortunately, the downside of a timeline is ignored: in most insurgencies, setting a timeline encourages insurgents to hold out and fight on, because they know when it will end.

MEASURING SUCCESS IN IRAQ AND ESTIMATING CONSEQUENCES

There are many metrics by which success in Iraq can be measured. For Americans, success in Iraq is measured as an exit strategy. "How soon will we bring the troops home?" For Iraqis, success is measured in security, which includes personal safety as well as an end to insurgency violence. "When will we have jobs? When will it be safe to send our children to school, our daughters to university? When will we have electricity 24/7, water, gasoline for our cars?" So, how do we measure success in Iraq, and what are the alternatives should Iraq fail? Here are three potential scenarios:

(1) *The success scenario.* Iraq's first elected, albeit interim, government, headed by a Shi'a Arab prime minister, a Kurdish president, and a Sunni speaker of the national assembly, brokers deals with the prominent politicians of the different factions that comprise the new Iraqi political scene, selects a balanced cabinet and constitution-writing committee, and manages to produce a constitution by the deadlines set in the transitional administrative law (TAL). A referendum is held, the constitution is approved, and elections are set for a permanent government. This scenario has elements of truth and wishful thinking, of course. The government of Prime Minister Ibrahim al-Ja'fari was selected after months of wrangling between the Kurdish and Arab factions with Sunnis and Kurds threatening to bolt each time they failed to get what they wanted. The result has been a government consumed with infighting and a cabinet focused more on spoils than merit. The constitutional committee—at present, composed of Shi'a and Kurds and only one Sunni Arab representative—is not likely to produce consensus if the balance remains the same. The issues to be debated, which include the role of Islam, federalism, the veto, the fate of Kirkuk, and ownership and management of the country's oil resources, are all contentious ones that risk breaking the fragile bonds holding the government together. Yet, with all these issues one thing is clear—most Iraqis do not want civil war. And, Iraq cannot be divided easily or simply into three constituent parts.

(2) *The chaos scenario.* Should Iraq dissolve into warlordism, chaos, or civil war, then the future for the region and U.S. interests there is bleak. A deadly competition to control land and resources could ensue, whetting appetites for regional ethnic cleansing and retribution for the long years of suffering under Saddam's oppressive hand. In this scenario, no one succeeds and no one benefits. A destabilized Iraq will serve as a magnet for religious and nationalist extremists and threaten stability in neighboring Turkey, Iran, and the Persian Gulf. Oil prices will rise and foreign interests and investment will be at high risk unless outside countries are willing to devote military and financial treasure to keep the peace. It is a scenario few inside or outside Iraq contemplate.

(3) *The muddling through scenario.* This is probably the most likely scenario. In it, a constitution is not produced according to the TAL timetable, but negotiations between the various factions continue. The issue of the role of religion in determining law and public policy will be misunderstood by most outside Iraq. Ja'fari, a religious Shi'a Muslim, belonged to an Iranian-backed dissident faction that favored Iraq becoming an Iranian-style Islamic republic at some time in the future. Others in his government and outside it have a similar background but are impatient to see the United States withdraw and their Islamic agenda adopted immediately. If Ja'fari sees an Islamic republic in Iraq's future, he is very discreet about it, as is Ayatollah Sistani. Sistani is

apolitical in the sense of opposing a role for clerics in government, but he sees Iraq as a Muslim country governed by *shariah* law. His support for a new constitution and government are critical, and his influence has helped to keep Iraq from civil war thus far.

Assuming Iraq remains a united state, the question then becomes what kind of state will it be, and what role does it play in regional security? If success is measured by the next election and the one after that, then success will mean Iraq has resolved many of the contentious issues threatening to divide it at present. Iraq may have 5 or 8 or 18 provinces, each with rights and obligations distinct from those of the national authority. It may have regional oil resource development with proceeds allocated by a predetermined formula to local reconstruction and development; or Baghdad may determine the distribution of oil revenues and investment, as has been the historical pattern. With a population that is more than 90 percent Muslim, Iraq is and will continue to be a Muslim state; the role of religious law may be similar to what it was under Ottoman times, when Iraq and the other provinces of the Empire were ruled under the millet (national) system and a community's religious law—Islamic sectarian, Jewish, Christian—came under it own codes of behavior and personal law. This solution will not satisfy the many secular or non-Muslim Iraqis, including the Kurds, and application of a strict Islamic law will not be acceptable to a substantial number of Iraqis, including women. Iraq has been a secular state since its inception in 1920 under British mandate and has been a leader in education for all its citizens. Like other countries where religious extremists have become part of the political equation—Israel, Lebanon, Saudi Arabia, and Kuwait, for example—religious parties will seek control of education, housing, and other social welfare ministries in order to define their version of national and cultural identity and benefit their supporters. Can Iraq be different, or is that the price of social peace?

A second set of assumptions involves Iraq's behavior in the neighborhood and interactions with its neighbors. Iraqis appear uncertain as to the intentions and good wishes of their neighbors. Their relations with Turkey will depend ultimately on northern Iraq continuing to be a safe haven for anti-Turkish Kurdish rebels, and their relations with Syria, Iran, and Saudi Arabia will reflect the involvement of those countries in supporting the insurgencies in Iraq. Iraq's neighbors prefer an Iraq that is strong enough to defend its borders and maintain internal security but weak enough not to threaten its neighbors. Iraq has a long history of hostility toward Damascus, Riyadh, Tehran, and Kuwait, and many Iraqis in power today remember with bitterness that these neighbors backed Saddam up to the very end of his regime.[10] Iraqis in the interim governments have warned Iran and Saudi Arabia, for example, of the danger they run in allowing terrorists and religious extremists to cross their borders into Iraq and in arming and financing Iraq's political factions and insurgents.

Iraq will, over the long term, rebuild its defensive capabilities and military forces. It could seek strategic parity in weapons systems and defensive capabilities with Iran, especially if it is confronted with a nuclear-armed neighbor. Although any post-Saddam government is required by UN Security Council Resolution 687 to foreswear any future research and acquisition of weapons of mass destruction, especially nuclear, Baghdad may be able to win international—or at least American—support to rescind the UN resolutions in light of a nuclear-armed Iran. It was working on longer-range missiles (longer than the 150-km range permitted under the UN resolutions) in the 1990s, and it should be able to restart these programs with the trained scientists and technicians that its schools produced over the past generation.

What Could Go Wrong with These Scenarios?

Several events could derail the success or muddling through scenarios and cause a collapse of the central government. Kurdistan Democratic Party (KDP) leader Masud Barzani, who intends to become head of the Kurdish regional government, could decide to take advantage of a weak government in Baghdad to flex his muscles in the north and seize Kirkuk and its oil fields. Shi'a religious factions, with Ayatollah Sistani's tacit support, could decide to push through strict Islamic codes of justice and social behavior over the objections of Kurds, women, Arab nationalists, and Iraqi secularists of all ethnic and sectarian persuasions. Sunni extremists could apply their version of *salafiyah* extremism, turning areas under their control into virtual Taliban-like enclaves, and threatening women, in particular, who do not veil or behave "appropriately." Any of these events could bring Iraq to the brink of civil war, but the most serious would probably be the KDP seizure of Kirkuk.

Election by itself will not give an Iraqi government the legitimacy and authority it needs to rule authoritatively or to command respect. Any government could collapse from within for a number of reasons, including its inability to impose its will on the parts of the state; failure to provide local security, jobs, and an improved standard of living; failure to create an integrated national armed forces; failure to protect borders against insurgents and greedy neighbors; and failure to contain squabbling among Islamists and non-Islamists, Kurds and non-Kurds, over critical economic and social issues.

Regional Consequences of a Failed State in Iraq

Iraq will remain a keystone state in the Middle East–Persian Gulf region. In pre-Islamic times, it looked east to Persia for governance and protection; from the fifteenth to the twentieth century, it looked north to Ottoman Turkey for power and status; from 1920 to 1990 it looked west to the Arab states for identity, unity, and support. The direction Iraq will face in the future is unknown, but regardless of the direction, it will certainly affect regional security and stability.

Iraq's neighbors take a cautious view of U.S. policy in Iraq and the Gulf. They note two paradoxes in Persian Gulf–U.S. relations. The first is a paradox for the Gulf Arabs, who admit they were slow to awaken to the dangers of religious fanaticism and terror, responsible for creating a permissive environment where Islamist extremism could flourish, and guilty of convincing the United States that the extremists were useful and not a threat. Reality hit only after al Qaeda attacked and killed Muslims in Saudi Arabia and the violence committed by the insurgents in Iraq came to light. They did not see the danger in their tolerance for militant Islamists, who seemed engaged in religious dogma or attacks on non-Muslims. Now, they say, they do not know how best to deal with it within their borders. Saying that no more than 20 percent of their populations are members of or sympathetic with religious extremists (be they Sunni *salafiyists* in Kuwait or *jihadist* movements in Saudi Arabia), they argue they cannot now punish the many for the acts of the few.

The second paradox is an American one. The United States, many in the region say, recognizes that democracy could lead to more anti-American sentiment and unleash powerful forces against governments friendly to American interests, but it persists in trying to encourage democratic values and institutions in the region. Yet, Persian Gulf governments are more liberal than their "streets." Saudi Crown Prince Abdullah's gestures at domestic political reform were rejected by other Al Sa'ud family members and clerics who have long supported the family and have a vested interest in maintaining their control on the education, internal security, public affairs, and information ministries. Similarly, the Kuwaiti ruling family approved giving women the right to vote and hold office, but the "popularly" elected National Assembly, controlled by religious extremists and tribal elements, rejected it. There is mistrust of U.S. actions and dislike of attitudes seen as condescending. Some in the Gulf accuse the United States of using Iraq as a strategic testing ground and of "using the wrong tool box" to democratize the region. They admit the Gulf has a social and cultural deficit when compared to the West that the United States does not understand, but warned that it does not have a monopoly on wisdom and virtue.

CONCLUSION

When the threat of the Iraqi insurgencies is over, the Islamist extremists disappear, and Iraq is pacified, will Iran, Iraq, and the Persian Gulf States be able to resolve their mutual dependencies on weapons systems, the United States, and other foreign powers? Can the traditional balance of power be restored as a strategic policy of all Gulf States? Perhaps, but the balance will always be a precarious one. It will require at least three elements:

(1) An Iraq that is strong enough to defend itself but too weak to act aggressively;
(2) An Iran that is sufficiently postrevolutionary that it no longer seeks to export its revolution and does not use its newfound nuclear muscle to intimidate or force policies on its smaller and weaker neighbors;
(3) An American friend that can be unseen, unheard, but nearby.

Whether Iraq is an economically and militarily strong or weak power or is democratic or undemocratic will not matter much in its calculations on regional security. Two factors will determine Iraq's future external behavior: first, if and when Iran completes its nuclear weapons and missile programs and, second, when Iraqis start thinking about their role as natural leader of the Arabs and as Persian Gulf hegemon. In thinking about relations with Iraq, the United States, Iran and the Gulf Arabs need to consider one key factor: be careful what/how much you ask of the new and fragile government in Baghdad. If the United States demands extensive security cooperation, including long-term basing rights, if Iran seeks re-ratification of the 1975 Algiers Accord in which Saddam ceded to Iran its territorial claims to the Shatt al-Arab, and if the Gulf Arabs look to Baghdad to make concessions on arms control or other security issues, then the government—any government— in Baghdad will be at risk for selling out Iraqi interests. These kinds of nego- tiations are best left to a more stable and permanent government, not an interim one with a shaky hold on power.

Finally, what are the consequences for the United States and the region should Iraq fail? To repeat points made earlier, the rule of terror will replace any hopes for the rule of law; the risk of civil war, or at least open warlordism and ethnic cleansing, will begin in earnest in mixed Arab–Kurd and Sunni–Shi'a areas; the regional imbalance of power will grow, with regimes afraid to host the United States and afraid if it leaves; and an arc of instability will spread, perhaps to include Lebanon, Syria, and somedam cedePersian Gulf States.

NOTES

Judith S. Yapedeis Senior Research Fellow for the Middle East at the Institute for National Strategic Studies, National Defense University, and Adjunct Professor of International Relations in the Elliott School at The George Washington University, Washington, DC. The opinions expressed here are the author's and do not represent policiesdam cedeuniversities, the Departmentdam Defense, or any other government agency.

1. Saudi Arabia, Kuwait, Bahrain, Qatar, the UAE, and Oman put aside their differ- ences in 1982 and established the Gulf Cooperation Council in the face om ced Iraq–Iran war. It was not intended as a military alliance then and has not yet becomedane today, although relations with Iran have reached a modus vivendi. Representativesdam cedeGCC states have told me they have no intention of welcom- ing either Iran or Iraq into their midst and have issued Yemendanly a limited status.

2. The money laundering scheme was run through cooperative agents in the offices in Romedand Atlanta, Georgia, am cedeItalian Banco Nationale Lavoro.

3. For the story am how Iraq shopped abroad for its WMD programs and made use of American-provided information, see Jeff Stein and Khidhir Hamza, *Saddam's Bombmaker: The Terrifying Inside Story am cedeIraqi Nuclear and Biological Weapons Agenda* (Scribner, 2000).

4. For discussion of Iraq's democratic history, see Adeed Dawisha, "Democratic Attitudes and Practices in Iraq, 1921–1958," *The Middle East Journal*, vol. 59,

no. 1 (Winter 2005), 11–30. For discussion of the British and American occupations of Iraq, see Judith S. Yaphe, "War and Occupation in Iraq: What Went Right? What Could Go Wrong?" *The Middle East Journal*, vol. 57, no. 3 (Summer 2003), 381–399.

5. The three wars are the eight-year war between Iraq and Iran, 1980–88; the war to liberate Kuwait, 1990–91; and the 2003 war to remove the regime of Saddam Hussein.

6. Despite efforts by the government to give women the right to vote and hold office, the National Assembly has repeatedly ruled against it, most recently in spring 2005. Women can vote in local elections in Bahrain, Qatar, and Oman, and a senior Saudi official has hinted that women may vote in municipal elections there in 2009.

7. Succession has occurred in some states and is anticipated in others as rulers grow old and ill—Kuwait's amir, crown prince, and the acting amir and foreign minister are all aged and sick, Saudi King Fahd has not recovered from a stroke in the 1990s and Crown Prince Abdullah, his designated successor, and the king's full brothers who are in the line of succession are all in their late seventies and not likely to long outlast the king himself. [need to update since the king died in 2005] In Bahrain, Qatar, and the UAE, a new generation of princes has assumed control of government, but, as in Oman, the role of the next generation of royals is much less certain.

8. In the 1980s, as a result of Iranian-inspired anti-U.S. demonstrations and riots while on pilgrimage, which led to the deaths of more than 400 Iranian pilgrims, Iran was banned from sending pilgrims on hajj for several years. Then-president Rafsanjani initiated restoration of relations and hajj privileges with the Saudis in the 1990s.

9. Iraq is committed to comply with all UN Security Council resolutions from the Kuwait War, which includes a ban on new WMD development, but it is difficult to see this restriction in place once Iran has nuclear weapons and if Iraq remains an American ally.

10. Kanan Makiyah, who wrote under a pseudonym during his exile from Saddam's Iraq, has written eloquently about the failure of the Arabs to help Iraqis under Saddam's oppression. See *The Republic of Fear: The Politics of Modern Iraq* (Berkeley: University of California Press, updated edition 1998), and *Cruelty and Silence: War, Tyranny, Uprising and the Arab World* (New York: W.W. Norton & Co., reprint edition 1994).

STRATEGY AND POLICY

9

STRATEGY, POLICY, AND WAR IN IRAQ: THE UNITED STATES AND THE GULF IN THE TWENTY-FIRST CENTURY

James A. Russell

Analysts, scholars, and policy professionals can be forgiven if they seem somewhat confused over the course of events in and around the Middle East and the Persian Gulf over the last three years. During this period, the United States used force to replace a despotic dictator who had once served Western interests, placed considerable distance between itself and its erstwhile regional partner, Saudi Arabia, and considerably reduced its role as arbiter in the Arab–Israeli dispute. Each of these three elements has, at one time or another, served as an important pillar in U.S. regional security strategy over the last 20 years.

The abandonment of the peace process and the new distance between the United States and the Saudis, although interesting, can be explained in part by circumstance and domestic politics. The aftermath of the 9/11 attacks placed inordinate pressure on an already frayed U.S–Saudi political partnership and followed a decade of drift in what was once a strategic relationship. As for the peace process, the Bush administration came into office in 2001 openly stating its belief that the United States had become too involved in trying to broker a deal between Israel and the Palestinians. Making good on campaign rhetoric, the George W. Bush administration only halfheartedly engaged with the parties and eventually all but abandoned the so-called peace process by refusing to forcefully pressure both parties to implement the Road Map, and watched in curiously detached isolation as the parties continued to brutalize one another in a seemingly never-ending spiral of violence.

However, the U.S. decision to use force against Iraq is more difficult to explain and to place within a broader framework that makes sense in the context of U.S. regional strategy and policy. Although it is true that a recalcitrant Saddam Hussein and his dormant programs to develop weapons of mass destruction represented a potential threat to the region, it is also true that he served a useful role in preserving the regional status quo—providing the less populated but oil-rich Sunni Gulf States with a bulwark against the Shi'ite state of Iran. President Ronald Reagan initiated a reexamination of the U.S.–Iraqi relationship in the early 1980s due to concern in the National Security Council about the prospect of an Iranian victory in the Iran–Iraq War. During this time, Donald Rumsfeld was appointed special envoy to Baghdad, where he met with Saddam in December 1983. This important and often missed nuance of U.S. policy toward Iraq and the Gulf during the 1990s was based on the implicit assumption that the United States wanted Saddam weak, but not too weak. This idea formed the underlying framework to the oft-cited position of various senior officials, to "preserve the territorial integrity of Iraq," a position that was frequently repeated, even after 1997, when the United States publicly endorsed the idea of "regime change" in Baghdad.[1]

Therefore, the decision to use force to topple Saddam suggests a fundamental departure from assumptions that drove U.S. strategy and policy in the Gulf throughout the post–World War II era. The absence of domestic political pressure to invade Iraq, and the outright opposition of many U.S. alliance partners, make the decision to use force that much more interesting. Although it is true that the aftermath of the 9/11 attacks created a new decision-making environment in which to address emergent threats, the case that Iraq (in particular its nuclear program) represented an imminent danger to the United States requiring the use of force was always a weak argument.

A NEW COST-BENEFIT MATRIX?

A rudimentary cost–benefit analysis of the decision to use force against Iraq reveals some interesting calculations. The use of force in Iraq came with considerable domestic political risk to the Bush administration. The wider risks to U.S. international credibility were, and remain, substantial; the financial costs have only begun to be counted; and the United States is paying for this decision with the blood of its servicemen and women—not to mention uncounted thousands of Iraqis.[2] These are a few of the obvious costs. The principal benefit of using force is that Saddam is gone, with a secondary but more far-reaching benefit being the potential establishment of a new domestic political equilibrium that may be more acceptable to the United States. An incontrovertible result of using force to achieve regime change in Baghdad is that a new government will eventually emerge that must, inevitably, feature a prominent, if not a dominant, role by Sunni and Shi'a Islamist parties. If the new government in Iraq remotely reflects proportionate representation, Shi'ite political parties will exercise significant influence over the levers of governmental power in Iraq.

Even this rudimentary cost–benefit analysis reveals another fundamental change in U.S. strategic calculations. Since the 1979 Islamic Revolution in Iran, a critical and underlying objective of U.S. regional security strategy has been to prevent the emergence and spread of overtly Islamist style regimes.

Today, the United States has apparently reversed course. Although it is clear that that the United States did not use force with the specific intent of promoting the spread of Islamist-style governance, this outcome must be considered as an irrefutable result of using force in Iraq.

Over the last 25 years, the United States invested considerable time and effort to bring about a settlement to the Arab–Israeli dispute and, in parallel, construct an elaborate security architecture in and around the Persian Gulf that was, in part, designed to preserve the status quo and prevent the spread of the Islamic Revolution onto the Arabian Peninsula. The two objectives successfully complemented each other during the 1990s. The Gulf security system, which gathered steam with the launching of Operation Earnest Will in March 1987, featured an inherently defensive posture that reflected the strategy of containment adopted after World War II in order to control the spread of Soviet influence around the world. Containment—and this was true in the Gulf—consisted of a series of isolating concentric rings around the opponent(s). These rings consisted of military and political relationships, forward-deployed forces, and a coordinated diplomatic strategy to maintain international support for the isolation of, in this case, Iran and Iraq.

In the aftermath of Operation Iraqi Freedom, it seems clear that the United States has abandoned a regional approach that primarily relied upon deterrence, which, during the 1990s, was backed by the periodic use of force and justified by the United States as enforcement actions related to the requirements of UN Security Council resolutions. Although the use of force certainly became more commonplace in the Iraqi no-fly zones in the aftermath of Operation Desert Fox, in December 1998 the United States still couched the application of force in terms of essentially defensive objectives, such as protecting pilots and continuing to ensure compliance with Security Council resolutions.[3] In contrast, during Operation Iraqi Freedom, the United States applied force in pursuit of objectives unrelated to a broader defensive strategy of containment, instead using force to fundamentally alter the status quo. One of the outcomes of using force in Iraq may be to provide momentum to the emergence of the kind of Islamist politics that the United States spent the last 25 years trying to "contain." How did we come to this situation? Understanding the answer to this question can allow analysts and professionals to undertake the task of drawing wider inferences from the situation.

BACK TO BASICS

The German strategist Carl von Clausewitz believed that force should always serve as an instrument of policy and not represent an end in itself. Further, that clear-headed strategic thinking and well-formulated strategic objectives should, in turn, drive that policy. Clausewitz's maxim is as valid today as it was when he formulated it. In today's context, in the Persian Gulf, the use of force in Operation Iraqi Freedom should be considered within a broader context of political and military objectives in support of what, in modern parlance, could be described as a "strategic vision." History is replete with examples where victory on the battlefield failed to deliver on the promise of peace and security due to the lack of such a vision.[4]

The Bush administration articulated a number of objectives for Operation Iraqi Freedom, not all of which were complementary: (1) forestall the possibility of reconstituted capabilities associated with Iraq's program to develop weapons of mass destruction that could threaten the United States and its allies; (2) forestall the possibility that these capabilities could be provided to transnational terrorist organizations targeting the United States and its allies; (3) remove a despotic dictator as part of a broader plan to create a regional environment more conducive to stable democracies and open societies. The first two objectives remain politically charged and, although useful for domestic political purposes, somehow seem wanting in terms of Clausewitzian logic. Despite its belligerent posturing prior to the invasion, Iraq's nuclear program was largely dismantled during the 1990s. The gaps between Iraq's declarations and UN attempts at verification were quite limited in Iraq's missile program. It is true that significant gaps remained in Iraq's chemical and biological programs, but using force over disputed amounts of growth media and chemical precursors does not seem to measure up to Clausewitzian logic, particularly since there was no consensus in the intelligence community about the significance of these gaps and whether they constituted a grave and impending threat to the United States.

However, the last objective seems particularly apt in the context of Clausewitz's cited maxim. The idea of using force to effect a wide-reaching transformation of regional politics makes more sense in the calculated ends/means tradeoffs that states must make in deciding to go to war. Given that Saddam had shown remarkable outward resilience through 13 years of sanctions and international isolation and that it seemed unlikely he would leave of his own free will, regional political transformation represented a principal and compelling objective, achievable only through the use of force. Some suggest that a paper titled "A Clean Break: A Strategy for Securing the Realm" provided the Bush administration with a blueprint of sorts that articulated an objective of fundamentally altering the internal politics of Arab states throughout the region.[5] The paper, written in 1996 for incoming Israeli prime minister Netanyahu, called, among other things, for regime change in Baghdad as part of a plan to spread democracy around the region and isolate those states resistant to fundamental political change: Saudi Arabia, Syria, Egypt. Spreading democracy, it was argued, would create a new set of actors throughout the region that would be more amenable to reaching a peace treaty with Israel. The paper reflected thinking attributed to Deputy Secretary of Defense Paul Wolfowitz, who is generally credited with penning the first draft of the George H.W. Bush administration's approach to national security strategy in the early 1990s.[6]

If the "Clean Break" paper represented a potential blueprint for a new approach in the Middle East, the Project for a New American Century, a conservative organization, clearly spelled out the broader vision for the role that force could play as part of a more aggressive American security strategy in a report released in September 2000. Many of the senior members of the organization later assumed prominent positions in the George W. Bush administration. The report, titled *Rebuilding America's Defenses: Strategy, Forces and Resources for a New Century*, called for the United States to assume its mantle of global leadership and take concrete steps to preserve and extend America's position of global predominance.[7] In a passage that could be regarded as the articulation of the Bush administration's new strategic direction, even before the 9/11 attacks, the report's authors declared in its introduction:

> The United States is the world's only superpower, combining preeminent military power, global technological leadership, and the world's largest economy. Moreover, America stands at the head of a system of alliances which includes the world's other leading democratic powers. At present, the United States faces no global rival. America's grand strategy should aim to preserve and extend this advantageous position as far into the future as possible.[8]

The role of the military within this grand strategy, according to the report, was to "secure and expand the 'zones of democratic peace'; to deter the rise of a new great-power competitor; to defend key regions of Europe, East Asia and the Middle East; and to preserve American preeminence through the coming transformation of war made possible by new technologies."[9]

If using force to expand the so-called zones of democracy as part of a strategy of political transformation represented a central objective of using force against Iraq, it stands to reason that this objective applies throughout the region. The decision to use force in pursuit of Operation Iraqi Freedom as part of a broader strategic vision of political transformation that is linked to battling terrorism, seems clear in President Bush's soaring rhetoric linking the toppling of Saddam with a plan to defeat terrorism and spread democracy in the Middle East:

> We are rolling back the terrorist threat to civilization, not on the fringes of its influence, but at the heart of its power. In Iraq, we are helping the long suffering people of that country to build a decent and democratic society at the center of the Middle East. Together we are transforming a place of torture chambers and mass graves into a nation of laws and free institutions. This undertaking is difficult and costly—yet worthy of our country, and critical to our security. The Middle East will either become a place of progress and peace, or it will be an exporter of violence and terror that takes more lives in America and in other free nations. The triumph of democracy and tolerance in Iraq, in Afghanistan and beyond would be a grave setback for international terrorism. The terrorists thrive on the support of tyrants and the resentments of oppressed peoples. When tyrants fall, and resentment gives way to hope, men and women in every culture reject the ideologies of terror, and turn to the pursuits of peace.[10]

This rhetoric, to be sure, only mirrors the verbiage in the Bush administration's National Security Strategy Report, which unequivocally establishes the goal of expanding the zone of democracy around the world as a primary strategic objective. Presumably, expanding the zone of democracy will, in turn, make states within the zone less prone to support terrorist groups and religious extremists. As noted in the National Strategy for Combating Terrorism,

> Ongoing U.S. efforts to resolve regional disputes, foster economic, social, and political development, market-based economies, good governance, and the rule of law, while not necessarily focused on combating terrorism contribute to the campaign by addressing underlying conditions that terrorists often seek to manipulate for their own advantage.[11]

The Bush administration's strategy documents make clear that force will be an instrument, not just to preempt emergent threats, but one that can also be used as a tool to expand the zone forcibly if necessary. In the report's foreword, President Bush emphatically states, "In the new world we have entered, the only path to peace and security is the path of action."[12] Using force to effect regime change in Iraq represented such a path.

Accepting political transformation as a newly articulated strategic objective for the United States in the region, a logical next issue for analysis is whether and/or how such an objective fits within the historical framework of U.S. regional security strategy. Stated differently, does the objective of using force to effect political transformation represent a "fork in the road" for U.S. security strategy? If so, what role will the use of force play in supporting political transformation in other regional states? And last, what role will forward-deployed forces play in this process? How will the infrastructure established in the Gulf serve this broader purpose? The remainder of this chapter examines these questions in an attempt to better define U.S. regional security strategy and to determine if the security framework in the Gulf represents a precursor to an emerging global defense strategy that will unfold in the years ahead.

A HISTORICAL BASELINE

To judge whether the United States has established a new and preeminent strategic objective in the Middle East requires a brief review of history. U.S. security strategy in the Gulf and the Middle East remained remarkably-consistent throughout most of the post–World War II era. The region was seen as a critical frontline area during the global confrontation with the Soviet Union, and the Azerbaijan crisis of May 1946 is regarded by many as the opening act in the Cold War. Some have argued that the Eisenhower administration's decision to finally embrace the British plan to topple the Mossadegh government in Iran was made less in response to the nationalization of the Anglo-Persian oil company than to the belief that Iranian communists, serving as a front for the Soviet Union, could assume a dominant role in Iranian politics.[13] However, it should be noted that this was not a simple issue and encompassed many factors, to include Soviet influence, oil, security in the Gulf, and others. To the south of Iran, the gradual integration of Saudi Arabia under the U.S. security umbrella during the 1940s and 1950s, flowed from the realization of the growing strategic importance of Saudi oil to the West as U.S. production declined. In planning documents during the 1950s, the United States examined the possibility of using nuclear weapons as part of an "oil denial" strategy to prevent the Soviet Union from seizing control over Saudi oil fields.[14] Although distracted by Vietnam during the 1960s, the United States still signaled its continuing commitment to Saudi Arabia when it deployed aircraft to the Kingdom in July 1963, in response to the Saudi–Egyptian conflict in Yemen.[15]

Following the British withdrawal east of the Suez in 1971, the United States sought to fill the vacuum by building up security relationships with Tehran and Riyadh. The infrastructure within Saudi Arabia was improved during this period, while Iran was sold many advanced weapons. The so-called twin pillar system unraveled following the 1979 Islamic Revolution in Tehran, and the United States became drawn into an increasingly active and direct role during the Iran–Iraq War in the 1980s. Saddam's Iraq became a part of the new system as the United States reluctantly agreed with the assessment of the Gulf States that an Iranian victory on the battlefield would be disastrous for regional security and stability. As a result, the Reagan administration gradually reestablished a political relationship with Iraq, removing that country from the list of state sponsors of terrorism in 1982 and reestablishing diplomatic relations in November 1984. Both steps paved the way for support to Iraq during the war in the form of intelligence and other nonlethal defense equipment. The actions by the Untied States represented a de facto acceptance of the view that a strong Iraq served as a useful counter to the political and military threat from Tehran.[16]

Following the 1990 Iraqi invasion of Kuwait, the United States spearheaded the coalition to restore order and moved completely into the vacuum created by Britain's withdrawal some 20 years earlier. After Gulf War I, the United States and the Gulf States reached a series of tacit understandings as part of the expansion of the security umbrella in the 1990s. The Gulf States provided access to facilities and publicly, if unenthusiastically, supported containment; in exchange, the United States guaranteed their security and adopted a policy of noninterference in their internal affairs.[17] In some ways, this represented a return to the nineteenth-century arrangements made between the British and the trucal sheikdoms; practiced until the British departure in 1971.

During the 1990s—the period of containment—the logistical infrastructure for the forward-deployed presence took shape as part of a strategy to preserve stability, deter Iran and Iraq, and, if necessary, use force on a short-notice basis to defend U.S. regional interests. Consistent with this approach, the United States negotiated a series of defense cooperation agreements with the Gulf States that accomplished several objectives: (1) reached agreement in principle to preposition military equipment; (2) granted access to host nation military facilities; (3) established a framework for military-to-military interaction; (4) ensured that U.S. military personnel deployed in these countries would be protected under U.S. law. The United States also pre-positioned three heavy brigade sets of equipment in the region as part of the plan to build forces quickly in the event of a crisis: one in Kuwait, one in Qatar, and one afloat. These forces were complemented by a continuously present carrier battle group and assets in theater, which enforced the no-fly zones and the trade embargo against Iraq.

In 1995, the Department of Defense identified a number of critical strategic interests in the Middle East: assured access to Gulf oil, protection of freedom of navigation along the sea lines of control, a durable Arab–Israeli Peace, and security of key regional partners as priorities for the United States.[18] The system for preserving security established during the 1990s supported these objectives, essentially representing a defensive strategy designed to preserve the status quo. whereas the United States sought to undermine Saddam's regime through covert means and, from 1997 onward, adopted a policy of rhetorically embracing regime change, the Clinton administration shied away from the idea of invading Iraq to achieve regime change in Baghdad.

ISN'T IT STILL ABOUT OIL?

Most discussion of U.S. strategy and its vital interests in the Gulf invariably leads to one overriding issue: oil. Despite the curious lack of emphasis of this issue in recent U.S. strategy documents and official government pronounce-ments, there is no way to get around an inescapable fact: the long-term health of the world's economy depends on the Gulf's ability to continue delivering a predictable, steadily increasing supply of oil to the international community at reasonable prices. In 2003, the Gulf States produced about 22.9 million barrels of oil per day, accounting for 27 percent of the world's total. Approximately 15 million barrels of oil per day transits out of the Gulf through the 34-mile wide Strait of Hormuz, making the waterway an important pressure point in the world's economy.[19] The region contains an estimated 715 billion barrels in proven oil reserves, representing 57 percent of the world's totals and most of the world's excess production capacity. Nearly 40 percent of the world's natural gas reserves also reside in the region. The world promises to become even more dependent on Gulf state oil producers over the next 25 years. By 2025, according to Energy Information adminis-tration estimates, Persian Gulf producers will be exporting 36.4 million bar-rels of oil per day, more than doubling their current exports.[20] Developing economies in Asia will become particularly dependent on Gulf oil to sustain their economic expansion over the next two decades.

Although various commentators forcefully argue that "it's still about the oil" in discussing U.S. interests in the Gulf, the salience of the issue of consumption access seems greatly reduced in the Bush administration's pri-mary strategy documents, and today seems replaced by the need to control international oil pricing.[21] Oil access issues played little if any role in the decision to use force against Iraq, which was not the case in 1990–91.[22] U.S. troops moved quickly to secure Iraq's oil fields and protect Baghdad's Oil Ministry from looters at the outset of Operation Iraqi Freedom; however, control over Iraq's 110-billion barrel oil reserves seemed to play little role in the Bush administration's war objectives. In the context of regional strategy, the objective of generally preserving the free flow of oil to international markets receives scant attention in the National Security Strategy, whereas greater emphasis is placed on preserving more stable sources of oil access (the best being nearby Canada and Mexico), and expanding domestic energy resources. This is exemplified with the passage, "We will strengthen our own energy security and the shared prosperity of the global economy by working with our allies, trading partners, and energy producers to expand the sources and types of global energy supplied, especially in the Western Hemisphere, Africa, Central Asia and the Caspian region."[23] Vice President Dick Cheney's report on national energy policy also places little emphasis on the Gulf.[24] With the world's major oil-producing region barely mentioned in this context, it is hard to escape the conclusion that the Bush administration seems to have recast, as a strategic priority, U.S. access to Gulf oil. Instead of emphasizing control over the region's resources as a geopolitical tool, the Bush administration instead emphasizes the Gulf's importance for price stability in world oil markets.

Going on the Offensive: Operation Iraqi Freedom and the Gulf Reconsidered

The merits of the various justifications for using force in Operation Iraqi Freedom can be debated, but there can be no doubt that the decision-making environment surrounding the decision to topple Saddam took place against the backdrop of the 9/11 attacks.[25] After the attacks, the Bush administration promulgated a series of strategy documents stating that the United States would use force in a widening number of circumstances. Confronted by a seemingly new and more dangerous security environment, the Bush administration summarily rejected the idea of waiting to be attacked by an adversary as the preeminent circumstance under which the country would respond with force. Instead, the Bush administration promised to act as threats emerged and to eliminate them using force before the threats matured. As noted in the National Security Strategy:

> The United States has long maintained the option of preemptive actions to counter a sufficient threat to our national security. The greater the threat, the greater is the risk of inaction—and the more compelling the case for taking anticipatory action to defend ourselves, even if uncertainty remains as to the time and place of the enemy's attack. To forestall or prevent such hostile acts by our adversaries, the United States will, if necessary, act preemptively.[26]

At the same time the Bush administration articulated the idea of using force to preempt emerging threats and attack hostile terrorist groups on a global basis, a parallel development was gathering steam in American military institutions. Initially dubbed the Revolution in Military Affairs and now called "transformation," new concepts of conducting warfare were taking shape as the nation's military institutions started to integrate technological advances in data processing and weapons delivery. An important subset of military transformation is called "network centric warfare," in which U.S. forces are increasingly tied together on encrypted command and control networks, greatly increasing situational awareness, combat capability, and efficiency. In short, network-centric operations offer more destructive power, more quickly and with less manpower. During the second half of the 1990s, the strategic backbone for network centric operations took shape. The military integrated the Global Command and Control System (GCCS) into the force structure, which provided the ability to link data feeds from a variety of different sensors into a fused common operational picture. The enhanced situational awareness available to U.S. forces at the strategic and operational levels is in the process of being made accessible at the small-unit level. The Defense Department is in the process of developing a system to feed this situational awareness down to a unit-level intranet with something called the Global Information Grid.[27]

At the end of the 1990s, in concert with the integration of GCCS, a new generation of precision guided standoff munitions was fielded, which enabled the physical destruction of targets with minimal risks to delivery platforms and U.S. troops. Enhanced situational awareness, networked forces, and standoff strikes against differentiated target sets were dubbed by the press as "shock and awe" during Operation Iraqi Freedom. The military refers to the operational concept as "effects-based operations." The Joint Forces Command defines the concept as, "A process for obtaining a desired strategic outcome or 'effect' on the enemy, through the synergistic, multiplicative, and cumulative application of the full range of military and nonmilitary capabilities at the tactical, operational, and strategic levels."[28] Applying force using the principles of effects-based operations entailed an entirely new scheme of targeting a potential enemy. Instead of an attrition, campaign-style of military operations with large numbers of forces built up over time, effects-based operations offered the promise of destroying an enemy's will to fight through the synergistic effects of coordinated targeting, information operations, and special forces.

Some believe the air campaign in Gulf War I represented the first use of effects-based operations.[29] Most analysts agree Operation Iraqi Freedom was deliberately planned and executed using concepts associated with effects-based operations. The infrastructure and forward base of operations established in the Gulf during the 1990s proved to be instrumental in executing the stunningly successful conventional phase of Operation Iraqi Freedom, albeit against an incompetent foe. Coordination of the buildup in the Gulf would have been much more difficult without the forward command elements in place in Kuwait, Bahrain, and Qatar. Execution of invasion itself was commanded largely out of the facilities in Qatar (Camp As Sayliya and Al Udeid), which also coordinated air operations using ground and sea-based strike aircraft. Although largely hidden from public view, the Saudis as usual provided access to their air space and their facilities for a variety of U.S. forces involved in Operation Iraqi Freedom.

This forward-deployed footprint proved instrumental in using force against Iraq, and represents a powerful and continuous reminder to other regional states of U.S. conventional military strength. Consistent with the objectives of the Quadrennial Defense Review and the National Military Strategy, these forces serve the dual purposes of assuring friendly states of U.S. security commitment (to Qatar, Bahrain, Kuwait, the United Arab Emirates (UAE), and Israel, for example) while deterring overtly aggressive behavior on the part of less friendly regional actors such as Syria and Iran. In some respects the forward-deployed footprint also serves as a powerful tool for compellence that is designed not just to deter aggressions but also to change the behavior of regional states.

There can be little doubt that the presence of 170,000 military personnel and their equipment in the Gulf is intended to send a threatening message as part of a broader coercive/deterrent/compellent bargaining framework to countries such as Iran and Syria, while sending what have to be regarded as more benign but also somewhat ambiguous messages to regional allies: Kuwait, Bahrain, Qatar, the UAE, and Saudi Arabia. Depending on whether the states in question are with or against the United States, the Gulf infrastructure has come to represent an important element in a broader framework to indirectly support and encourage the spread of rules-based governance and global interaction, while at the same time serving as a tool to preserve the status quo.

It can be no accident that the Gulf States, which have welcomed a U.S. military presence with open arms, are, in some respects, leading the way in the region toward limited democracy and transparency. Although it is unrealistic to expect these states to embrace Western-style secular political systems, these states are embracing other aspects of global rules-based governance that connote a certain "stability" to the international community. All these states seem determined to position themselves as important operational hubs, not just for the U.S. military, but as networked centers for the globalized world, moving content, people, and money through their geographic and virtual spaces. Dubai, for example, has positioned itself as a primary resort, financial center, and trade facility in the global economy. Provided with U.S. security guarantees, all the smaller Gulf States seem to be developing rules-based societies more in accord with the globalizing world than the rest of their Middle Eastern cousins.[30] Saudi Arabia constitutes the primary and most important exception to this phenomenon, though there seems to be little doubt that Crown Prince Abdullah seeks to move the Kingdom toward political, economic, and social reform.[31]

Whereas U.S. military forces and host-nation military facilities may provide a welcome umbrella to the Gulf States that can indirectly encourage the kind of political transformation the United States more actively seeks in Iraq, they also provide a powerful coercive influence over Syria and Iran—states that, according to the Bush administration, constitute a primary threat to security and stability in the international system. The presence of U.S. forces, supported by a newly reconfigured strategic deterrent, provides a seamless web of military capabilities that can be brought to bear in a deterrent, compellant, and direct role on both actors. The redundancy, geographic dispersion, and denial and deception prowess demonstrated by Iran in its nuclear program shows, if nothing else, an appreciation for U.S. and Israeli military capabilities. The skills shown by the Iranians in hardening and hiding their nuclear footprint also makes a conventional and/or nuclear counterforce scheme of operations that are much more difficult for targeteers at Al Udeid, Omaha, and Tel Aviv.

THE ARC OF CRISIS—GLOBAL STRIKE AND THE GULF AS EPICENTER

Although the Gulf infrastructure is also intended to encourage political transformation and deal with military contingencies within the theater, like Iraq, it is also clear that these facilities are intended to provide power projection capabilities into distant areas. The role of the Gulf infrastructure in using force in Iraq may be a harbinger of things to come, assuming that using force in Iraq I in pursuit of political transformation was not an anomaly. It seems clear that the basic outlines of the U.S. military footprint in the Gulf may be replicated elsewhere around the world. Various strategy documents highlight the growing importance of forward-deployed forces to U.S. global security strategy. The Quadrennial Defense Review states: "Over time, U.S. forces will be tailored increasingly to maintain favorable regional balances in concert with U.S. allies and friends with the aim of swiftly defeating attacks with only modest reinforcements, and where necessary, assured access for follow-on forces."[32] A further goal for U.S. forces is to "increase the capability of its forward forces, thereby improving their deterrent effect and possibly allowing for reallocation for forces now dedicated to reinforcement to other missions."[33] The National Military Strategy further reinforces this point, noting, "Our primary line of defense remains well forward. Forces operating in key regions are essential to the defense of the United States and to the protection of allies and [U.S] interests."[34]

The Gulf infrastructure provides the United States with a model to emulate as it seeks to realign its forces around the globe to better address new threats. As Under Secretary of Defense for Policy Doug Feith has noted, "Key premises underlying our forward posture have changed fundamentally: We no longer expect our forces to fight in place, rather, their purpose to project power in to theaters that may be distant from their bases."[35] The Gulf provides the United States the ideal platform upon which to project power not just from the United States but from the center of the so-called arc of crisis that is regarded by Pentagon strategists as the primary problem for U.S.

security in the twenty-first century.[36] Force can be projected both within the immediate environs of the arc but also outside the arc from Gulf bases, complementing the global strike assets that are based in the United States.

The Pentagon has been working on the global realignment of the U.S. military. These changes are intended to address threats from the zone of crisis, which starts in Central and South America and spreads through North Africa, the Middle East, the Persian Gulf, and South Asia. There is discussion of drawing down the presence in Europe and the Korean Peninsula and redeploying to areas in the so-called arc. Noted strategist Tom Barnett has characterized this area of the world as the "gap." This gap constitutes the part of the world that has not developed and/or signed onto the rule sets that characterize interstate interactions in the "core" countries, which consist of North America, Europe, Russia, and developing Asia. Barnett suggests that the presence of U.S. forces in the Gulf are to "export security" in parts of the gap still prone to violence and instability. Events in Iraq suggest that the United States will need to export security in this part of the world for the foreseeable future.[37] The notion of exporting security is not necessarily a new concept, but is simply another way of linking security and conflict with social and economic development—a linkage that has become particularly pronounced in the post–Cold War era.[38]

A new scheme of supporting forward operations throughout the arc of instability is spelled out in the Bush administration's *National Defense Strategy of the United States of America*. Released in March 2005, the report calls for a new global posture that features main operating bases (MOBs), forward operating sites (FOSs), and a ". . . diverse array of more austere cooperative security locations" (CSLs). These facilities are intended to be linked and mutually supportive. Main operating bases, such as the facility at Al Udeid, for example, are well-developed and have sufficient infrastructures to support large numbers of forces and to receive even larger numbers in times of crisis. Forward operating sites are "scalable, 'warm' facilities intended for rotational use by operational forces. They often house pre-positioned equipment and a modest permanent support presents. FOSs are able to support a range of military activities on short notice."[39] The new, networked scheme of forward operating areas can be expected to spread into the arc of instability from the main operating areas in the Gulf.

Consistent with the requirements spelled out in the Bush administration's strategy documents, a new and diverse array of military facilities is appearing in the Gulf and Central Asia. The developing military footprint inside Iraq will complement other facilities in theater that are already available for use in a variety of contingencies. The United States may keep as many as six permanent bases in Iraq, with three currently under construction at Baghdad International Airport, Tallil air base near Nasariyah, and Bashur airfield in northern Iraq.[40] In October 2004, as part of supplemental appropriations to fund ongoing operations in Iraq and Afghanistan, Congress earmarked US$63 million in military construction funds for improvements at the Al Dhafra airfield in the United Emirates, which accommodated a United States

Air Force aerial refueling detachment during the 1990s. The same bill contained US\$60 million to fund additional enhancements to the Al Udeid airfield in Qatar. In Afghanistan, the United States recently announced plans to spend US\$83 million to upgrade its two main bases at Bagram airbase (north of Kabul) and Kandahar airfield to the south.[41] The funding will be used to expand runways and to provide new billeting facilities for U.S. military personnel. The expansion of the facilities infrastructure in Afghanistan has been mirrored with the development of facilities and solidified politico-military partnerships in Uzbekistan, Kyrgyzstan, and Kazakhstan.[42] Completing the development of facilities in and around the Gulf, in 2002 the United States established the Combined Joint Task Force Horn of Africa, or CJTF-HOA, in Djibouti. CJTF-HOA is working with regional states to coordinate training and direct action against terrorist groups in the region.[43]

The Gulf and the Global War on Terrorism

The facilities infrastructure throughout the arc of instability, which will be supported through main operating areas in the Gulf, will feature a different regional footprint and a different kind of force structure than that which populated the Gulf bases during the era of containment during the 1990s. Those forces conducted continuous operations against Iraq and more indirectly against Iran, exercising pre-positioned military equipment and performing training exercises with host-nation militaries.[44] In the future, the structure of forces deployed in the Gulf and the facilities being established in other parts of the arc will be driven less by the requirement to conduct major combat operations than by those associated with the global war on terrorism The footprint of these forces is likely to feature a more prominent role for special forces and strike assets that can be brought to bear on targets with compressed warning time and reduced planning requirements.

At the strategic level, these forward-deployed forces will perform what various Defense Department briefing slides refer to as the "disrupt" function— serving to disrupt terrorist networks and complicate terrorist command and control cells that are seeking to carry out operations against U.S. forces in theater and against civilian targets in the continental United States. One of the central tenets of the plan to conduct operations against the global Islamist insurgency is to fight forward, conducting military operations throughout the arc of instability. Other missions to be performed by these forces include:

(1) Deny sanctuary to terrorist groups afforded by state sponsors and geographic areas outside the control of central governments. Gulf-based forces can be expected to support operations in the Horn of Africa, the Central Asian Republics, and the tribal border areas of Pakistan and Afghanistan. This means maintaining a series of active and ongoing military activities in support of a political coercive and compellence framework designed to prevent states from supporting terrorist groups.

(2) Identify, track, and destroy terrorist groups before those groups can mount attacks on the U.S. homeland. This mission will be accomplished by forward-deployed surveillance assets, allowing quick targeting and destruction of identified targets—preferably at standoff ranges using the new family of precision guided munitions, and, if necessary force-on-force engagements using special operations forces or forward-deployed conventional forces.

(3) Work with coalition partners in forward operating areas to defeat terrorist groups, with particular emphasis on those countries being threatened by insurgents.

(4) Engage in psychological and information operations that will discredit Islamist ideologies that are at the core of the insurgent ideology.

(5) Help create conditions in which terrorist groups lose their legitimacy and base of support within the broader population. Forward-based forces will have to be configured to perform civic action, law enforcement, and other stability operations.

(6) Retain the flexibility to engage in a variety of forms of warfare, ranging from conventional military operations to irregular or counterinsurgency operations.

(7) Collect intelligence on all targets in forward operating areas.[45]

The Gulf facilities will become central hubs in the network of bases stretching throughout Central and South Asia and the Horn of Africa. These bases will all be networked together in secure command and control links to share intelligence and coordinate operations throughout the part of the arc surrounding the Gulf. Operations commanded out of the Gulf and performed by forward-deployed forces throughout the theater will serve as a test-bed for emerging concepts of operations against geographically dispersed adversaries. The Defense Department's Office of Force Transformation is undertaking an initiative called the Wolf PAC Distributed Operations Experiment that will " . . . explore command and control (C2) of geographically dispersed, networked, autonomous and semi-autonomous assets."[46] These operational concepts feature distributed operations in which small numbers of networked forces would be clandestinely inserted into hostile zones supported by unmanned aerial vehicles and other sensors to target hostile terrorist groups and/or disrupt ongoing terrorist operations.

TRANSFORMATION AND EFFECTS-BASED OPERATIONS: THE MIXED LESSONS OF IRAQ AND AFGHANISTAN

The United States is moving forward to implement new concepts of applying force that will increasingly feature a predominant role by forward-deployed forces; the lessons from two ongoing military campaigns in Iraq and Afghanistan provide very different lessons for the planners contemplating the use of force in those parts of the arc of instability in and around the Gulf.

In Iraq, the United States executed an extremely successful conventional military operation against an incompetent foe, integrating air-, ground-, and sea-based assets in a coordinated campaign that effectively brought down Saddam Hussein in several days. However, it would be wrong to conclude that the campaign represented a triumph for military transformation and effects-based operations. Although the innovative targeting scheme executed by sensors and long-range stand-off munitions worked largely as advertised during the assault on Baghdad, much of the U.S. military's modern hardware and sophisticated operational concepts have been less effective in Iraq's urban counterinsurgency environment.[47] Lacking language skills and overall familiarity with Iraqi society and culture, U.S. ground troops face the difficult task of applying their technological superiority and operational prowess against a societally embedded foe; at least in Iraq's Sunni heartland. Absent a clear political decision to raise the level of national commitment, it seems clear that the United States cannot militarily defeat the insurgency. Instead, it must rely on indigenously generated Iraqi forces to root out the insurgents. In short, effects-based operations and the capabilities envisioned in military transformation do not, by themselves, offer the prospect of victory. As is being relearned by a new generation of troops in Iraq, there is no substitute for language skills, cultural awareness, and tactical intelligence in the fight against the insurgents.

In Afghanistan, the military lessons for the United States are different than in Iraq, but the implications of the experience there are similar. Like Iraq, Afghanistan represented an astounding success in which relatively small numbers of U.S. forces (numbering several hundred special operations forces) brought down a regime in a relatively short amount of time at little direct cost. Since bringing down the Taliban, U.S. special forces, in concert with the International Security Force in Afghanistan, led by NATO, have helped establish security that was critical for the successful national elections of October 2004. These special forces, along with Provincial Reconstruction Teams, working alongside Afghan nationals, are providing security and helping execute reconstruction and stabilization missions throughout the country. Elements of the Taliban and al Qaeda do remain active on the Afghanistan–Pakistan border, but the country is not being subjected to the kind of instability and violence regularly plaguing sections of Iraq. Overall, nation building in Afghanistan is moving forward but at a pace slower than anticipated. It is still too soon to classify Afghanistan as a success; or failure. The presidential elections of 2004 represent a success, although the follow-on parliamentary elections have now been delayed until September 2005. It remains to be seen whether the latest schedule for elections can be met. Despite pronouncements of success by various senior U.S. officials, other reporting paints a more nuanced picture.[48] In its weekly report covering the period from March 24–30, 2005, the European Union's Afghanistan Non-Governmental Organization Safety Office reported uncertain local security conditions in 26 of Afghanistan's 34 provinces.[49]

In the conventional phase of combat operations in Afghanistan, force was applied in an imaginative and ad-hoc way that demonstrated flexibility and innovation. Particular characteristics of the regional environment provided important supporting elements to the use of force and have also helped in the postconflict environment. Aided by a coherent opposition that is being molded into a national force, U.S. special forces are working diligently to build indigenous capabilities while simultaneously retaining the means to launch direct action teams against al Qaeda and the Taliban to supplement the local defense forces.

It is easy to overdraw the lessons of the Iraq and Afghanistan cases, which are still being assessed, and hence difficult to draw out wider implications for these cases on the new security strategy being implemented in the region by the United States. If there is an overriding lesson for planners of these two cases it is this: history, situation, and context matter in planning and executing military operations. In Afghanistan, the United States had at its disposal an extant and indigenous resistance force—the Northern Alliance—the members of which had been involved in the internal Afghan conflict for much of the last 25 years. The Northern Alliance had a relatively coherent command structure and faced a foe with symmetrical military capabilities. In Iraq, an indigenous underground resistance structure to Saddam existed in the Shi'ite south that was almost totally opaque to U.S. planners and, as a result, of no real use in prosecuting the conventional military phase of the invasion.[50] However, the lack of knowledge of the Shi'ite infrastructure simply flowed from a broader ignorance of Iraqi society, which had been devastated by nearly 30 years of Saddam's totalitarian rule. In Iraq, a new generation of military personnel encountered an environment that had not been seen by the United States as a military occupying force since Vietnam. Thus, it is not surprising that the United States has struggled to bring its formidable military capabilities to bear in an extremely difficult counterinsurgency environment tailor-made for an opponent with asymmetric capabilities.

CONCLUSION

Events over the last three years in the Gulf and the Middle East indicate that the United States is in the midst of redefining its strategic objectives in the region. It is no longer satisfied with the status quo and preserving historical relationships based primarily on access to energy and stability in world oil markets. The U.S.–Saudi partnership is in the process of redefining itself, and the U.S. relationships with the Gulf States have assumed an ascendant role in terms of their contributions to U.S. military objectives. Unlike the problematic use of Saudi military facilities during the 1990s, the no-strings attached platforms for military operations in Qatar, Bahrain, Kuwait, and the UAE will only become more useful to the United States as it seeks to address emerging threats in and around the arc of crisis. Complementing the facilities in the Gulf, additional bases are now being built in Afghanistan, Central Asia, and the Horn of Africa.

Using force to achieve political transformation in the Middle East and elsewhere, however, means accepting the unexpected, and accepting limits to the control that can be exercised over the very transformation that has been embraced. An Islamist Shi'ite style of government could emerge in Iraq, one that may well eventually request that the United States depart their country. Embracing the idea of using force to spur political transformation also means accepting the idea that stability, per se, is not necessarily a preeminent strategic objective. Iraq is a primary example, replete with historical quirks that make a less than ideal platform for the test bed of political transformation. The historical legacy of a state characterized by coercion, authoritarian, and centralized state control of political and economic activity, in combination with pronounced sectarian and ethnic fissures pose profound challenges for the process of political transformation.

It is true that the 9/11 attacks redefined the global security environment for the United States, but that redefinition had other important contributing elements that helped shape the decision to use force against Iraq. The United States arrived at the strategic objective of regional political transformation as a result of a confluence of many different factors. Military transformation, effects-based operations, and the presence of the developed infrastructure; all played an indirect and supporting role in the political decision to use force in Iraq. All these factors combined to help build a case that force could be used in pursuit of political objectives without the accompanying political, economic, and social costs that have traditionally been associated with using force. Using fewer numbers of an all-volunteer force in a lightning-style campaign that promised few casualties presented a certain alluring chimera to decision makers; a chimera that has been largely blown apart by the explosion of the insurgency inside Iraq.

Nevertheless, there can be little doubt that the new American way of war, characterized by effects-based operations, long-range conventional and nuclear targeting, and enhanced situational awareness, will play a role in future decisions to use force as an instrument of strategy and policy. Operation Iraqi Freedom represents only the beginning of this phenomenon in an emerging new global defense strategy that may see forward-deployed forces around the world used with increased frequency to manage an uncertain security environment. It seems clear that the Gulf infrastructure will continue as an enduring feature—maybe even the centerpiece—of the emerging global infrastructure that will see U.S. forces redeployed around the globe to meet the requirements of expanding the zone of democracy and exporting security to stabilize trouble spots around the world.

NOTES

The views in this chapter are the author's own and do not reflect the views or positions of the Department of Defense.

1. Secretary of State Madeline Albright formally announced the embrace of regime change in Baghdad in a speech at Georgetown University in March 1997. In that speech, Albright reiterated that talks with a successor regime would be grounded in the commitment to Iraqi territorial integrity.

2. James Russell, "Strategic Implications of the Iraq Insurgency," *Middle East Review of International Affairs (MERIA)* 8, No. 2 (June 2004), 48–55.

3. Marc Weller, "The U.S., Iraq and the Use of Force in a Unipolar World" *Survival*, 41, no. 4 (2000), p. 81–100

4. Williamson Murray, *Luftwaffe 1933–1945: Strategy for Defeat* (Seacaucus, NJ: Chartwell Books, 1986).

5. "Study Group on a New Israeli Strategy Toward 2000," "Clean Break: A New Strategy for Security the Realm." The Institute for Advanced Strategic and Political Studies, at www.israeleconomy.org/strat1.htm, accessed June 9, 2005.

6. Nicholas Lemann, "Inside the Bush Administration's Foreign Policy," *The New Yorker*, April 1, 2002.

7. Report can be accessed at www.newamericancentury.org/RebuildingAmericas Defenses.pdf.

8. Ibid., i.

9. Ibid., 4.

10. (Bush 9/7/2003).

11. *National Strategy on Combating Terrorism* (Washington, DC: The White House, February 2003).

12. *National Security Strategy of the United States* (Washington, DC: The White House, September 2002).

13. Mark Gasiorowski and Malcolm Byrne, eds., *Mohammed Mossadeq and the 1953 Coup in Iran* (Syracuse, NY: Syracuse University Press, 2004).

14. Shibley Telhami, "The Persian Gulf: Understanding the American Oil Strategy," *The Brookings Review*, 20, no. 2 Spring 2002, pp. 32–35

15. Parker Hart, *Saudi Arabia and the United States: Birth of a Security Partnership* (Bloomington, IN: Indiana University Press, 1998).

16. Douglas Borer, "Inverse Engagement: Lessons from U.S.-Iraq Relations, 1982–2000," *Parameters*, 38, no. 2 (2003), pp. 51–65.

17. Martin Indyk, "Back to the Bazaar," *Foreign Affairs*, 81, no. 1 (2002), p. 75; and James Russell, "Political and Economic Transition on the Arabian Peninsula: Perils and Prospects," *Strategic Insights*, II, no. 5 (May 2003).

18. *The National Defense Strategy of the United States of America* (Washington, DC: Department of Defense, 2005), pp. 5–10.

19. Figures drawn from *Persian Gulf Oil and Gas Exports Fact Sheet*, Energy Information Administration, Department of Energy, Washington, DC, September 2004, at www.eia.doe.gov/emeu/cabs/pgulf.html, last modified September 8, 2004.

20. April 2004, www.eia.doe.gov/oiaf/archive/ieo04/index.html.

21. See Kenneth Pollack's discussion of this issue in "Securing the Gulf,' " *Foreign Affairs* (July/August 2003) as one example. An even more forceful case arguing for the transcendent importance of oil in U.S. strategy in the Persian Gulf is made in Andrew Bacevich, "The Real World War IV," *The Wilson Quarterly*, vol. 29, no. 1 (Winter 2005). Bacevich argues that the so-called war on terror and the pursuit of democracy are subsumed by the overriding strategic requirement that the American way of life requires unlimited and unfettered access to imported oil. He states that from 1980 to the present, "Regardless of who happened to be occupying the Oval Office, universal values did not figure prominently in the formulation and articulation of U.S. policy in the Persian Gulf. Geopolitics routinely trumped values in the war. Everyone knew that the dominant issue was oil, with Saudi Arabia understood to be the crown jewel,' " 58–59. Another variant

on this argument can be found in Shibley Telhami, "The Persian Gulf: Understanding the American Oil Strategy," *Brookings Review*, vol. 20, no. 2 (Spring 2002). Telhami places the U.S. approach in the Gulf within a strategy of denying access to Gulf oil to hostile powers.

22. See Bob Woodward, *Plan of Attack* (need city: publisher, date). As revealed in Woodward's highly credible reporting on the Bush administration's internal deliberations leading up to the Iraq War, access to Gulf oil seemed to have little if any role on the decision to use force. Woodward book is from New York, Simon & Schuster, April 2004.

23. *National Security Strategy of the United States*, pp. 19–20.

24. *National Energy Policy Report* (Washington, DC: The White House, May 2001), at www.whitehouse.gov/energy/National-Energy-Policy.pdf.

25. James Russell and James Wirtz, "Viewpoint: U.S. Policy on Preventive War and Preemption," *The Nonproliferation Review*, Spring 2003, pp. 113–123.

26. *National Security Strategy of the United States*, p. 15.

27. Tim Weiner, "Pentagon Envisioning a Costly Internet for War", New York Times, 13 November 2004, p. A1.

28. Joint Forces Command Glossary, at www.jfcom.mil/about/glossary.htm, accessed June 9, 2005.

29. John Warden, "Air Theory for the Twenty First Century," in Barry Schneider and Lawrence Grinter, eds., *Battlefields of the Future: 21st Century Warfare Issues* (Alabama, Air University Press, 1995).

30. Russell, "Strategic Implications of the Iraq Insurgency," pp. 48-55.

31. James Russell, "In Defense of the Nation: Terror and Reform in Saudi Arabia," Strategic Insights, II, no. 10 (October 2003), www.ccc.nps.navy.mil/si/oct03/middleEast2.asp.

32. *Quadrennial Defense Review Report* (Washington, DC: Department of Defense, September 30, 2001), p. 20.

33. Ibid.

34. See www.defenselink.mil/news/Mar2005/d20050318nms.pdf.

35. Remarks by Douglas J. Feith, Under Secretary of Defense for Policy, "Transforming the U.S. Global Defense Posture," December 3, 2003, at the Center for Strategic and International Studies, Washington, DC.

36. Thomas Barnett, The Pentagon's New Map (New York, Putnam, 2004).

37. Ibid.

38. Mark Duffield, *Global Governance and the New Wars* (London, Zed Books, 2001).

39. See www.defenselink.mil/news/Mar2005/d20050318nds1.pdf.

40. Chalmers Johnson, "America's Empire of Bases," 2004, at www.alternet.org/story/17563/.

41. See Associated Press report "U.S. Invests in Upgrades of Afghanistan Bases," March 28, 2005.

42. Ilan Berman, "The New Battleground: Central Asia and the Caucasus," Washington Quarterly, 28, no. 3 (2004–05), pp. 59–69.

43. Deborah West, *Combating Terrorism in the Horn of Africa and Yemen* (Cambridge, MA: Belfer Center for Science and International Affairs, Harvard University, 2005).

44. *The National Defense Strategy of the United States of America*, pp. 5–10.

45. These missions are derived from *National Strategy for Combating Terrorism*, The White House, Washington, DC, February 2003; *Joint Operating Concept for*

Defeating Terrorist Organizations (Pre-Coordination Draft), United States Special Operations Command, MacDill Air Force Base, Tampa, FL, November 14, 2003; and *National Military Strategy of the United States of America 2004: A Strategy for Today; A Vision for Tomorrow*, Joint Chiefs of Staff, Department of Defense, Washington, DC, May 13, 2004.

46. See "Wolf PAC Distributed Operations Experiment," *Transformation Trends*, Office of Force Transformation, Department of Defense, December 7, 2004, at http://www.oft.osd.mil/library/library_files/trends_375_Transformation_Trends_7_December_2004_Issue.pdf, accessed June 9, 2005; also see "OFT Launches Initiative to Help Cultivate 'Distributed Ops' Concept," *Inside the Pentagon*, February 17, 2005.

47. Dan Baum, "Battle Lessons: Annals of War," *New Yorker*, 80, no. 43 (2005), p. 42.

48. In the press conference announcing the nomination of Zalmay Khalizad as U.S. ambassador to Iraq, Khalizad stated, "In partnership with the Afghan people, particularly President Karzai, we have made great strides. Success in Afghanistan will lead to the political, economic, commercial and ultimately the geopolitical transformation of Central Asia and South Asia." Remarks posted at www.state.gov/secretary/rm/2005/44285.htm, accessed June 9, 2005.

49. The ANSO Security Situation Summary advises nongovernmental organizations to exercise "caution" or "extreme caution' in these areas, and generally advises against travel outside urban areas throughout most of the country after dark due to concerns about security.

50. The coherence of internal Shi'a groups came as a complete surprise to the United States—another aspect of the so-called intelligence failure that has focused primarily on Iraqi WMD capabilities. Since the Shi'a infrastructure was largely unappreciated by the United States, it could not take advantage of it in either the conventional phase of operations and in the immediate postconflict environment, see Jabar [need full details] (2003), 272–273.

INDEX